I Have Never Failed...

But I do have extensive experience with things that absolutely won't work

Bill Stork, DVM

LITTLE CREEK PRESS®
AND BOOK DESIGN
MINERAL POINT, WISCONSIN

Dedication

In his best-selling memoir *Hillbilly Elegy,* author JD Vance credits his grandmother for his success, if not his very survival. He concludes that the biggest single difference between those who make it and those who fail, is to have someone who believes in them. A proposed title for this book was Tailwinded. (I thought it was cool that spell-check didn't recognize it, but my wife thought it sounded too much like Long Winded.) Faced with me having to repeat my first year of veterinary school, Dad asked if I had done my best; Mom asked how they could help. That moment has been the wind beneath my wings for thirty years. So, this collection of short stories is dedicated to all who have nurtured, mentored, guided, or held accountable—Tailwinded—a young person in need. Q

Table of Contents

I participate in a live storytelling group called The Moth. I tell stories that are often adaptions of the chapters from *In Herriot's Shadow, Stepping from Herriot's Shadow,* and *I Have Never Failed.* Since early March I've been telling stories to the back of my iPhone and posting them on YouTube. I asked Kristin at Little Creek Press if we could include the scripts for these chapters in the book. She either thought it was a good idea, or knew I'd do it anyway, and agreed.

Next, I wondered how we might get folks from the scripts to the YouTube videos, hence, the QR codes. So, the last five chapters of the book are rough drafts of stories told live at Moth events. Above the title will be one of those funny little boxes you see on everything from beer to fabric softener. Hold your phone over them in camera mode, and they'll download me, down by the lake, on the stage at Anodyne Coffee in Milwaukee, or out back at sunset, telling the story.

Peyton

Historians have hypothesized for decades as to the disposition of Adolph Hitler's right testicle. A Polish priest and amateur historian named Franciszek Pawlar corroborated the story of an army medic who reported it lost to a rogue piece of shrapnel in the Battle of the Somme during the First World War. More recent accounts suggest the elusive organ never descended from the German dictator's abdomen.

Whether it was his monorchidism or his mother paying more attention to his brother that drove him to commit such atrocities is pure speculation and of little relevance. What I have found is that the presence of a *third testicle* will render a nine-year-old German Shorthaired Pointer gregarious and charming beyond words.

Peyton Schroeder's second puppy visit was June 5, 2007. In the patient notes, I wrote: "Peyton doing quite well. He did not jump up and fell asleep on the exam table. Curiously calm."

It was the first and last documented occasion that Peyton was not moving.

Though we've already violated HIPAA laws, this story is endorsed by Jackie and Steve. Peyton's medical record was thick as a Chicago phone book and weighed like the title for Johnny Cash's Cadillac. Thankfully, there was never anything catastrophic.

In 2009, he endured an episode of extremely intense localized pruritus. That was resolved with a lubed and gloved index finger. Much to Jackie's disgust, he went through a period of maniacal coprophagy, which thankfully lasted less time than a high school kid experimenting with marijuana. There is at least one episode each of scratching, vomiting, diarrhea, and limping in Peyton's nine-year odyssey.

Every dog has a superpower. Peyton has two: growing toenails and lipomas.

If powdered German Shorthaired Pointer nail trimmings are ever found to supplement liver health, delay memory loss, or increase blood testosterone, Jackie and Steve are in the money. His chart includes at least fifty-two appointments for nail trims, and each one pushes our techs to the limits of their athleticism, flexibility, and creativity. Distraction techniques have included touch training and the Peyton Special Busy Bowl (PSBB). The PSBB is canned food, squeeze cheese, and braunschweiger smeared in the bottom. We sprinkle in Charlee Bears and freeze-dried liver, then freeze it overnight. Initially, Steve attempted to hold Peyton on his lap for the duration of the pedicure. He likened the effort to the Hotter'N Hell Hundred, a century bike ride across central Texas in August.

Our staff at the Lake Mills Veterinary Clinic have flirted with the notion of paperless records for at least fifteen years. We remain old school. On the front of the paper chart is a lump map. At the risk of sounding morbid, the lump map looks like a chalk outline at a police scene. When we discover a dermal mass, it is drawn on the sketch with a line attached to a dialogue box detailing the date, dimensions, and results of in-house cytology.

Peyton's lump map looks like flight plans out of O'Hare on Christmas Eve. Thankfully, they have all been cosmetic, benign, and not in the least bit threatening. Each entry was labeled "lipoma," "skin tag," or "wart."

Things got serious on Wednesday, May 4, 2016.

Peyton was due for a leptospirosis vaccine and his heartworm and tick-borne disease blood test. Jackie wanted me to check a new mass that had developed rather quickly. I lay on the floor like an auto mechanic checking for leaks on Peyton's differential. She was not exaggerating. High on the medial aspect of his back leg was a firm but fluctuant ovoid mass that measured two and a half centimeters, like half a

BILL STORK

deviled egg. Experience has taught me to dignify the client's concern, regardless of how convinced I may be that the dog is in no danger.

The Schroeders knew the drill. The technicians were all handling telephone calls, prescriptions, and setting an IV catheter. I extracted a sample from the mass and excused myself to stain and analyze it.

I was back in minutes. "Another lipoma, Dr. Stork?" she asked.

The crease in my brow absolved her levity in a heartbeat. "Jackie, the first thing you need to know is that Peyton is going to be just fine, but it is not just another lipoma. This just goes to show that if you practice long enough, you'll see everything," I laid it on thicker as I went. I was half asleep in theriogenology lecture in vet school, but Dr. Randy Ott explained to us there are rare circumstances—even in animals that are neutered or castrated at a young age—where there can be ectopic foci of testosterone-producing cells often near the kidney. At a site of a bruise or contusion, those cells can be mobilized, multiply, and organize into a full-formed organ.

"Jackie," I deadpanned, "Peyton has grown a third testicle."

"But, Dr. Stork, Peyton was neutered nine years ago, when he was a puppy. You did the surgery," she pleaded.

Still without expression, I launched into an alternate explanation. "Jackie, there's a condition in horses called 'high flanker.' There are testosterone-producing cells far up the spermatic cord, above where we place our ligatures. Even after gelding, those horses can act like stallions."

I had nearly convinced even myself when my technician Kelly pushed open the pocket door and blew my cover, "Dr. Stork, was the lipoma on the microscope from Peyton?" ꝙ

Sticks and Stones

Corporate America has cashed in on the feel-good of children and dogs for years. Think of Buster Brown* shoes and the Coppertone kid. In his painting titled *Boy and Dog*, Norman Rockwell features a lanky lad with rolled up blue jeans, straw hat, and a long, thin stick across his shoulders. At his bare feet, a Shepherd cross wags and bounces with expectant eyes.

Damn, I hope he didn't throw that stick for fear the pup would end up on the operating table, like my friend Kiya.

Joe Trytten may be one of the most unassuming folks you'll ever have the pleasure to know. With some regularity, he can be found at the Tyranena Brewing Company in Lake Mills, Wisconsin. Before I knew his last name, we simply identified him as "kindly old Joe." He refers to himself as "permanently unemployed."

We've bonded over a shared love of old-school Chicago blues and a songwriting farmer from Northern Ontario named Fred J. Eaglesmith. Joe lives in a hundred-year-old cottage with the finest sunset views on Rock Lake, but it lacks central heating. So, when the snow starts to pile on the roof, he retreats to his permanent residence in Sleepy Hollow, Illinois. Possibly a product of his dual-citizenship, Joe experiences episodes of dissociative identity disorder. He is a Jordan-era Bulls and diehard Bears fan who can recite the starting offensive line for the Green Bay Packers. We're going to have to agree to disagree when it comes to the Cubs versus Cardinals. From finance to bluegill fishing, Joe knows. Someday I'll find a topic he doesn't have at least conversational, if not extensive knowledge of.

Though my own deficiency is only a few decibels behind Joe's, I found myself frustrated with Joe's hearing deficiency. In a crowd he needs to

 BILL STORK

be positioned with his good ear out, and you need to speak directly. We were leaving a Dave Alvin concert when I asked if his hearing was a casualty of rock and roll.

"No, I was a gunner in Vietnam." I looked for the smallest crack in the sidewalk to crawl into.

When he was discharged from the service, Joe went to Iowa State University. He took math classes randomly. What he did not know was that he was taking graduate-level classes. By his junior year of undergraduate study, he had run through all of the PhD-level math classes. <insert your favorite Iowa joke here>

Then Joe went to the University of Iowa, followed by the University of Illinois at Urbana-Champaign. After blowing through every math class in the big ten, he became the COO of Southwest Airlines.

When I'd spring my dad from the nursing home, Joe would listen to his stories, laughing on cue like it was the first time.

On the business end of a slack leash looped around Joe's wrist will be a seventy-pound chocolate Lab with legs like Lolo Jones and eyes kind as a nanny. She's the dog little kids take for a walk around the beer garden, and who quashes Tugger to the ground with her neck when he's being a three-month-old Catahoula puppy. If something were to happen to Joe, I'd take Kiya in a heartbeat. She's *that* dog.

Their union was love at first sight.

Joe was on a bike ride when she barreled across the yard and into the road. Faced with flight or fight, he stopped his bike to say hello. He reached with an up-turned palm, which Kiya instantly licked.

Her owner hobbled across the yard, apologizing. Exasperated, he made a grand wave and an offer: "If you like her, you can take her."

Kiya is not without her vices. She has an addiction without an antidote: tennis balls. She can jump from Joe's dock halfway across Rock Lake when Joe chucks them into the water. She will not return without two. Throw a ball into a stack of leaves the size of a VW microbus, and the pile will explode like a toolshed in a tornado.

Which darn near killed her.

On the surface, Joe was amazingly calm. "I think Kiya is going to need a few stitches."

I reckon compared to battle wounds in the jungles of Southeast Asia, it was a flesh wound, but in Lake Mills—to one of our most endearing hounds—this was a certified 9-1-1. In hot pursuit of a tennis ball, she flew into a mound of maple and oak leaves. At the base was the stump of a sapling, cut at a perfect forty-five-degree angle. It skewered her like a bayonet, piercing her at the thoracic inlet, deflecting off her sternum, slashing past her elbow and penetrating to her eighth rib.

It did not slow her retrieve by a step.

Somehow, Dr. Clark and staff managed to extract the shrapnel, reconstruct, and reassemble her chest against the onslaught of an already insane Saturday.

Kiya and Joe are the ultimate illustration of human-animal interdependence. Though her first home was fine, she was a bit too much pup for the elder dog in residence. Life with Joe is as good as a girl can get.

A cursory knowledge of anatomy and applied physics suggests that a few centimeters cranial or caudal, or a few degrees closer to vertical, and Kiya could have bled out from a lacerated jugular vein or collapsed a lung.

This is not an incident that only happens once in a lifetime of practicing. Unless Rockwell's boy had an arm like Aaron Rodgers and his dog ran like a fifteen-year-old Basset, the dog's going to get to the stick, just as it lands. If the ground is soft, the stick can protrude like a javelin. In hot pursuit of their next retrieve, we've known a Goldendoodle who lacerated her esophagus and a Dalmatian his soft palate.

So, as opportune and quaint as it may seem, if you're going to play fetch, please get a ball.

Google the Buster Brown logo. The little round-headed dog looks to be rabid. I'm not sure which is more frightening, him or the Gerber Baby. ໓

  BILL STORK

CNA

The thirteen-inch TV suspended over the resuscitation cabinet in the ICU at Decatur Memorial Hospital showed lines of folks stretching from the checkout counter to the ice cooler, all shifting like schoolboys outside a confessional, clutching scraps of paper. Behind the beautiful blonde ten o'clock local news anchor, a computer graphic blasts *Power Ball Mania*—a burst of stars tails off the *a*. From the tiny speaker next to the nurses' call button, blondie exclaims, "Saturday's estimated jackpot is up to $422 million!" like it's the Second Coming of Jesus Christ.

CNN reports live from the 2016 DNC in Philadelphia. Carol Costello breaks down a seating chart at a champagne brunch hosted by Hillary Clinton. Donors who have given less than $750,000 are seated at card tables in the side room like the ugly cousins at Thanksgiving dinner. To sit close enough to toast the Democratic presidential nominee, donors must have raised $1.5 million or more. Senator Elizabeth Warren assures us our country is not broken. She knows this because there are CEOs of American companies making tens of millions of dollars per year.

In the sterile, stainless, and tile room below the squawk box lies my dad. Registered nurses attend to the sodium chloride infusion in his right arm and the heparin drip in his left. Doctors Patel, Trachtenberg, and Collins order contrast MRIs, sonograms, and EEGs to confirm the diagnosis and localize the lesions. Demyelination and beta-amyloid proteins have conspired to rob him of the laser clarity and steady hand that allowed him to deftly place 450 tons of nuclear fuel rods with a quarter-inch clearance from the seat of a Manitowoc tower crane. A rogue blood clot in his left femoral artery renders his clutch foot cool. Three more in his brain cost him control of most basic human functions. For how long, and to what extent, is the great unknown, to a son apposing his faith vs. his father's quality of life.

One core faculty that was never in jeopardy was his dignity. For that we have to thank an indefatigable, hyper-compassionate army in green scrubs.

They are the Certified Nursing Assistants.

There is a hierarchy in health care. Physicians diagnose and prescribe treatments, and insurance companies fight not to pay for them. Registered nurses ensure said treatments are administered on time and accurately, and patients are monitored in real-time. Finally, at the very heart of care are the CNAs. At times when we are as dependent as a newborn, they are more helpful than I thought humanly possible.

Their job description reads like the list we dread as our parents age and inevitably decline.

I've watched them in nursing homes and hospitals. Their work is always physical, organic, unsightly, and often at god-awful times of the day.

I've taken it as a mission to find a complaint, curled lip, or a syllable of frustration, as they changed soiled bedclothes for the fourth and fifth time, in one shift. And I have failed.

They earn less than a cashier at a Kwik Trip, with fewer benefits. O'Meka is a thirty-five-year-old mother of three boys; all are fixtures on the high honor roll and excel in three sports. She's been a CNA for nine years. She blushed when I thanked her, "Oh, you're welcome, Mr. Stork. I just want my patients to get the kind of care I would want for my own mother."

Dear Senator Warren, I differ, and I will not beg with you to do it. CEOs earning hundreds, if not thousands, of times more than working men and women is criminal. Aspects of this country are broken, and we will be approaching some sense of equity the day people who have taken care of *my* family like O'Meka, Stephanie, Carol, Karen, and Christie earn enough to support *their* families. ꕥ

BILL STORK

The Pike County Jesus is a Packers Fan

Lose the wrap-around shades and Guinness t-shirt, cloak him in a long, white robe, and Shawn Burdick is a dead ringer for Diogo Morgado from the 2014 movie *Son of God*. While he's never hung from a cross outside the gates of Jerusalem, he's had a tough go from day one. Born with multiple challenges, if he'd been a dairy calf, Shawn would have never been weaned.

I sat across from Shawn at the family table in June 2015, at the wedding of Erika Edmonds and handsome Joe Hefler. Erika is the eldest daughter of our friends Gary and Diane. She and her sister, Melanie, are beautiful, mature, and polite.

Owing partially to his demeanor and largely his appearance, Shawn was known to folks around his hometown of Pittsfield, Illinois, as "Jesus." Being born with his intestines everted and a heart murmur were challenging, but long before his recollection. Thanks to a divorce and settlement that broke his heart and his bank account, the last ten years had been a tough go.

While the wedding dance floor looked like a tryout for the Dallas Cowboys Cheerleaders, a few feet away, Shawn sat in quiet resignation, sipping Mountain Dew, periodically checking his watch. It was a two-and-a-half-hour drive from Peoria back home to Pittsfield, and he was looking to save the expense of a hotel.

Motivated by pride, divorce debt, and medical bills, he worked as an auto body technician and landscaper. He helped manage Gary's rental properties and looked in on his mom several times a week. Scrubbing the religious allusions for this one sentence, Shawn was my friend—Gary's savior.

Then came a revelation.

Anytime I travel south of Rockford, Illinois, I inadvertently fall back to my native tongue. I call it "central Illinois mushmouth." After growing up in the hometown of the Chicago Bears, Shawn knew I had moved north. Though standardly polite to a fault, he asserted, "So now that ya'll have been in Wisconsin for twenty years, you are Packers fans?"

Shawn was born and raised ninety minutes from St. Louis and had never crossed the Cheddar Curtain. Yet, the Pike County Jesus was a Packers fan.

For better than a decade, Shawn had been encumbered by the adage about nice guys. We HAD to get this man to Lambeau Field. I do not have the means to absolve his debt, but an afternoon in the south end zone, surrounded by 78,000 green and gold brothers and sisters, could make him forget for at least three hours.

Wedding reception resolutions often don't make it past the hangover. This one we were going to take to the foot of the fourteen-foot bronze statue of Vince Lombardi. Not to mention, I'd yet to go to a Packers game when the high temp was in the double digits.

The date was set—September 25 vs. the Detroit Lions. There are occasions to look for a blue light special from the scalpers outside the Resch Center during the last verse of the national anthem, and there are times to hold the ticket in your hand before preseason even kicks off. In hindsight, if I'd waited until after the Packers rolled over and wet themselves in the second game of the season against the Vikings, I could have saved a week's worth of grocery money.

Dad always kept a few bills in the back of his wallet and tucked away in his toolbox. He called it "hideout money." It took all that and my carwash quarters, but I secured seats 19 through 23, row 42, section 136. When they arrived, I snapped a photo and sent it to Gary.

I filed them securely next to the estimated tax vouchers on my desk.

When Shawn crawled back under the '59 GTO he was restoring to original factory imperfection on Monday, it was not going to be without the full Lambeau experience. For insurance, I called in a ringer.

  BILL STORK

Catholics facing their Confirmation have sponsors. Jess O'Connor was by my side the first time I entered the hallowed halls of Lambeau. He taught me when to stand, sit, kneel, and yell, "GO PACK, GO!"

Jess hasn't missed a home Packers game since Bart Starr was a baby. "Jess, when you leavin', and where are you tailgating?"

"I'm not sure, Bill," he replied with the urgency of a CEO to his board of directors. "Let's go to The Grist, have a beer, and figure it out."

In the time it took to drink two Nebraska Brewing Company IPAs, we had a plan. Jess, Ken, and Al would lead the way. It's a two-hour fifteen-minute drive and a noon kickoff. They'd leave at five forty-five to stake a claim for two vehicles. Shawn, Gary, Diane, and I would trail twenty minutes behind. The meeting was adjourned at 10 p.m., and we all dispersed to get some rest.

Like a six-year-old boy on Christmas Eve, sleep would be broken at best. By four-thirty, I gave in. Silent as a two-hundred-pound mouse (with ataxia), I loaded the cooler, chairs, and canopy. The Coast Guard had issued a small craft warning on Green Bay, and AccuWeather had a ninety percent chance of rain, beginning shortly after kickoff. I placed my displaced uterus repair uniform (Helly Hansen Alaskan Fishing Boat Issue rain gear and rubber farm boots) under the topper for easy access.

I worked with Gary on the hog farm for three years, and he was never a minute late. I feared the years in the insurance industry may have softened him, so at four forty-five, I rattled some pans and hit the button on the Mr. Coffee. By five, there were four plates of road-kill brisket omelets on the table. Just as I drew breath to give a John Humphries mountain-man coffee-call, light appeared beneath their door.

No Lambeau pilgrimage is to be attempted without an obligatory pit stop at Kwik Trip for a twenty-four ounce Cafe Karuba and a *Wisconsin State Journal*. Three-quarters of a tank would surely get us there and back. In my first premonition of the day, I topped off the tank.

There's nothing like a plan that comes together. We turned north off County Road A, and I regaled my three dozing passengers with a Cliffs

Notes version of two decades of love, loss, betrayal, and derechos that have conspired to splinter residents of Milford Township. A spectacular magenta sunrise was quickly consumed by black, grey, and pea-green cumulonimbus clouds and towering thunderheads roiling above the bean field horizon.

By eight thirty, we were just past the Kaukauna exit when the phone rang. I yelled at my headset to answer the call. "Hey, Doc, we're in the First Bank parking lot, just past the Shell station on Lombardi." Thirty years in the cockpit of 747 jumbo jets had left Jess deaf as my dad.

Jess had squatted a parking spot next to theirs. We set up camp chairs, fired up the grill, and poured our first Bloody Mary. This was no amateur operation. By 9 a.m., Jess was best friends with our neighbor with the snow-white goatee and number sixty-six Ray Nitschke jersey that matched his.

We had three solid hours to absorb the full-on Lambeau, pre-game ritual.

The sun would dip behind the clouds, and an east wind blew a chill off the bay, just ten blocks to our east. I took a second sip from the alcoholic breakfast buffet in a cup and returned to the truck for my fleece, gloves, and raincoat.

I had a realization as I rifled through the pile of foul-weather gear:

By age fifty, every man comes to expect that, in relatively predictable intervals, he will make colossal miscalculations. Author and social scientist Bruce Feiler calls them lifequakes. He thinks, plans, and strategizes to minimize the impact and frequency, but to think they will not happen is denial. It is more adaptation than concession to plan his response. The young man reacts with fury, the elder with resignation.

The four tickets were still in Lake Mills, on my desk, next to the tax deposits, exactly where I'd left them. I was so sure that I didn't even rifle through the glove box or look above the visor.

There would be a solution, but it would not come in the next five minutes. I paced the parking lot to calm the electrical storm raging in my brain and find a porta-potty. I had not yet settled the whole-body trembling when I went to work.

BILL STORK

Aaron Rodgers can diagnose a full-on blitz at the line of scrimmage, audible, and find an open receiver in six seconds. I had 170 minutes.

I was surely not the first. Here in 2016, there has to be some technological end-around that can negate my blunder and get us to section 136 by noon.

With the efficiency of a teenager on Snapchat, I pulled up the emails congratulating me for logging on to Vivid Seats, thanking me for my order, surveying my customer satisfaction, assuring me they were processing the order, and that they had shipped. A half-dozen clicks later, I had the order confirmation, and I chose to download and print the tickets. No matter how many times, how hard, how crisply I tapped that damn screen, the computer algorithm would not let me un-ring that bell and send them to my screen.

The Vivid website emphasized how important it was that I was completely satisfied with my transaction. I dialed the twenty-four-hour courtesy line. While I was on hold, they offered me tickets to everything from the Chicago Blackhawks to Celine Dion. They did not mention $250 worth of handling fees.

In minutes that seemed like hours, the uber-friendly agent asked, "How can I help you?"

Customer service can fix anything. I felt a moment of relief, followed by reality. Though she was looking at my order on her computer, the most she could do was email the original sellers of the tickets. I had visions of ninety-year-old season ticket holders in a condo in Boca, playing pickleball.

It was time to launch plans B, C, D, and E.

I paced the parking lot, Googling and making phone calls.

Plan B: Sheila and Sarah were going horseback riding in Mountain, Wisconsin. They were to leave near ten, which would route them within a half-hour of Lambeau by noon. They could grab the tickets, and I could arrange an intercept on the interstate. Realizing Healy standard-time and the unpredictability of horses, I quickly searched for a more certain option.

News had spread back to the tailgate. Sipping on apple cider and moonshine, Ken weighed in from the Department of the Obvious, "You know, Doc, what do we say before we ever get in the car?"

"You show me yours, and I'll show you mine!" the entire parking lot responded in unison.

The urge to strangle him did not even break my stride.

There are friends, and there is Jess. We were not going to resolve this pickle from the First Bank parking lot, so Jess and I headed for the stadium, calling and emailing as we hobbled. The ticket window at Lambeau opened at ten. I had my face on the bulletproof glass as the lady lifted the shade. On my knees, figuratively and literally, I bowed to speak into the microphone. I owned my ignorance and pleaded my case, "My friend, the Pike County Jesus, has come from seven hours south to see the Packers for the first time." I began as if she knew Shawn from birth.

Marge was not amused.

"My friend Gary was run over by a tractor in June (it was really a spray rig). The *only* thing that got him through was the promise of this game." I couldn't tell if it was sympathy or disbelief, but her brow began to soften. I had one more round. "After the accident, they didn't have enough money for a lift or a high-rise commode, and Gary's wife, Diane, tore her hamstring picking him up off the toilet."

I pointed to my Samsung S7. "I can have pictures of the tickets sent to my phone, and the ushers can scan them. No one else will be able to use those tickets."

Without further expression, Marge excused herself to fetch her supervisor. "This guy has a bunch of cripples from Illinois, and he forgot their tickets," she condensed my plea.

Irene stepped up, "The problem is, sir, we need the paper so that if you misbehave, security can mark it and eject you."

I stepped back and removed my hat. Bald and wrinkled, I looked as threatening as Ron Howard. "He looks like he's on leave from assisted living himself," I heard them say from behind the glass.

There was a brief pause. "Sorry. Next!"

I was feeling both poor and stupid.

As Jess relieved himself of his first IPAs of the day, my nephew, Sam, called. I had dispatched him to the clinic, thinking he could take pictures of the tickets and send them to my phone.

"They won't take the pictures, Sam," I relayed.

There was a very specific reason I asked Sam to use the hidden key to let himself in the clinic and take the pictures of the tickets.

Sam has had an infatuation with flying since grade school. He once built a plane from conduit and two motors repurposed from a weed trimmer. When it nearly made it off the ground, Ned thought it would be safer to buy him lessons.

"That's no problem, Bill. I'll just fly them up," he said as if he was walking a cup of sugar across the street.

Jess wasn't sure Sam could get clearance at Austin-Straubel Airport among the corporate jets on game day.

"Alright, Sam. Let me know with a solid ETA."

For the Illinois contingent to miss a single play as a result of my ignorance was not an option, so long as Jess didn't run out of money.

We weaved through the blacktop on the east side of the stadium. The motorhome and Mercedes crowd were in full-throat. We grabbed samples of the sweet potato and curry chicken mini-quiche and goat cheese as we sprinted like OJ through an airport. We ducked between the trombone and tuba player spray-painted green in the Packers Backers New Orleans Brass Band, as they blasted "Roll Out the Barrel" to a contingent doing the polka with abandon.

We waited for the rent-a-cop to signal and crossed. The corner of Oneida Street and Armed Forces Drive is the Packers equivalent of Maxwell Street meets The Salvation Army. I thought, "It would be fascinating to know how many times a ticket changed hands."

Vendors had recycled cardboard signs, hanging from US Navy lanyards, "Want Tickets/Need Tickets" front and back, in thick, black marker.

We intended to secure Shawn's seat and see how much money we had left. Individual tickets are often a bargain. We were able to get him in row thirty-seven on the forty-five-yard line.

I never expected to hear back from Vivid, or the original ticket sellers, and a lame horse had delayed Sheila's departure. My ace in the hole was Sam, and we hadn't heard a word.

I had sixty dollars to my name and was ready to head back to the tailgate. Jess is nothing if not persistent.

"Hey, Doc, I found an extra thirty bucks in my left pocket. Let's just see what we can get for Gary and Diane, just in case Sam can't get clearance to land."

We learned a valuable lesson in ticket economics. The first three vendors hawking pairs laughed, and the next two just turned to keep selling. Finally, a haggard gentleman in a Goodwill Patriots jersey selling two tickets in the north end zone paused.

"C'mon man, I gotta have another twenty," he agonized.

I everted both pockets and offered him thirty-five cents and a handful of freeze-dried liver treats I'd been training my dog with.

"Damn," he relented.

Seventy-five minutes before kickoff, we made tracks back to the lot. I was feeling indebted to Jess and foolish, but relieved. The flatland Packers fans *would* get in the gate.

I grabbed a naked brat from the pile on the endgate as the phone rang.

"Hey, Uncle Bill, it's Sam. I couldn't get clearance into Green Bay, so I'll meet you in Appleton in forty minutes."

I threw Gary and Diane their raingear and fired up the Dodge. With the window rolled down, yelling "'Scuse me, pardon me," I scattered Weber grills, Easy Ups, and beanbag games like Bo and Luke in the General Lee, roaring through a flea market ... backward.

There is no outbound traffic on Interstate 41 before the game. Satisfied there was nothing more I could screw up, I listened to Mark Tauscher do the pregame for the thirty-minute drive to Appleton.

BILL STORK

If the Healys' plane were an Oldsmobile, it'd have collector plates. As I turned off Prospect Avenue into the Platinum Flight Center, I looked skyward to see the green and yellow underbelly of the forty-year-old Cessna growing larger.

Either Homeland Security isn't an issue at the Appleton International Airport Field Base Operations, or there are goons having tickets flown up for every home Packers game. I screamed through the circle drive and left the door wide open. I did my Herman Munster hop-and-run toward the tarmac. The security guard waved me through, never taking his eyes off the screen.

Sam's little brother Vincent on his skateboard drew a wide arc across the cement and did a tail-drag to slow just enough to put the elusive envelope in my hand like a relay baton. "Have fun, Uncle Bill."

Northbound once more, the clock read 11:20. I called Jess.

"Sell the tickets back, and meet me at the corner of Lombardi and Oneida in thirty minutes."

There was little traffic eight minutes before kickoff. Being the youngest and fleetest of foot, the Pike County Jesus stood on the corner. I rolled the passenger window down and passed the envelope to him.

I watched the first two Packers touchdowns on the Jumbotron from Lombardi Avenue as I approached the stadium. Having surrendered my last scrap of cash to the scalpers, I swiped my Mastercard for a Leinenkugel Oktoberfest en route to the bleachers.

After looking like Super Bowl contenders in the first half, the Pack snuck out a victory in the face of a furious fourth quarter from the Lions. Just as we merged on southbound route 41, the monsoon hit with fury. As the wipers tried to keep up, Gary asked, "So, Willy, how do you decide what to write about?"

Just Call Me Rick

We are all products of our environment, upbringing, and interactions. Chance encounters leave snapshots stored deep in our hard drives. Jen Rodriguez says that we come away from every human interaction changed. For several consecutive weeks, I wandered off my path to buy the Sunday paper from the Fort Atkinson Kwik Trip and an uber-friendly clerk named Kurt. His every move, dress, and diction were as crisp as a cadet.

Then, some folks come into our lives at a time of weakness, vulnerability, or need. They bring perspective, strength, or energy that serves us every day of our lives, from that minute forward.

John Humphries is one of those characters. John is a cycling guide and a spirit. Together we have ridden the Continental Divide through Colorado and the Burr Trail in the deserts of Utah. From him, I've developed perseverance on Lizard Head Pass. The mountain in full raging monsoon pushed me to what I had perceived was the point of failure, only to turn the pedals a thousand more times. Layered in polypropylene, smart wool, and rubber, we lived the Norwegian proverb: there is no such thing as bad weather, just a poor choice of clothes.

In a decade and a half of touring with John, I've met a shuttle bus load of exemplary people (and Howie). None have been more memorable than Hendrick Boyd Barner. Having retired from a fifty-year career, Hendrick was encouraged to try cycling by his neighbor Barret. Though Hendrick and Barret lived at or below sea level in St. Louis, their first ride was a high-altitude sufferfest called Ride the Rockies. I met Rick on his second bike trip out West. It was a five-hundred-mile trek from Lake Powell to Bryce Canyon through the white rocks of Utah. Rick was seventy-five.

BILL STORK

Sunrise on day one of a Lizard Head Cycling tour looks like some combination of a mobile bike shop and a flea market. Guides check pedals, saddles, and derailleurs. Guests gather windbreakers, water bottles, and goo shots while checking Strava segments and AccuWeather on their phones. Thirty, or maybe ninety minutes past the announced time of departure, the meeting is called to order.

Guests gather in a semicircle while John lectures like Jimmy Fallon teaching yoga.

"All right, everyone. The hardest part of the trip is now over. You're here," he opens.

To follow are tips on self-preservation, hydration, nutrition, and rules of the road. "If you're in front of the guide, you're no longer on a guided bike tour. If in doubt, chicken out."

Finally, we're asked to introduce ourselves. A rack of unsold copies of the *Herriot's Shadow Collection* in the basement has cured my aversion to self-promotion. "My name is Bill. I'm a Packers fan from Wisconsin, a full-time veterinarian, and a part-time author."

Last in line is Hendrick. "Please, just call me Rick. I'm recently retired," he nearly whispers.

Early in the spring, John floated some options for the 2016 installment of our cycle-born brotherhood: "Big Bend National Park is surreal, our trans-Utah chubby bike tour is epic, and we're doing a Nova Scotia–Cape Breton tour," he left a pregnant pause to lead my decision, "which will be Rick Barner's last ride."

Just call me Rick walked softly and spoke quietly, yet he rode multi-day bike tours through the most spectacular landscapes in the land, oblivious to headwinds, horizontal rains, or a nine percent mountain grade. As we departed the Hell's Backbone Grill in Boulder, Utah, he and Barret quietly deposited their luggage by the rig and pedaled off into the mountains, an hour or so before the group. I cringed that the gravel at the end of the drive might throw him like a tyke losing his training wheels.

Diffracted by the October sun off the desert blacktop, forty or so miles into a ninety-mile day, a meandering mirage would appear in the distance, his front tire drawing a sine wave across the fog line. You were well served to break pace and ride a stretch with Rick. Between gasps, he'd ask about your parents, children, and profession. If you managed to turn the conversation, you'd find out that before he retired, Rick was an MD. I'd pedal and chat with him for a half-hour, wish him well, and ride off.

Somewhere between post bike ride IPAs and hors d'oeuvres, he and Barret would roll up the drive. The gauntlet of guests cheered like the Tour de France. Rick responded like Walter Payton scoring a touchdown; it was his job for the day. He started long before the group and finished well after, but he rode EFI* every day.

You're only a guest on a Lizard Head trip for about an hour before you become family.

One of the premier tours offered by Lizard Head Cycling traverses a famous section of the Lone Star State. The swath of god-forsaken tumbleweed and cow pastures that run from Dallas to San Antonio, glancing just west of Austin, is known as the Hill Country. It covers an area twice the size of the Eastern European countries that many of its famously stubborn inhabitants immigrated from. It is not called the Mountain Country of Texas.

Still, in the spring of 2016, at age eighty-two, a four percent grade into Blanco must've seemed as daunting to Rick as Cottonwood Pass in Colorado.

Thank God for Jim.

Jim and Sue live in Boulder. They are the adult version of Pebbles and Bamm-Bamm. On a tandem bike, they are known to wave slow-moving cars out of their way. Sue is a research consultant, and Jim installs well components. Judging from his forearms, he uses a pick and shovel. Recognizing that Rick was starting to fade, Jim would ride handlebar to handlebar with his hand on Rick's back and push him up the Texas hills.

When John leaked it could be Rick's last, the Lizard Head Cycling tour of Nova Scotia became a family reunion. The focal point of the tour was Cape Breton. It reminded me of a mountain, sticking out of

 BILL STORK

the North Atlantic. Where rugged sea cliffs meet forests of maple in full fall foliage, it is an artist's wet dream. Transit on bike or a car is by way of 198 kilometers blacktop called Cabot Trail. It is one of the ten top cycling destinations in the world. Thankfully, the drivers are pathologically polite because seldom is there a proper shoulder, and often there is road construction, avalanche repair, and fog.

While the CT is not exactly the Swiss Alps, it ain't Illinois. Pebbles and Bamm-Bamm knew it would be more than Rick could ride. If this were to be his last, his legacy of EFI, or even MEI, would remain intact. They rented a tandem bicycle in Halifax. When the bike shop in Nova Scotia sold the rental tandem bike before they arrived, they bought one in Boulder, boxed it up, and sent it to Canada.

For the six days in the saddle over five hundred kilometers, Jim was captain and engine. Sue trailed, reminding Rick not to lean and to pedal hard into the hills. Sometime after lunch, Rick would relinquish his stoker's saddle so that Jim and Sue could have some time together. They'd drop the rest of us like a Lamborghini pulling away from a Prius.

Google Hendrick Boyd Barner, MD. The man who begs you to *Please, just call me Rick,* has authored 133 research papers, contributed to multiple medical textbooks, and pioneered the brachial artery harvesting technique for greater coronary artery bypass surgery.

As the gale force winds rocked our bikes on top of the rig just outside, we gathered for breakfast on day three in Antigonish. The waitress escorted Rick to the head of our tables with a gentle hand on his arm, which he thanked her for. We chanted, "Good Morning, Rick," to remind him we were his people.

The hands that had once deftly bypassed occluded coronary arteries, and whose procedures may have saved my grandfather in 1974, now struggled with a plastic butter knife and a packet of strawberry marmalade. I handed him an open one.

Back in Halifax, we tipped our guides and hugged our goodbyes. Rick shook my hand and pulled me aside.

"Bill, it was a pleasure to ride with you, and thanks for helping me with the marmalade." Ɋ

Howard

A month spent toggling between hope and resignation did nothing to prepare me for the morning of Tuesday, September 7, 2004. A boot-width from the fieldstones next to the driveway, Herb Altenburg winced just to put one foot in front of the other. He picked up his head only to find the door handle.

I laid my forearms across the counter, crossed my hands, and met his gaze. "Any word, Herb?" I asked the question I feared the answer to.

He closed his eyes hard and twitched to the right. "Nah, Doc. I'm gonna need you to come out and check the cows."

Twelve years ago, few would have predicted today's drone's-eye view of 5680 Highway S to be that of a tie-stall barn, dog pen, and a swing set in the backyard.

Five-thirty in the morning, muted by the condensation from forty-eight lazy crossbred cows, the six west windows threw a fluorescent glow across the old cow yard like an OPEN sign at the café on Main. The tenor moan of the little six-horse milk pump spoke in tones as hushed as Howard himself. Inside, he scraped manure into the gutter and fed silage from a fifty-bushel electric cart. A two-inch stainless steel line carried milk to the receiver jar and bulk tank.

Ask Howard how long he's been milking cows, he's not sure. He figures he's been full-time since age twelve when he was first tall enough to dump the Surge buckets through the strainer in the bulk tank about the size of a four-person hot tub. He'd probably hung his first unit between fifth and sixth grade.

Ask him how much time he's had off. He'll tell you, eighty-eight days.

For ten years after he graduated high school, Howard would be in the barn by four in the morning, milking and feeding cows, so that he could be on time for his day job. After eight hours of feeding, cleaning, and breeding mink, he'd be back for evening chores on the farm. In 1985, he went farmin' full time.

If ever there was a push-button factory farm, the Altenburg farm was not. Feed was pushed in a wheelbarrow from the silo room to the manger. The barn cleaner was the fork and bicep variety. Howard would throw cornstalks and manure onto a 150-bushel spreader drawn by a John Deere 2020 or Allis D-15, the only tractors small enough to drive through the twenty-nine stanchion, hip-roof barn.

With nary an able-bodied high school football stud to be found, he'd mow a dozen loads of second-crop hay solo between morning and evening milking.

As a bachelor farmer and man of few words, early signs were subtle. In retrospect, Wendy and Dennis at Lake Mills Feed and Grain recall they couldn't make out whether he was asking for grass seed or calf feed in late July of '04. Some speculated he got hit in the head with a chain; others figured it was silo gas. Either of which is a day in the life of your average farmer.

Then he showed up for a doctor's appointment that didn't exist and was found downtown with his shoes on the wrong feet. On August 4, 2004, he was in St. Mary's Hospital in Madison, Wisconsin, unresponsive and comatose. How he got there, no one knows.

Coach Mike McCarthy touts his "next man up" philosophy. When a farmer goes down, friends, family, and neighbors circle the wagons. Brother Herb can fix anything with green paint; cows are not his first love. Keith Fulk is a man who's taken a few wrong turns, but when a friend is in need, he asks when and where. Thanks to Herb and Keith, the calves never missed a meal, the cows never missed a milking, and mangers were full of fresh feed. Never mind they had their own farms to run. Herb's wife, Pam, ensured Howard's bills were paid.

There were radiographs, CT scans, and organ panels, but the diagnosis did not come until hematologist Dr. Roby Rogers reviewed one of his many CBCs.

Thrombotic thrombocytopenia purpura is a disease that affects fewer than five people in a million. The patient's platelets aggregate to form clots. Initial signs are similar to a stroke: impaired cognition, balance, and vision. The course of the rare disease is defined by the organs where the rogue clots take up residence. Howard was kept alive by feeding tube, IV fluids, and a procedure called plasma exchange. His prognosis was guarded, at best.

Howard had lost forty pounds and a quarter of his right lung. His prognosis was descending toward grave. Doctors and social workers advised Herb and Pam to get his affairs in order. Henry Miller, the family lawyer, was called to establish power of attorney.

It was early September, and Herb and Pam sat in silence at Howard's bedside. He had not spoken a word or wiggled a toe since August 4. He opened his eyes and asked, "How are my cows?"

Thirty-six years of farmin' had rendered Howard thin as a strand of number nine wire and strong as a gate post. A month in a coma had reduced him to the constitution of a Raggedy Ann doll. Like a forty-eight-year-old toddler, he struggled to sort red and green blocks. With the expertise of physical and occupational therapy, and German tenacity, he would progress from Hoyer lift to walker and finally stand on his own.

Howard was discharged from the hospital on September 27, 2004. It would take a leave of absence and a month of Pam's home cooking to get him strong enough to get back to the barn.

The day Howard awoke from his coma was Tuesday, September 7, 2004, the same day Herb came to the clinic to disperse the herd.

For some, it was karma or one helluva coincidence. For others, divine intervention.

Merry Christmas. Ⱡ

Life Without Art

Years before the "don't call 'em millennials" in their trucker hats and civil war beards were old enough to shave, Rob Larson was building Legendary Wisconsin Beers in his kitchen. Twenty years ago, he opened Tyranena Brewing Company. His ales, pales, and barrel-aged porters are masterpieces. The micro, nano, and pico breweries who are new to the party only hope to come close.

The walls of the public space at TBC feature portraits of Chief Black Hawk and Cal, the original Bitter Woman, namesakes of his flagship porter and India pale ale. There are a handful of high-tops, a dozen barstools, and an eight-by-eight space in the corner for live music. You're only a stranger once, or by choice. Given the cast of characters who routinely gather to hoist a pint and exchange philosophy, the tasting room can be *Fox and Friends* vs. *New Day* or *Sportscenter*, any given evening.

Rob has master's degrees in chemical engineering and business administration. He tends every detail from parts-per-million of yeast in his lagers, to which groove the chairs line up on. He also programs the house music. You will find no orchestrated remakes of Beach Boys classics. Ranging from Katharine McPhee to The Cash Box Kings, it would take a dozen Spotify channels to cover the range. Most selections are from artists who've played the tasting room and beer garden or are someone's favorite.

Fifteen years ago, I offered Rob a copy of *It Came from Nashville*, the 1992 release from Webb Wilder and the Beatnecks. A couple of weeks ago, Tim Sprecher and I toasted the approach of a new year just as the computer picked "Poolside," cut number ten from that album. Webb wears high-waters, suspenders, and a pocket protector and has dubbed himself "two hundred pounds of swaggering bulk and an electrifying performer." And he is.

Donny "The Twangler" Roberts gave Webb a vocal break to dictate the "Poolside" rules in his gut-bucket baritone: "No running, no jumping, no profanity, and no dogs."

Then Donny jumped back into another searing rockabilly riff on his purple Fender Flying V and took it to the bridge. Early in his career, Webb was asked if he had any words of wisdom to close an interview. Without hesitation, he responded, "Work hard, rock hard, eat hard, sleep hard, grow big, and wear glasses if you need them." Just like that, the Webb Wilder credo was born.

Tim paused to absorb this wisdom while watching the replay of Russell Wilson escape a full-grown defensive end and throw a bullet to Doug Baldwin in the end zone. Tim admitted that as much as he loved music, his taste was largely secondhand, borrowed from his niece or plucked from conversations like this.

I responded by sharing what I thought was a fairly novel notion, "You know, Tim. I think we are surrounded by poetry, art, and beauty. Regrettably, we're often too busy, blind, or numb and end up walking right by."

I was working on a quote from "Mamas Don't Let Your Babies Grow up to Be Cowboys," to make my case when Tim trumped me silent.

"You know, Bill. Without art, life as we know it would cease to exist."

Tim Sprecher exudes competence. His three-quarter-ton Ford is showroom-spotless and backed into the middle of a parking spot in the back forty, with the rearview mirrors folded inward. It had 300k on the odometer before the first scratch. He dresses like Orvis meets Eddie Bauer, is well-spoken, and really tall. Tim shows up in work gloves at 8 a.m. the Sunday after every Storkfest to help with cleanup, so I consider my response specifically not to offend. I've got my favorite potters, painters, authors, and guitar pickers, but altering the course of civilization seemed a stretch. I went back to the big screen, pretending to watch the Seahawks vs. Rams and gave it some thought.

It has been said, and I can confirm that "blues music is all about feelin' good about feelin' bad." Thirty years ago, I danced with abandon with my friend Barb, as The Mudhens helped us celebrate the commencement of real life and graduation from the University of Illinois. Then, in December 2007, I was driving from a milk fever to a dystocia when the FCC broke into The Dave Mathews Band to announce the New York Stock Exchange had been closed mid-session to halt a free fall of the markets. For the years to follow, businesses struggled to keep their nostrils above water. Our clients had to choose between the health of their pets and supper. During that time, the family court commissioner of Jefferson County ruled that my kids were better off an hour away.

Two beers and a Saturday night at the Crystal Corner Bar with The Cash Box Kings were one of the few pleasures that could relieve the vice that crushed my temples.

Brad Wells is a bipolar blackbelt, college linebacker, prison guard, dog trainer, karate instructor, Tai Chi master, potter, and friend. Twenty-five years ago, I stopped to have a sandwich in his basement studio in Cambridge. Without breaking conversation, he bellied up to his wheel and threw a hunk of mud in the middle. Like an eighth-grade boy gawking at a poster of Farrah Fawcett, I stared as he imposed his soul on the pound of Paoli clay. My whole head tingled like I'd taken off my stocking hat with a full sweat in the middle of a blizzard as he pressed his thumbs to his fingers, and a vase rose from the amorphous grey lump. I've served three dozen Valentine's, birthday, and cheer-up bouquets of red roses and wildflowers from that teal green and earth tone vase. It is featured prominently above a salt-glazed piece from my friend Bruce Johnson and below a pitcher made for my mother by Mark Skudlarek.

As I arrange the next line of this story in my head, I sip from a mug Paige duped me into choosing for Father's Day 2004. She told me it was for our friend, Sarah.

There are three pictures over our mantle. In the center hangs a portrait of a puppy napping on a pair of cowboy boots. Purchased from the trade show at National Finals Rodeo, it ensures I'll never forget my first Christmas with Sheila. Our second year was marked by the arrival of a Wyoming Cattle Dog, Token. To the left is a sketch by my brother, Glenn Fuller, of Token and her sister, keeping Remmi forever on our mind. A cowboy on a Quarter Horse riding a line fence through a blizzard hangs in the corner. It may be the only piece in the house created by a hand I haven't shaken. It caught Sheila's attention at a benefit raffle for a friend. A patch of black ice cost him thousands in medical expenses, and his girl. The piece made its way to our wall Christmas 2015.

It is inarguable that art enhances our lives. But the stock market would have recovered if I'd spent those Crystal Corner Saturday nights at home playing Scrabble. I look forward to my cup of Cafe Karuba from Mark's mug every morning, but coffee is ninety milligrams of caffeine per cup, Styrofoam, or hand-thrown clay. The plumber who fixed our toilet wouldn't know Benny and Luck's portrait by my friend Rod Mellot from a velvet Elvis.

"Without art, civilization as we know it would cease to exist," still seemed a stretch, but Tim's got cred.

So, I pulled in Merriam-Webster's definition of art: skill acquired by experience, study, or observation. Thus, there is an artist in backhoe operators, welders, and HVAC technicians. There is an art to sales, conversation, plowing snow, and making friends. My commute is eight miles through the country past houses, farms, and fields. Every ditch is mowed like the fairways at the country club. Paul Kalanithi speaks to the art of brain surgery in his best-selling posthumous memoir *When Breath Becomes Air*.

Finally, Jamie Manix brought in her ten-year-old Miniature Schnauzer, Lilly.

Lilly is Jamie's last living thread to the elderly neighbor who owned her first and to her recently deceased husband, Tim.

Lilly's going to live until she's thirty.

Once we'd assured Jamie the lesion on Lilly's side was a small laceration from the icebergs that lined her path while in hot pursuit of a chipmunk, the air in the room lightened. Years removed from

BILL STORK

her childhood in the Volunteer State, Jamie's diction is soft as the first warm rain of spring. Tim played banjo and shared her love of bluegrass music. Jamie leads a dance group that entertains at nursing homes and assisted living facilities. She spoke of how hands slap the chair rails and heads bob at the sound of Sinatra, Como, or the King.

I thought of my mom, who had passed nine years ago that day. She'd grown up in central Kentucky. Her cousin had played banjo with Bill Monroe; bluegrass was in her DNA. In July 2006, dementia had reduced her to skin, bones, and selfless core. In the ultimate expression of "'til death do us part," Dad had singlehandedly taken care of her. I sent him with Glenn to the truck and tractor pulls at the Jefferson County Fair for a three-hour break. Five virtuoso pickers, known collectively as The New Pioneers, regularly gathered at the Café Carpe in Fort Atkinson. My mom's shoulders slumped like Raggedy Ann, and she stared at the floor. Though she didn't know me from John Glenn, her toe came to life at the first note of "Foggy Mountain Breakdown," tapping in imperfect time.

Jamie nodded, "You know, Dr. Stork, every time my folks heard 'Tennessee Waltz,' whether it was on a car radio, record player, or Patti Page singing it live, they'd stop what they were doing and dance. Every time I hear that song, I think of my parents."

Without art, life as we know it would cease to exist.

Yup. ꧂

The Quilt of Many Colours

It's been said that if you enjoy what you do, you'll never work a day in your life. As if being a Holstein Rectum Ranger is not rewarding unto itself, I always walk away enlightened by the herdsman, hired hand, or farmer. Especially at the Haack farm.

Rolling east over the hill on Holzhueter Lane, I'll wave at Russ Dahl turning into his drive with an empty spreader. In my head, I'll be repeating the day's quote from Margaret Thatcher, Winston Churchill, or the origin of Superman, tendered by Ryan Haack, sure I'll never forget it. Ryan once shared that when he has a good thought comin' on, he'll stop milking just to write it down.

"Ah, so you don't forget," I surmised.

"Yeah, and to make room for the next one." On Ryan's suggestion and necessitated by an accumulation of birthdays, I dried my hands and pulled out one of the half-dozen drug company notepads I keep in my console.

On Friday, January 20, 2017, the topic was quilting.

The Haack herd check has been on Thursday mornings since 1992. This week we moved to Friday so that the family could attend the funeral of Ryan's Aunt Beth. With no ongoing arrhythmias or murmurs, she had passed away suddenly. Beth was fifty-nine years old—three years past the age the thirteen Parrell siblings silently fear; their father died at fifty-six.

Serendipitously, or by the grace of God, Beth's daughter had given birth a month early. She was able to spend three weeks with her first grandchild.

Beth worked for the State of Wisconsin and the Department of Veterans Affairs. Without a lick of formal schooling, she was their go-to information technologist. With thirty years seniority, and faced with training a generation of colleagues preoccupied with the next ping, engaged in Snap-Book, and looking to be spoon-fed, she retired in June 2016. Ryan's mom, Cathy, and Aunt Beth share the same git-'er-done and social butterfly genes. In six months at home, she had the house painted, carpeted, roofed, and resided. Since walls don't talk and the dogs only listen, she was ready for people and productivity, so she took a job with the Village of Black Earth doing office and computer work. Rumor has it only once was there was someone in her office she didn't already know.

I had just one, but I suspected the void is no less when you have more aunts than elementary school teachers. I asked what defined Beth. Ryan is known for his contemplative pause. His response can come in the space of two cows or two separate farm visits. This time there was none.

"Her quilts."

Sheila had already caught me on Pinterest; I was down to my last man-card. For two guys to be overheard in a free-stall barn talking about quilting, next comes the Newberry knife. (Google it if you dare.)

For the next six cows, there was silence.

If I have a skill, it is sleeping. When it comes to bedclothes, the Princess and the Pea, I am not. In 1988, a grieving family brought their ten-year-old St. Bernard to the Brush College Animal Hospital. A splenic tumor had rendered him lifeless and in pain. They donated the blanket he rested on; the very sight would be too much for them. The teal green, queen-sized comforter followed me from home, through eight years at the University of Illinois, and across the Cheddar Curtain.

As Ryan and I worked our way through the cow barn to the heifers, we became enamored with the whole idea. It's been said the best thing about firewood is that it gets you warm twice. So, what about a quilt?

I asked Ryan if his mom would be willing to talk about her time spent quilting with Beth. "In forty-two years, I've never known my mom to pass on an opportunity to talk."

Beth's father, Martin Parrell, was told his heart wasn't good enough for the United States Army. His parents sold the family farm to his brother, thinking he wasn't strong enough for a life of milking cows, cleaning barns, and baling hay. Not to be deterred, Martin bought his own farm (literally over the hill and through the woods from the Haack farm). He and his wife, Mary, farmed and raised thirteen children, the eldest being Ryan's mom, Cathy. She learned to play Cowboys and Indians with three younger brothers. She was seven before Beth was born.

I had this *Little House on the Prairie* vision of Mom, Grandma, and the Parrell sisters huddled around a roaring fire in the old farmhouse on River Valley Road. With frozen fingers and a cast iron pot on the woodstove, they meticulously stitch together stray pieces of fabric. Meanwhile, Pa and the boys are dragging logs with a team of horses and splitting and stacking wood against a raging blizzard.

Not so much.

Eldest sister Cathy was in St. Mary's School of Nursing when the brood of middle girls were in elementary and junior high school. She was known as "that girl who shows up on weekends." By the time Beth's first daughter, Paige, was born, Cathy was on number three. Popular wisdom in those days advised that babies be woken in the middle of the night to be fed, and Beth confessed she was exhausted. A nurse, big sister, and working mother, Cathy calmly assured her it was okay to let sleeping babies lie.

Martin and Mary Parrell have 105 grandchildren. When the grandchildren began to start their own families, the aunts came together. The gift registry at Kohl's just wouldn't do.

In advance of every niece's or nephew's wedding, Pat, Donna, Beth, and Cathy would pick a pattern, collect the material, and gather in someone's kitchen on Saturday and Sunday afternoons. They'd cut, stitch, sew, and talk. There were times when the last stitch had barely cooled when the couple said, "I do."

For the first time in thirty-five years, the sisters became friends.

Wedding quilts may have been the beginning, but Parrell girls are more productive than a Chinese shoe factory. Cathy raised six kids, milked cows, fed calves, and drove combines on the farm. (One famous autumn, she picked corn until she had broken water.) She also worked as a full-time nurse. She and her sisters made quilts for the family and also to give to the police department, homeless shelters, and hospitals for children who were victims of abuse, neglect, and tragedy.

Project Linus is a worldwide organization that collects handmade quilts to give to any child in need of a hug—many with life-threatening congenital diseases, including childhood cancer. They've donated thousands of hours, hundreds of quilts, and heart.

For a kid to close his eyes on a day's troubles wrapped in a garment made by the hands of strangers who care is warmth you can't buy at Bed, Bath, and Beyond.

Bloomingdale's sells duvet covers made of 400-thread-count batiste cotton and comforters of hand-plucked European duck down. They're guaranteed to keep a couple warm for the price of a reliable used car.

But after "'til death do us part," clinking glasses, and the "Chicken Dance," when a newlywed couple comes to rest beneath an Aunt Cathy, Pat, Donna, and Beth quilt, they do so wrapped in the warmth of the family that embraces their union. ꝅ

Club Coprophagy

I called *In Herriot's Shadow* "a 264-page assault on the notion that you never get a second chance to make a first impression." This is not to say that we don't make them; it's human nature.

In the process of getting to know new clients, I'll glance at the parking lot. I'll pick up the pace of conversation a couple of beats for the young mother being dragged by a new Lab puppy with a car seat hooked in the crook of her right arm, wet wipes, and a Cheerios dispenser falling out the sliding door of the Grand Caravan.

We'll save the recommendation of purple, glittery Soft Paws and pheromone dispensers for the second visit when the good ol' boy in an F-250 shows up with an eight-week-old kitten nestled in the breast pocket of his bib overalls.

We ask place of employment or profession on our registration form for those who choose to share. It helps us make better conversation during tough blood draws, awkward anal gland expressions, and waiting for lab results. Not to mention, people do fascinating things. We've met folks who help orchestrate the extraction of core ice samples from 150 miles below Antarctica, and actuarial scientists*. It also helps us relate. I felt like a circus clown at a Catholic funeral when I launched the "rock in the stream" analogy to explain a brand-new heart murmur in Tom Kreje's eleven-year-old retriever. Tom raised his hand just above the table, creased his brow, and winced. He is a professor of anesthesiology at Northwestern University School of Medicine.

We avoid the most subtle hint of profiling. But in an effort to deliver the most appropriate information to our clients, we'll take a look at their family configuration, lifestyle, and the make and model of their pets.

 BILL STORK

Still, there are conversations that you simply do not expect to have with certain clients.

Before walking into exam room one with Ilene Isthmus and her daughter, Abby, you tuck in your shirt and lint roll your khakis. You'd as likely expect her Volvo hybrid SUV to be parked at Whole Foods or Dragonfly Hot Yoga studio. The tone is set when six-year-old Abby asks if I prefer the low dose dexamethasone suppression test or urine cortisol to creatinine ratio as a screening test for Cushing's disease. I feared they had been waiting too long. She'd been skimming from the January edition of the *Journal of the American Veterinary Medical Association* she'd picked up off the counter. Her eight-month-old Anatolian Shepherd, Bernie, looked as if he'd just been called out at Westminster. His paws never left the floor when I slid open the pocket door. He promptly parked his hinder on the linoleum when I raised my hand to scratch my chin.

The chances of finding an abnormality during my physical exam of this magnificent animal seemed as likely as Rob Larson with a Bud Light. Maybe I could find a fleck of pigment in his iris or a spot of dirt in the vertical canal of his ear. I asked anyway, "So, Ilene, any lumps, bumps, lameness, coughing, vomiting, head shaking, or accidents in the house?"

I checked the boxes on our physical exam sheet ahead of her answers.

I'd have to go back and circle *abnormal* at number six.

"Oh no, none of that," she responded. "Our only problem is he will not stop eating his poop."

I take pride in my ability not to respond. I may have let the team down.

My pat response, when faced with a coprophagic puppy, is to try and lighten things up. "Well, Ilene, this starts a most absurd conversation on how to make your dog's poop less appealing."

Ilene's body position and conspicuous lack of expression suggested I save the attempt at cornball comedy and throw the full resources of the Lake Mills Veterinary Clinic at this situation.

To address the topic of coprophagy in a comprehensive fashion requires a tectonic paradigm shift.

Dog poop is on the receiving end of more jokes than a hundred-dollar lawyer in a polyester suit. It is the standard metaphor for underachievement: "We played like shit." "The high school cafeteria's tuna casserole tastes like shit." "When I had the flu, I felt like crap." "He looks like shit."

Bernie Isthmus, my dog Tugger, and a significant percentage of all dogs think differently. To them, a steaming pile (yes, they prefer fresh) is better than unlimited trips to the Sunday buffet at Ponderosa.

A skilled sommelier can describe the most intricate nuances of a fine wine. "Ah, yes, the 1999 Chateauneuf-du-Pape, produced in a diverse array of styles, the rebound reds share the common characteristics of fresh red and black cherries, strawberries, kirsch (whatever that is), black pepper, black raspberry, spice, earth, and herb. Literally translated, 'new castle of the pope,' this French masterpiece is heavy in the nose, with a silky mouthfeel and a most satiating finish."

If they could only speak. A dog's olfactory alone is at least a hundred times more sensitive than our six senses combined. Howling like Big Mama Thornton, a Beagle or a Bloodhound can follow a week-old rabbit track through six inches of snow while running twenty miles an hour. One whiff of a steaming pile of yesterday's Fromm's, and they can tell you the breed and birthday of the chicken sacrificed for that kibble and what state the wheat was grown in.

In a recent visit, I was stopped short by a hyper-polite client as I offered his dog a freeze-dried turkey heart. "Please don't," he asked. Twelve hours after Sampson eats freeze-dried treats, his other dog, Chewy, gets obsessed with his piles, like hungover college students after chicken Kiev.

The onset of coprophagy in an adult dog is serious medicine. It can be a sign of exocrine pancreatic insufficiency, inflammatory bowel syndrome, hypothyroidism, intestinal parasites, vitamin B12 deficiency, malabsorption syndrome, and malnutrition. The best medicine is to perform a CBC, chemistry panel, TLI, PLI, folate, cobalamin, intestinal biopsies, and an MRI.

BILL STORK

In young, healthy dogs in excellent body condition, on good diets, with normal stools, poop is a delicacy. Theories vary as to how the behavior starts. Some speculate it is an attempt at cleanliness, an imitation of their mother at birth, or territorial behavior. Like many behaviors, it can be inadvertently perpetuated by appropriately dramatic owners: "Good God, Gus. Put down that pile of poop!"

So, what is a dog owner to do?

The aversion approach.

Rendering the stool less appealing makes for lively exam room conversation, and we're obligated to include it. It is seldom effective. First, you have to identify the dog who's producing the doo-doo that is being dined on by your dog. Then you have to feed that dog a substrate that will render their stool less appetizing to your dog.

"Hello, Mrs. Nelson. Sorry to interrupt in the middle of your book club, but I was wondering if you might feed this bag of peppermints to your dog, Roger, over the next couple of weeks, as Tugger has developed a taste for his poop."

Other popular recommendations include pineapple and a product called For-Bid (available from our online store, only $18.69 for a twelve-pack).

The topical treatment approach.

Fearing that she was losing her tenuous grip on sanity, Ilene did not want her neighbors to become suspicious. After dark, she donned her Petzl LED headlamp and went on a scavenger hunt with an industrial-sized can of cayenne flakes, peppering the piles as she found them.

A continuation of the aversion by fire approach is to treat the piles with hot sauce. One wonders if there are breed-specific recommendations, Cholula for the Chihuahuas, Tabasco for the Catahoulas, and Sriracha for the Chows and Chins.

Desperate clients call on old-school wisdom: "Put it in a bag and tie it around their neck for a few days. That'll fix 'em." (It won't. It's gross, and you could create severe behavior issues. So just don't.)

At the Lake Mills Veterinary Clinic, puppy visits are scheduled for forty to sixty minutes. The first part of the conversation usually revolves around crate and house training, and then we discuss socialization in detail.

Research says that around sixteen percent of puppies eat poop. Club Coprophagy is a fraternity no owner wants to join. We have every reason to assume this statistic is under-reported. Anonymous support groups come to mind. "Hello, my name is Fletcher. I've been eating poop since I was a pup."

Should we add coprophagy counter-conditioning to the initial puppy visit? In doing so, we'd surely have to push every puppy visit to at least seventy minutes, an hour and a half if Mittsy is involved. If it is in the best interest of our clients and patients, we're happy to do that, but business is business. We'd have to find a way to market that service. Since her arrival nine years ago, our staff behaviorist, Mittsy Voiles, has been helping to guide us in making veterinary visits as stress-free as possible. The industry is now catching up. Fear Free has now become a certificate designation for veterinary clinics, complete with a governing body to ensure compliance.

After an exhaustive literature search (I googled it), I was unable to find any such governing body to ensure proper dissemination of information having to do with canine coprophagy aversion (CCA).

Should the Lake Mills Veterinary Clinic blaze the trail?

There will be questions. How will social media embrace this? We've always enjoyed a collegial relationship with our neighboring practices. Will being designated the county's only CCA clinic create an unfair competitive advantage, or would we absorb the hardcore addiction cases others would be happy to turf? Would we need to bring more trained staff on board and expand our facility?

You gotta look before you leap, lest we risk the fate of Bill VanAlstine.

Highlighting the ludicrousness of a decade when bell bottoms and disco were in fashion, pet skunks were popular in the '70s. Thinking he'd discourage the business, my mentor Doc V. charged $750 to de-scent a client's Pepe Le Pew. He instantly became the de-facto skunk guru of Macon County, Illinois.

We've established that (excepting malnourished and adult dogs with serious GI issues), CCA seldom has a medical basis, and grandpa's "rub their noses in it" approach may actually encourage the behavior.

So, seriously, what is an owner to do, and how do we blame this on Donald Trump?

The solution is easier to explain than it is to execute. Think of the three Cs: cleanliness and counter-conditioning. When he poops, pick it up. If you need to go tech or engage your eighth-grader, download the Puppy Potty Log app (seriously). And, you distract him. All the more reason to establish a solid recall from day one. The minute he squeezes one off, you call him to your side and reward him with an even higher value treat.

Plan B: Embrace the behavior.

Our dog Tugger is a Catahoula Leopard Dog. We call him camo dog. Sheila and I live on a seven-acre wildlife swamp where, on any given day, you can find evidence of deer, cats, raccoons, possum, and groundhog. And of course, the pièce de résistance—frozen horse poop. He loves to run the farm while Sheila and I do chores.

Tugger is also very social.

If he hears the neighbors laughing or the chickens cackling, he'll disappear like the friend that owes you twenty. We've come to know our neighbors by way of Tug. I once brewed a pot of chili as a peace offering to compensate for Tug's culling of their aging flock of layers.

We clipped one of Calvin's headlamps with a flashing red light to his collar to mark the little ghost through the endless months of darkness in the Wisconsin winter. There is a cadence when you're doing chores. You feed grain, check for Tug. Feed hay, locate Tug. Drag the hose to the water tank... . You have to keep an eye on him at all times.

That is unless he's locked on to a pile of scat. You don't want any kisses for an hour or so, but you know exactly where he is.

*I was all geeked out when I found out Erik Huth was an actuarial scientist, "You do know what we do, don't you?"

Under This Old Hat

John B. Stetson invented the cowboy hat in 1865. Ironically, the man who designed the icon universally associated with all things rugged and west was from New Jersey. Stetson was on a trek to Pike's Peak. In those days, the hats worn by cowboys and vaqueros were made of straw. Born of necessity, his signature model, The Boss of the Plains, was made of waterproof felt. The four-inch brim kept rain from running down his back all the way to a cowboy's crack and shaded his eyes when the sun shone. The crown formed a built-in bucket to pull water from a stream for his horse. The brim curled nicely to form a cup for the cowboy. I'm assuming they went upstream from where they'd just herded the cattle through the creek.

With thumb and middle finger clutching the crown, the rig was large enough to fan embers into flames for the chuckwagon or turn a thundering herd of cattle when waved above the cowboy's head.

The original design set forth by Stetson more than 150 years ago remains intact, untouched, and celebrated by card-carrying cowboys and country singers.

The most ear-splitting cheer of the night at a Garth Brooks concert will be in the middle of the third verse of "I'm Much Too Young to Feel This Damn Old." He'll sing, "Competition's getting younger, tougher broncs, you know I can't recall." The Oklahoma cowboy will pause with his hat over his heart. "A worn-out tape of Chris LeDoux, lonely women and bad booze, seem to be the only friends I've left at all."

LeDoux was a high school intercollegiate and National Finals Rodeo bareback riding champion. To make expenses of a travelin' rodeo hand, he turned to the lucrative craft of writing songs. In the early seventies, he met the woman who would become his wife. In declaring

 BILL STORK

his love for her, he wrote: "Under this ol' hat is the head you turned around."

It must have worked. They were married for thirty-three years and had five kids.

In "This Cowboy's Hat," LeDoux describes an encounter in a coffee shop. A biker having a bad day poked fun at his friend's Stetson. Looking to keep the peace, his buddy shared with the misguided motorcycle man the significance of his hat, the band that circled the crown, and the eagle feather he wore.

Chris LeDoux died in 2005 of liver disease. Garth volunteered to donate a lobe.

Lyle Lovett sings from experience. On his first post-Julia Roberts album *The Road to Ensenada*, he sings, "You can have my girl, but don't touch my hat." Clearly, a cowboy hat trumps the pretty woman.

I did not even recognize Tim McGraw as Sean Tuohy in *The Blind Side*. In khakis, loafers, and an Oxford, he could pass for a Walgreens pharmacist. Throw a microphone in his hand and a black Bullhide Shantung Panama Straw Western hat on his head, and he'll have women half his age swooning all the way to the cheap seats, ten years of CrossFit and $1,200 jeans, notwithstanding.

It's not all about cowboy hats.

I dedicated the better part of the eighties to book learning. The education involved four years in the College of Agriculture, followed by another stint at the College of Veterinary Medicine. (After graduation, Dad concluded that it'd take him six months *out back* to make me worth anything again.)

Summers, holidays, and spring breaks were spent working at the University of Illinois Swine Research Center. The summer of 1988 was an epic drought. It didn't rain for nearly three months, and I couldn't get a date to save my soul. My good friend Gary and I would start weighing pigs and cleaning pens at six in the morning. By three in the afternoon, we'd be on Lake Decatur carving an imaginary slalom course sixty-five feet behind a twenty-one-foot, under-powered towboat christened *The Cat Dancer*. Gary was out-skiing the old wooden slalom with a rear toe loop. He laid down four hundred hog-farm dollars for a new carbon-fiber, double high wrap, competition Connelly slalom, and two black corduroy hats. The second of which he gave to me.

One would assume that our farm tans and chiseled physiques would be all it would take when it came to courtin', but it never hurts to have a pitch. Minus boneyard creek and the borrow pits around the bypasses, Champaign–Urbana is landlocked. Since you can't exactly carry your slalom ski and tow rope into a bar, we figured the hats would surely draw campus coeds looking for a day on the lake like Winnie the Pooh to a pot of honey.

Not so much. It must've been the pig smell that kept them at bay.

That black Connelly corduroy hat was given by a brother. Without his support, there's no proof I could have gotten through the rough patches. Between agonizing over a left-shifted leukogram and an elevated ALP on a clinical pathology retest in vet school, I could adjust the brim and take a mini-mental excursion to the lake.

I refused to attempt any major academic challenge without that hat on my head and size twelve Red Wing Supersoles on my feet. After twenty-eight years of academia and dependence, I turned my tassel on May 15, 1992. I loaded the Bronco and crossed the Cheddar Curtain into Wisconsin. The cords had long since worn smooth. After a million or more agonizing adjustments while fretting over carbon rings in the Kreb's cycle, cardiac physiology, and muscular insertions and origins, the plastic brim cracked and gave up its Mosati curl*. After damn near a decade under the summer sun and classroom fluorescent fade, the red-to-yellow embroidered Connelly was legible only by memory. The hat rests in state, safely in a box in the basement.

For all the aspiring self-published authors out there, I offer some sales insight. The *New York Times* bestseller list remains just out of reach, and I still haven't heard from Oprah, but the pallet of books in my daughter's closet is slowly shrinking. First, whenever your book is done, release it in September or October. Books make the perfect Christmas gift. Second, don't miss a small-town holiday market, dog fair, or pet wellness expo. The booth fees can usually be covered with

BILL STORK

the sale of fewer than ten copies, and you meet a lot of really cool people. (Pro tip: request your booth between the fudge and kettle corn guys.)

There is an art to sales.

I have an eight-foot banquet table and a red and white checkered tablecloth given by my sister Sarah. It feels like Sunday dinner at Grandma's house. I cobbled together double-decker repurposed barnwood bookholders that display each of my two books, exposing front and back covers. Readers will approach slowly and go straight for the back-cover synopsis.

Anyone old enough to be grandparents or receive AARP junk mail will recognize my titles' association with *All Creatures Great and Small*. I have fourteen-by-seventeen cardboard images of the two book covers displayed on music stands. I cut down an art easel to hold a three-by-four repurposed barnwood bulletin board with an old picture of my dog Cooder, front and center. When the legions who love Labs pause and ooh, I'll tell them about the time he donated blood to save the dog of a boy in a wheelchair. I've stapled pictures of Calvin, Dad, and me at the John Deere Pavilion and views from the peak of Crested Butte around the periphery. A shot of Chief the Great Dane tilting his head like a goof has pulled folks across the aisle for a better look.

Shoppers want the courtesy to not be engaged if they're not interested. They walk by in stealth mode on the first lap. The art is not to make eye contact while making enough observations to relate to them. I have a camp chair and a book. I pretend to be reading. I peer over the top as dog lovers and holiday shoppers side-shuffle down the aisle, looking for clues and cues. T-shirts, sweatshirts, belt buckles, and most frequently, hats. Without fail, folks will wear their allegiance on their head—Packers, Brewers, Ranger Bass Boats, Trek Bicycles, New Belgium Brewing.

My favorite is to go for the guy in the John Deere hat who got dragged along by his wife. I'll have a bookmark on the page with a story about my Uncle Con, who saved the farm with eighty acres of popcorn and a two-cylinder John Deere Model A. For those with an Outdoor Life camouflaged lid, I have a Cliffs Notes version of "Buck," about an old

Chocolate Lab. There will always be guys and gals with a gold fish hook clipped to the brim who go for "Fishin' Magician," about my dad and his one-armed buddy, Harry.

At the 2015 Fort Atkinson Holiday Market, my booth was in the hallway between the rectory and gymnasium at St. Mark's Church. I saw him first in the bright light streaming through the clear pane of stained glass. Though he fit right in among the farmers, woodcarvers, and artists, his posture was out of place like Pa Walton at L'Etoile. He buried his hands in the pockets of his faded bibs. With his head pointed at the floor and his eyes slowly rising, he politely declined free samples from the salsa man and the kettle corn guy in the booths next to me.

Slow as a sundial, he rounded my easel. I knew his eyes would never rise. "Steamfitter?" I asked in his general direction.

His shoulders separated, back straightened, and his eyes briefly met mine, "Well, yeah."

"Looking for something for your wife," I took no chance at all. His face softened and eyes relaxed.

"We just bought a place out in the country, so money's a little tight, but I wanted to get her something nice."

"What do you have?"

"Ah, right now, just a half-dozen chickens, couple of dogs, and a goat. But if I let her, she'd have a whole zoo."

I asked him what she did for a living. "She's a nurse."

Ricky Van Shelton crooned inside my head as I thought of the woman who married this gentle giant. "She wears a gold ring on her finger, and I'm so glad that it's mine."

I pulled down my sloppy copy of *In Herriot's Shadow* and pointed to "So Thankful" and "Kim Kardashian," two short chapters about an uber-sweet herdsman and a kindly client we've known at the clinic for years. I acknowledged that after setting catheters and soothing patients all day, then building goat fence 'til dark that a gal wasn't

gonna last long in the La-Z-Boy with *War and Peace.* Dad's cousin reviewed my collection of short stories as "*a good one for the shitter.*"

I dropped my head, put my pen to the inside flap of the book, thanked her and her profession for their compassion and care, and signed my name. I'd be humbled if either one of them read a chapter.

He shook my hand as I handed him the book, then paused two steps from the table. "How'd you know I was a steamfitter?" I put my finger on my temple. He adjusted the short brim of his red and white polka-dot hat and smiled.

My family and friends had all gathered on the porch of our rental to celebrate the miracle of my graduation. Someone with a Kodachrome on the high side of the street took a drone's-eye view of the event. My first reaction was a moment of denial. My buddy Wes, the World War II veteran barber, called me Duroc for the wiry auburn mop he'd fashion into a flat-top. Either he wasn't tall enough to see the top of my head, or as a courtesy of the profession, he failed to mention—like a low spot in the middle of an Illinois bean field was an oval of lily-white flesh.

In the years to follow, I wrestled with rationalization and overcompensation, which have since settled into resignation. That I'm bald does not so much bother me as how I'm bald. I look at this old man in the mirror. There sits a homogenous ovoid globe of wrinkled flesh on my shoulders. Michael Perry famously calls it crop failure. Though I still won't wear them at the dinner table, or in church, I've taken to wearing hats as a lifestyle.

It really wasn't that much of a stretch.

I have written extensively on the purpose, fashion, and function of the touk. I keep fewer than three in constant rotation depending on outside temperature, how badly they smell, and my ability to find them when heading into the winter. I will seldom be seen without one from Halloween through Easter. The Connelly hat has been retired to the museum and replaced by a grey special occasions lid from my personal utopia, Camp 4 Coffee, just off Elk Avenue in Crested Butte, Colorado. (In small letters over the strap in back: Coffee, it makes you poop.) Seven years ago, when Dad pre-inherited Sheila and me the John Deere 2520, he got two free hats from the Sloan Implement dealer in Assumption, Illinois. Those two are getting faded and fit just about right for the sweat, grease, and cowshit occasions. Being a cradle flatlander, I'll be seen in a Packers lid that's been through the wash a few times, so my allegiance never comes into question.

I've always wanted the hat to complement my "I'm not on call" underwear, and so the maître d' doesn't ask, "Table for you and your daughter, sir?" when I'm out with Sheila.

Sheila and I were on a four-day weekend in Nashville. I lingered by Goorin Bros. hat store, trying not to be caught, like a pimple-faced eighth-grade boy in a Victoria's Secret. Finally, Sheila took me by the arm. Looking like a tattooed and pierced 2016 reincarnation of Janis Joplin, the clerk listened, "I'm looking for *the* hat." She understood. Though shopping of any sort makes me crazy, hats are infinitely more efficient to try on than pants. In a flurry of minutes that seemed like hours, I found myself standing in front of a three-direction mirror in a pea-green flat newsboy cap. Like Pitt or Clooney, I turned my chin two ticks to the right and a couple degrees up. I creased my left eye for a moment and nodded. "That's it."

The jury is still out on the hat, but before we parted, I asked Janis for a music reference. She looked at her watch and declared herself on break. It was the middle of a Thursday afternoon on South Broadway, and there were a dozen aspiring young songwriters with acoustic guitars strumming bar chords for tips. She led us past them all and straight to a bar where her friends, The High Jivers, were playing. They were a rockabilly bad-ass breath of fresh air and had us swing dancing with abandon at three o'clock in the afternoon.

There are hats I will not wear.

If someone helps me saddle him, and he's damn-near bomb proof, I can ride a horse. I've never faced the fury of a two-year-old green colt or roped a coyote at a dead run. I do not wake up every day, kiss my family goodbye, and place myself in harm's way to protect my community. I've never dragged a hose into a burning building or dodged flames to save a baby or a kitten. I can barely make a

bubblegum weld on two flat pieces of steel with a stick welder. I have never volunteered four years of my life in the protection of my country.

Therefore, I'll not be seen in a Stetson, police, fire, welding, or Army hat.

I have a hat I wear once a year. I have a hard-wired respect for the purpose and productivity of the blue-collar working men and women. I've never seen a student loan bill, thanks to a long-boom crane operator. Every Labor Day, I wear a white hat with the emblem of the International Union of Operating Engineers, Local 965.

Dad never missed a minute of overtime or a high school band concert. He shined his shoes and washed the '76 Mercury Marquis he paid cash for before taking Mom and me to a steak dinner. When he retired, he took Mom to New York City, because she said she wanted to go. In the ultimate expression of 'til death do us part, he cared for Mom until her last three months.

Old age, loneliness, and a dozen rogue blood clots have reduced my git-'er-done dad to a wheelchair. He has a navy blue Seabees cap featuring a pissed-off bumblebee clutching a machine gun that I put on him when we go out to eat and to church. His shit-eatin' grin is gone, but there is a momentary flash of pride when the cashier at The Family Restaurant offers her hand and thanks him for his service. ꝗ

Thanks, Maw

My daughter has taken to calling me every Sunday morning. She is finishing her third year of college in Burlington, Vermont. Paige is an officer in Engineers Without Borders. She's watched the sun rise over Machu Picchu and travels to Finland for the summer with less luggage than I take to a B&B in Cedarburg. For her to hold a Wisconsin address again is as likely as the Packers trading Aaron Rodgers for Jay Cutler.

Paige reads. Though she'd never be caught with a copy of the *Herriot's Shadow* series, she has penetrating insight and a keen perspective that an old guy could benefit from an injection of now and then. Since I failed to get her hooked on fishing and wood splittin', I'm always searching for fodder for our Sunday morning talks.

Her most recent suggestion was *Hillbilly Elegy: A Memoir of a Family and Culture in Crisis*, by J.D. Vance. Vance was born in Jackson, Kentucky, surrounded by abject poverty, addiction, and Mountain Dew. His family migrated up the Hillbilly Highway. U.S. Highway 23 is the route taken by southern folk in search of jobs that do not involve crawling into a dark hole or marketing corn by the quart. His family settled in Middletown, Ohio. While there were opportunities aplenty in the Rust Belt, the culture changed little.

Vance makes no attempt to portray himself as the Golden Boy. He dabbled in drugs, did poorly in school, crossed the law, and fought when he had to. He moved from one broken home to another, as his abusive and addicted mother bounced through countless violent relationships in search of a father figure for J.D. and his sister. In one poignant scene, she demanded his urine so she might pass a drug test for her job as a nurse. By way of happenstance or happy accident, he ended up in the United States Marine Corps. Those four years would prove to be transformative and earn him a ticket to The Ohio State University. He would graduate from arguably the most prestigious law school in the country. In his hand, he carried a shingle from Yale Law School; on his head, he wore the stigma of having grown up hillbilly like a crown of thorns.

Released in August 2016, *Hillbilly Elegy* brought attention to his people in the final rounds of a tempestuous election cycle, and landed Vance in the crosshairs of politicos, and on the couch of countless network news programs. At the time of this writing, *Hillbilly Elegy* had been on the New York Times Best Seller List for twenty-five weeks. Social scientists and politicians raged as to whether the Hillbilly condition was a case of mass under-motivation, failed policy, or a regional epidemic of learned helplessness.

When I finished, Paige asked for my review. I enjoyed the book but felt it was a bit redundant at times. Speaking with the authority of an author who once sold fifty copies at the Lake Mills Winter Market, I remarked, "I appreciate the authenticity of his voice but thought his language was a little loose at times."

Paige has less tolerance for my rhetorical ramblings than Sheila. She cut me off early. "Dad, that's because we're not the target audience for this book."

The challenges of working-class whites are a foreign concept to so many blue-blood elected officials. Inside The Beltway, *Hillbilly Elegy* was a revelation. Inside the Lake Mills Veterinary Clinic, it was a pretty good read and 261 pages of insight into the hillbilly among us.

Today, many of you know Mittsy as the indefatigable saint in the Subaru who has saved Freddy the Bassett from amputating the hand that feeds him, a legendary Lab named Guinness from inflicting undue embarrassment upon one of our favorite friends (due to his hobby of straddling visitors), and countless others.

I met Mittsy Voiles at a Humane Society of Jefferson County Spring Rabies Clinic. For those who have never attended, it is akin to a family reunion of *Duck Dynasty*, *American Pickers*, *Swamp People*, and *Keeping up With the Kardashians*, with five hundred barking dogs. For four hours, Mittsy arranged the chaos with pointed commands of,

"Can you kindly sit, stay, or come this way?" always preceded by, "Please," and followed by, "Thank you." Yet her tone left little room for interpretation.

Though her expression varied less than the Queen's Guard, her diction was riveting. As the people ambled past like the security line at a Kid Rock concert, with their dogs lunging on choke chains and baler twine, I cherry-picked her conversations. I'd pluck a hardened German consonant followed by a softly drawn y'all (clearly enunciating the apostrophe) as she directed the hunter with the Coonhounds to the on-deck circle. Seconds later, she said, "Please bring your pom-a-labra-dini-dor this waye." The hard A seemed to be surrounded on both sides by a Y.

When the din settled, I made an introduction that I can only hope lasts a lifetime. With a drawn brow and a wild eye, I asked, "Who the hell are you, and where are you from?" Her posture did not suggest my bluntness put her off.

"My name is Mittsy. I was born in Tennessee, went to school near Boston, spent some time in Wisconsin, and the last several years in Australia."

She shared that she was in the process of navigating some life changes. Our conversation ended with a handshake and a standing offer. The Lake Mills Vet Clinic had not offered puppy or obedience classes for several years.

I had a hunch.

When the call came, we met at Water House Foods. I asked if she'd ever taught before. She described the programs she'd started in Australia. Anticipating her move, she'd designed a secession so that her programs could continue. When I asked if she planned to teach again, she pulled out the four-inch black binder, ran her index finger down the table of contents, and then deftly flipped the corresponding dividers. One could easily send their child to the military or university with half the paperwork. There were legal forms, an enrollment sheet, a pre-class interview to establish goals for each family's puppy, homework and curricula for each week, cancellation policies in the event of weather, famine, or nuclear war, and an exit interview.

BILL STORK

It is nigh on to ten years since that meeting. Mittsy has woven herself into the fabric of our clinic and community. She's been a veterinary assistant, receptionist, IT liaison, social media consultant, and raised our behavior IQ a hundred points. We were a stress-less clinic years before Marty Becker took credit for the phrase. Her reward and positive reinforcement-based methods of dog handling have not always been met with immediate acceptance by the callous and camo sect on the other end of the leash. Choosing to earn, rather than expect, respect, I've watched as she spent a half-dozen Zuke's and ninety seconds to park the most exuberant seven-month-old Labrador pup at her feet. In doing so, she converted an old-school pheasant hunter from "put your knee in his chest, that'll show 'em" to a student.

My dad is in an assisted living center, and I'm convinced he looks more forward to visits from Mittsy and her partner, Barb, than me. (Editor's note: This is not true. Although, Bill Sr. does occasionally attempt to recruit our assistance in liberating his driver's license and car keys from his son.)

On page 127 of *In Herriot's Shadow*, I wrote: "I was born a conservative cradle Catholic. Since, I've been impressed upon by people practicing acts of selflessness and kindness that are in no way bound by orientation, ethnicity, or race. I've come to define the family as a group of people loving without condition, mutually respectful, and universally supportive."

I would like to think I had moved past the tackle-store racism and hog-barn biases I had been exposed to as a kid. Mittsy has barricaded the paths of small-mindedness with dignity and tolerance.

Though the parallels aren't perfect, Vance's corner of Kentucky could just as easily been Rogersville, Tennessee. Her home may not have been the iconic tin-roof shack, but they grew tobacco, raised and canned every bite of food they put in their mouths, and had no running water. She had the benefit of a nuclear family, but there was no shortage of moonshine, methamphetamines, and misdemeanors.

Shocked to attention by *Hillbilly Elegy*, the political administration scrambles to assemble policy to at least get credit for attempting to up the plight of the working-class white. In his conclusion, Vance boils it down to a bullet point that transcends politics and policy:

The single greatest determinant of one's trajectory in life is the influence of at least one steadfastly supportive, unconditionally loving role model. Personal perfection is not a requisite.

Vance's father was elusive; his mother was mentally ill. His Mamaw was as blunt as a butcher. She smoked, drank, and cussed like a construction worker, but she guided, supported, and loved him unconditionally.

Mittsy may have scrubbed her speech of the y'alls and fixin's, but to say she has risen above her bringin' up would be a slight that she'd edit off this book in an instant. She's got an Ivy League college education and more stamps on her passport than most of her family has trips to Knoxville. Still, she attacks every endeavor with the tenacity, frugality, and resourcefulness that survival depends on back home in Honeycutte.

To every friendship, she brings love and loyalty that defines her and becomes a source of strength for those of us within her circle. This, I suspect, we can trace straight back to her mom, Janie.

On the back porch holding court, Janie could go through a pack of cigarettes and a gallon of sweet tea between dinner and sundown. Get crossways of her kinfolk and find yourself staring down the barrel of a whole heap of trouble.

It took several years of lung cancer and a half-dozen blood clots to get her, but 2017 will be her family's first Mother's Day without her.

For those of us who have lost, we will take a few moments to reflect on the components of our core that are thanks to our mother's DNA and demonstration.

For those who are still here, give 'em a hug. ⋈

Popeye

Belle was the waitress you'd expect in a roadside diner three miles west of Nowheresville, Iowa. With porcelain platters balanced up her right forearm, she stooped to pour a warm-up from a steamin' pot of Farmer Brothers. Pastel rouge spackled on her cheeks was unable to hide the years. The liner on her lashes was no disguise for the longing in her eyes.

The retired construction worker, fire chief, and banker who always came to town for breakfast on the last day of their crappie crusades bantered friendly, something about Belle collecting eggs and milking the cow before she mopped floors and brewed coffee. Without breaking stride, she cracked the automatic smile of a single mother, working for tips.

Her soft drawl and you y'all's suggested circumstance had driven her north of her comfort zone. Dad asked her, "Where's home?"

"Aw, just across the Ohio River from Cincinnati," she politely dismissed.

She paused when he asked, "Anywhere near Covington?" So he continued, "You ever hear of a little guy named LeRoy Summers?"

Belle froze.

"You know LeRoy Summers," she couldn't have been more awed if Dad name-dropped Dale Earnhardt.

Skipping the middle chapters of her life that'd left her shattered, "LeRoy Summers is the kindest person I've ever met. He saved our lives."

Safe places to live and schools were on the Kentucky side of the river; jobs were in Cincinnati. Belle told of the 1965 LTD that was her family's lifeline to earn enough in rust-belt wages to put food on the table. On a good day, it would barely limp across the bridge. When it wouldn't, LeRoy would tow the old Ford to his shop and cobble it back together. A down payment, a handshake, and a fresh loaf of bread were his only compensation for another late-night rebuild of their alternator, carburetor, or timing belt.

If he could've stood straight, LeRoy "Popeye" Summers was still well under six feet. He had one glass eye and forearms that would have busted a rusted nut off an exhaust manifold. LeRoy looked up at almost everyone. He was looked down upon by no one. By the time he'd shaken your hand and asked, "How you doing there, young man?" you'd been sized up.

Dad and LeRoy had been the best of friends since sixth grade.

Brush College II Elementary was fifty yards past the half-acre garden and fruit trees in my grandparents' backyard. After school, Dad and LeRoy would play ball, shuck sweet corn, or pick tomatoes for my grandpa. They were always together. In their junior year of high school, Dad took a fancy to a lawyer's daughter named Doris Jackson. Doris Jackson took a likin' to LeRoy, or so she said.

Dad worked in the Kilbourne Chrysler garage, the Sloan Implement dealership, and farmed all through high school. LeRoy drove a wrecker and worked in his dad's service station. In the midst of the Korean conflict, with the draft in full effect, they enlisted in the United States Naval Construction Unit in 1954. Although Dad started in Rhode Island, and LeRoy in San Diego, for the last three years in the Seabees, even Uncle Sam could not keep the boys apart. They were both assigned to a base in Newfoundland. After the service, Dad stayed in Decatur and joined the Operating Engineers Local 965. LeRoy moved to Covington and opened his own service station. As the ultimate manifestation of her commitment to Dad and her indomitable good nature, Mom and Dad traveled to California, New Orleans, and New Hampshire with LeRoy and his wife, Phyllis. LeRoy was famous for his good nature and charity; Phyllis was not. The boys fished together once a year. They talked about fishing every Sunday afternoon.

Summers' Service was at exit 23 off Interstate 65. LeRoy was your savior in Cintas, with a red shop towel in his back pocket and his name in cursive on a white patch ironed on his left chest.

The afternoon sun bleached the lot outside the two bays in front of Summers' Service. LeRoy torqued the last two bolts in the head of a carb job. With his chest on the fender blanket and his feet barely touching, he pulled out from under the hood at the sound of a chirping fan belt. Nursing the crick in his lower back, he wiped grease from the nine-sixteenths-inch Snap-on and squinted at the arrival.

A harried young mother turned to referee two six-year-olds' hand-slapping and finger-pointing in the middle seats.

Six purposeful strides after a car door shut, the glare was eclipsed by a six-foot figure in a CPO jacket and a weathered pair of Red Wings. In his right hand, a shotgun case.

In his twenty years of owning the station, LeRoy had been robbed on several occasions, though never by a construction foreman with his gun in the case and his wife in the car.

Fully anticipating the old mechanic's perplexion, the man gently laid the case on the trunk of the Chrysler and stepped back. Shoulder dipped, LeRoy rolled his good eye at the stranger, wiped his hands, and pulled a Benelli Super Black Eagle semi-automatic shotgun from the case.

As LeRoy rubbed the walnut stock, sighting the barrel, Darren spoke first.

"Mr. Summers, fifteen years ago, I broke into this shop, cheap wine drunk and high on pot. Before I could get my crowbar wedged in the cash register, I heard a crash and a cuss. I didn't get three steps before a muzzle flash and a burnin' in my ass. That night, I spent three hours biting a towel and screaming like childbirth while a doctor and two nurses wrestled four hundred #8 lead shot out of my backside. I had a come-to-Jesus revelation: the road I was on was no kinda career path. As soon as I could sit again, I applied to the plumber's union."

His wife rolled the window down and waved timidly. "As you can see, those three are the world to me. Thank you."

The two shook hands like angle braces on a corner post.

A high-tone woman will clean out your pocketbook and ache your head. A good friend will eat your mom's liver and onions. Back in high school, LeRoy suspected Doris Jackson was more looking for a ride in his '36 Ford Coupe than dating him. Dad was still afoot. LeRoy just told her, "Nah."

For some, doin' the right thing takes a gentle prompt from a twelve gauge. For others, it's just in 'em. ⊾

Chores: Expectations, Accountability, and Professions of Love

*C*hores: *noun. A routine task, especially a household one. Alt. An unpleasant but necessary task. A chewy, single-syllable word, with one muddy vowel in the middle. Whether spoken by a software engineer in Chicago mowing the boulevard of his bungalow with an electric Craftsman or a Wyoming Cowboy riding fence lines, it always seems to come out sounding Midwest-mushmouth, "I'll be ready to go, right after chores are done."*

The word may feel like a wad of used barn shavings in the mouth. Yet, there are few things we can learn more, teach more, or benefit from more than doing chores.

To a nine-year-old boy burdened by unloading the dishwasher, it's like dragging an anvil. "Mom says I can't play kickball until after I do chores."

They were the ultimate kids' currency, long before we knew a dollar bill from a Benjamin. Assigned according to age and ability and inversely proportional to attitude. I was every kid. My first jobs were to take out the garbage and help Mom dry dishes. If I did a good job and had my geometry done, then I could go play basketball or help Dad put a new muffler on the Chrysler. I spent weeks collecting conduit and plywood and scabbed the hard plastic wheels off an old shop cart to cobble together my first pull-behind bike trailer, all to tow my Toro to the neighbors or carry two beat-up galvanized garbage cans fifty feet to the end of the driveway.

My introduction to negotiation was the day I convinced Dad that I was big enough to mow the grass. My allowance jumped from $2.50 a week to $7.50 (Dad 1: Kid 0). The job was in jeopardy the day he came home from work to find the self-propelled mower chewing at the foundation of the house like a carnival car off its tether. I was nowhere to be found.

Mom had come out of the house to tell me my best friend had called. "CT says the dogs got out of the fence." I did three and a half miles on a Schwinn Varsity in nineteen minutes. His pair of Schnauzers were securely in the chain-link. (His dad made us dig the post holes before he took us water skiing.) CT lived across from the entry to Baker Woods Estate Swimming Club. "Dogs are out" was code for "Kim Chizevsky is two blocks from the pool."

I was ten or eleven when Mom and Dad left me home alone for a few hours while they went to visit a friend in the hospital. Looking to earn another increment of trust, motivated by some intangible ethic, I was one possessed pup. I mowed the seven-tenths of an acre tight as the fairways at Augusta and raked every apricot I could get to fall from the three trees out back. I washed the F-250 and swept the garage.

Forty years on, I have the image of them pulling onto the gravel at the end of the driveway in the piss-yellow '72 Chrysler Newport. I'd just finished hosing the concrete. I signaled Dad to roll down his window. "'Scuse me, sir. You mind wiping your tires before you pull in?"

I never felt pushed or pressured by my parents—just loved.

My brother, Scott, is an attorney in Chicago. He drives a BMW, lives in a condo in The Loop, and shares a health club with Oprah, Michael Jordan, and Barack Obama. Realizing the perceived conflict of concepts, he has the purest heart of anyone I know. He listened politely as I told him about Sheila.

I'd met her shortly after crossing the Cheddar Curtain eighteen years ago. When her name came up in tailgate conversations among the guys, there was simply "something about Sheila." I began to understand what that something was ten years later when fate and our friends Ned and Sarah conned her first to the beer garden

at Tyranena, then into the passenger seat of my Subaru. We were heading from The Kristy Larson Trio to see Joel Paterson and the Modern Sounds in Madison.

With St. John's Lutheran Church and Joe Spoke's farm tucked under the mist of a September sunset in the twin valleys south of I-94, a feeling came over me like the heated seats were on high as she talked of working in the family garden. Just past the Route 73 exit, I gazed out the driver's side to see the stocking hat of Ryan silhouetted by a single bulb in the vestibule of the Haack farm as she spoke fondly of her grandma. After swing-dancing until bar time, we parted in the parking lot at four on Sunday morning. I didn't risk a hug, so I extended my hand across the console and thanked her.

I fought the urge to tell her I loved her, a battle my mouth would win with my heart exactly one time.

Ask a girl out to dinner. If she says, "I don't know. I have to do chores first," you've either been given the country equivalent of the classic "shopping with Grandma" brush-off or been served a slow ball right down the middle of the plate. Your response is the difference between a table for two overlooking the lake and a seat for one at the bar.

I am not famous for my confidence, but this time I was swinging for the fences. I showed up with a pair of work gloves in my back pocket and a Leatherman.

To a guy, doing horse chores is the equivalent of picking up a gallon of milk or changing a wheel bearing after working ten hours. Just git 'er done. To a farm girl, being in the barn among her horses and cats is better than the finest Pinot and a Prozac. Spend an hour in the barn, and you'll learn more about her than Match.com, OkCupid, and DATCP combined.

There are times in life you find a mate by way of shared interests. Others, love comes first.

Eight years ago, I would never have thought the smell of horses and cedar shavings on a fall breeze and a freshly swept barn would trigger a full-on serotonin surge. The sight of her car in the drive sets me to singin' a two-line ditty only the dogs will ever hear.

I told Scott how Sheila and I feed horses, clean barn*, bale hay, and share our days. I explained that I had learned if it was eight below zero and she had to go back to the clinic at midnight to foal sit, I was well-served to hurry home and have chores done before she got there. If she had conducted staff reviews that day, make her a casserole and a whiskey old fashioned, send her to the barn, and stay as far away as you can.

Scott will stand in a courtroom before jury and judge and argue fearlessly on behalf of his client like an articulate pit bull in a thousand-dollar suit. Ask him to step through a two-strand electric fence, and he approaches like he'll be sticking his head in a guillotine. Standing in the middle of a pasture grazed tight by six horses, I turned to see Scott holding his shoes shoulder high. He had once stepped into the grass in Grant Park. It took him fifty bucks and an afternoon to get the stain off the white soles of his Adidas. He chose to sacrifice his socks.

He didn't get it.

"C'mon, Hick. You gotta get her the hell out of the barn for a while. Take her for some tapas. Buy her a nice bottle of Chateauneuf-du-Pape, and then lay some of your fancy words on her. You know, tell her the wine features her hair."

I explained to Scott that his resemblance to Tom Cruise, personality, pedicure, and skincare routine is clearly working well for him. Any one of Scott's dates could be plucked from the pages of the Colombian Cosmo.

Here in Wisconsin, you'll get more cuddle time on the couch if your hand fits a fork handle than the homemade ravioli and a twenty-five-dollar bottle of wine at Trattoria No. 10.

The woman who nurses a seven-dollar corn broom until the bristles meet the braid is the one to trust with your pocketbook. She who concocts soaked alfalfa pellets, soybean oil, and Nutrena Senior feed for her thirty-year-old Quarter Horse and spends more money buying Nike Airs to protect the thin soles of a big Bay named Boom Truck, than on her best pair of cowboy boots, is the one you want holding your hand the day the doctor finds a lump.

Chores act as the currency of accountability and expectations and sometimes a profession of love that will outlive any collection of daylilies and phlox plucked from the roadside.

This spring, I knelt in the mud at the site in the pasture where we hope our front porch will be and asked if she'd wear a white gold and diamond ring on her left hand.

Seven years previous, my first major play was also shiny, round, and galvanized. The carriage bolts were about to pull through the rusty, once-green bed of the True Value wheelbarrow she picked stalls into. Four three-quarter-inch fender washers bought us another couple of years.

My head gets warm envisioning the soft of Sheila's temple the evening she pulled it down on its wheel, the handles solid in her hand.

Allow me to interject a couple of observations for the single young men looking to land a farm girl:

1. *You can haul her muck bucket, clean the water tank, or scrape the yard, but only clean stalls if you can keep her out of the barn long enough for the horses to shit 'em up again. You could have a PhD in stall picking from Texas A&M, but you will not meet her specs.*

2. *Feeding hay: To a horsewoman, a flake is as precise as any metric measure of weight or volume. To us, it's the way the bale falls open and how much we can grab without getting chaff under our shirtsleeve. You'll get it wrong. On a good day, she'll just pick some up, add some, or move it ten feet to the left, without saying a word.*

Micah's Ritual

OCD.

Many will inject the acronym to justify a tendency toward order and organization. Upon arrival at the clinic, Claire will first ensure that the deposit book is bound by her yellow paper clamp, and the client records on her desk are aligned parallel to the counter. At home, Sheila arranges our canned goods in alphabetical order, labels facing out.

"I'm sorry, it's just my OCD," they'll apologize. I find organization admirable and enviable. It is a strength I was born without. I once contracted a company cleverly called Ducks in a Row. I was filled with hope when their receptionist assured me they could organize anyone and anything. In fifteen minutes, their best two agents went screaming from the building like Mormon missionaries from The Moonlight Ranch.

Those possessing obsessive tendencies are often precise and productive; we call them engineers, doctors, and managers. Yet, to watch someone who truly has OCD is to gain an appreciation for the potentially crippling effects. We could not understand how it took Mittsy half the day to count prescriptions. We convinced her that Georgie would get relief from her back pain an hour sooner if the Gabapentin capsules were simply thrown into the prescription bottle, without first arranging them with their serial numbers in order. *(Editor's note: This is somewhat of an exaggeration.—Mittsy)*

Obsessive-compulsive disorder: Obsessions are unwanted, intrusive thoughts, images, or urges that trigger intensely distressing feelings. Compulsions are behaviors an individual engages in to attempt to get rid of the obsessions and/or decrease his or her distress.

Those with OCD can be obsessed with organization. This is not limited to humans.

Lilly is a miniature Schnauzer with a hundred toys. She will play with every one of them, so long as they start each day in the proper place—her basket.

We've known cats obsessed with hygiene. Bella was a cat who would not use her litter box if there was so much as a drop of urine in the clay.

Artfully avoiding all frat-boy metaphors, there are cats with exaggerated sexual tendencies. Koal Shipley was neutered at five months of age, and yet he was obsessed with a certain stuffed animal and the need to perform. Whether a monthly meeting of the book club or Thanksgiving dinner, he would find the social center of the gathering and have his way with his special friend.

Scientists believe OCD is a brain disorder. I'm hoping there is no significant environmental or learned component.

Days short of her nineteenth birthday, I got the call. Ashley could no longer get up. She was a legendary German Shorthaired Pointer who had whelped six pups. Ashley was obsessed with birds, mammals, and right-leaning political news. She's buried peacefully overlooking a pond on Highway 89, but no one who hunted over her would bat an eye if she were to come crawling out of her grave at the scent of a pheasant or sound of a shotgun. Her longevity and durability we'll attribute to genetics and a steady diet of hot, buttered, whole wheat toast for breakfast. Her drive? I'm thinking a product of attitude and environment. Ash was raised in a heavy equipment fabrication, repair, and towing shop. The crew at Steve's can rebuild a rotted-out garbage truck from stock steel and welding rod or yank a Cat D6 bulldozer out of a swamp. They are not quiet or cordial. Ash spent her days resting in a cedar bed under a shop cart from daylight until precisely four thirty in the afternoon.

Steve, Jason, or Rick knew to let her out of the shop, into the house, and turn the TV to channel 7. There she'd peacefully watch the *Fox Evening News*. Leave her with ABC, CBS, or CNN, and you'd risk having your couch turned to leather strips and stuffing, topped off with a steaming exclamation point.

Mittsy's designation as a Certified Professional Dog Trainer, Knowledge Assessed, is a hard-earned punctuation. She's spent her life working to reduce the stress of every animal on earth and to understand behavior. She can explain body language and expressions, as well as how to enhance human-animal interdependence, while only occasionally borrowing from anthropomorphism.

I asked her about Micah.

In the exam room, Micah was a dream. He'd take Charlee Bears and freeze-dried goodness gentle as a baby's hand. As I knelt with a three-cc syringe and cotton ball, he'd offer his paw like he gave blood every day. Micah had a presence that moved you to tuck in your shirt, lint roll your jacket, and skip the weather and Packers banter. I'm sure he could balance the bank deposit at the end of the day.

I asked the history questions. "Have you noticed any new lumps and bumps, coughs, lameness, itching, and has he been eating normally?"

When I got to number six, they responded, "I guess it depends on what you consider normal."

I creased my brow, "Is he off feed? Does he vomit, have diarrhea, polyphagia? How much does he eat?"

"Well, he eats about two cups of food a day, but it takes him all day to do it."

I explained that it's not unusual for certain breeds to graze throughout the day.

"Yeah, but why in the hell does he have to make a mess of it first?"

They went on to explain.

At precisely 5 a.m. and p.m., Micah waits politely for his cup of kibble. He then picks up the bowl and dumps the entire contents on the floor. They've tried stainless steel and clay bowls, attempting to curb the behavior. One poured in concrete only resulted in a deep dent in the hardwood floor.

 BILL STORK

Then, he creates.

One kibble at a time, he'll make Micah's daily design. On sunny spring days, he may be whimsical, creating concentric circles or swirls. Dark days are more literal, with parallel lines: vertical, horizontal, or diagonal. His spacing is always perfect, and each kibble is oriented flat side down. Fascinated visitors have turned over a chunk, earning them a death stare until they apologetically restore his art to its intended form.

Ever since Lassie told Paul, "Timmy's fallen down the well," man has asked, "I wonder what he's thinking."

If I could know what any one dog was thinking, it would be Micah. ꔞ

Kickin' Back on the Merramec (and Fishin' With My Dad)

My friend Kevin Deforest sang, "I'll never catch a feeling, quite like the one I had,

Kickin' back on the Meramec, and fishin' with my dad."

On the first listen, I thought, "Man that's a good idea, but I've gotta mow the grass, clean out the truck, fix the fence where the deer went through, and knock down the back pasture before the burdocks come on."

Then I got Harry Chapin stuck in my head. "I've long since retired, and my son's moved away. I called him up just the other day. I said, I'd like to see you if you don't mind. He said, 'I'd love to, Dad, if I could find the time.'"

Dad worked twelve-hour days setting steel. He was never too tired to play catch. I picked up the phone.

I trusted that, at some point, the f'd up notion of nobility I fought to suppress would fade to silent. Dad put his family first every day of his life, taught me everything I know, and drove used pickup trucks to save money and help me pay for college. I recall one time he was laid off. He was painting our cantankerous neighbor's house before I got home from school, the same day. As if driving 250 miles south and taking thirty-six hours out of my life to sit in a boat with him oughta nominate me for the 2015 Son of the Year award.

Dad was never one to leap knee high and click the heels of his Wellingtons, but his lack of reaction was deafening. He nearly tried to talk me out of it, and not of the, "Aw shucks. I don't want you going through all the trouble," vein.

We've fished Lake Shelbyville since the day they dammed the Kaskaskia River in 1970. Father's Day 2015 near the crack of 7 a.m., Dad idled into the mouth of Coon Creek, cut the 150-horse Merc, and dropped the trolling motor. We sat gently bobbing in the lull of the wake of a '70s Ski Nautique dragging an old-school slalom skier. For forty minutes, not so much as a word was spoken or a tremble on the tip of my ten-foot fiberglass fly rod.

The U.S. Army Corp of Engineers established a three-hundred-foot buffer zone around Lake Shelbyville. There isn't a house on the twenty-six-mile man-made recreation and flood control mecca. My despise deepened for the US Cellular pitchman who boasts of his towers "out here" at the sight of a hundred-foot galvanized eyesore gashing the western horizon. The thought flew through my head, that if something were to happen, I'd be glad for five bars of reception. Or would I? If Dad could write his own encore, it'd be sitting in the bow of his boat with his Fenwick fly rod in his hand.

As if thirty years ago idled past my eyes, a young boy and his dad eased past us in the cove. Six years old with an orange puffy PFD framing his chipmunk cheeks, the boy absently drug the minnow net in the water. With the tiller of a ten horse Johnson in his hand, Dad scanned the shoreline and deadheads for the next spot that might be hiding bluegill or crappie to tickle his kid's bobber.

Dad's stoicism was striking. If I told him I had grass to mow and wood to cut on a weekend, he was the man who'd pull his red Ram into the parking lot of the clinic ten minutes before my eight o'clock appointment Friday morning, after driving from home and stopping for biscuits and gravy at Cracker Barrel in Janesville. I'd never known him to drop the first line more than ten minutes after sunrise, let alone 7 a.m.

One thing he had spot-on. "Son, when we've caught all the fish in this old lake, I'll take you to Dalton City. We'll have the best hamburger you've ever had from the ugliest bartender you've ever seen." With its smoker's shack out back, gambler's corner, and set against the backdrop of a dozen grain bins, The Shamrock Pub woulda made a fine episode of *Diners, Drive-ins, and Dives*. What Marge lacked in looks, she doubled in charm. Delivered in a plastic red basket, with a slab of sharp cheddar and a forkful of fried onions, the burger will be the cover of George Motz's second edition of *Hamburger America.*

The stretch alongside Highway 121 between Mount Zion and Mattoon is some of the most productive land in the nation's breadbasket. For better than a century, the farmers have had a friendly competition for braggin' rights on who can get their corn and beans in the ground first. Intent on taking in the high clouds and endless horizons of Race Horse Flats and maybe a seven-minute siesta, I politely declined all three of Dad's offers for me to drive his truck and boat home.

Any room for rationalization and hope was dashed as Dad swung wide of the drive at 54 Lynette Place. The man who could back the Queen Mary through a keyhole could not get his nineteen-foot Crestliner between the sweetgum tree and the gravel pad where it belonged. In the long straight-line of Highway 39 homebound, I came to grips with the notion that I was soon going to have to know how to load a grease gun, square a corner, and wire the lights on my own trailer.

On July 20, 2016, our cousin Jim called. "Bill, we've got problems. Your dad's driven out in the middle of a cornfield, and we can't find him." In the fourteen months to follow, we'd be through four hospitals and two nursing homes. Nights spent in a plastic recliner listening to the pulse of the fluid pump and the hiss of an oxygen mask give a guy time to do some thinking.

Once a man loses his dad, it is up to him. He's the one who's supposed to know all the stuff. I'm not sure I'll ever be comfortable with that.

Alzheimer's/dementia is a heartless bastard of a disease that eludes medical science and defies Mother Teresa. It robs a person of their personality and their mind long before their heart stops. Doctor Philbin was wonderful. She assured me there would be down days. I'd walk away thinking I oughta shine my shoes and press my funeral coat. Other days, I bought night crawlers to take him fishing, but I always knew there would be a time of imminence.

I knew whether it lasted a day or a month, the vigil would be a unique and beautiful time. I decided I'd open my ears, eyes, soul, and my pores and absorb.

I had no clue.

 BILL STORK

I was consoled by a one-handed dairy farmer who'd lost his dad over twenty years ago and a woman who'd battled breast cancer for two years. She never missed a workout and came out swingin' on the other side, training to be an EMT. One October morning, I euthanized a thirty-one-year-old mare for a woman who'd been by her husband's side every day since his catastrophic motorcycle accident two years previous. "She was my therapy horse," she spoke through the tears. "I lost both my parents within two weeks when I was thirty-six."

As I sat by Dad's side, I realized the CNAs and aides who helped feed, bathe, and administer his medication never knew my dad. I told them about the morning his neighbor set out to dig a foundation for a new deck with a shovel and wheelbarrow. In an hour, Dad returned with a Cat tractor backhoe. The job that could have taken the banker all summer was done by noon. I told of him selling a well that belonged to a 6 foot 5, 240-pound retired rodeo hand, Marine, and construction worker, to a green young laborer who'd bought a place in the country five miles away. I shared with them how I learned to drive. After working sixty back-breaking hours of construction, Dad would take us camping. Once off the state highways, he'd turn the wheel of the Ford three-quarter-ton and twenty-one-foot boat over to his thirteen-year-old son. He'd recline in the passenger seat with his right arm out the window and his left clutching a PBR.

And I listened.

It hurt to watch Karen walk. You could see the swelling in her left knee through her scrubs. Yet, she worked two full-time CNA gigs. She would sit with Dad, holding his hand and kissing his forehead as she told him she loved him. When I thanked her, she shrugged, "Oh, I'm just taking care of my friends."

And then there was Rainbow Hospice Care. In support of the staff at Lilac Springs, they labored to ensure that as the end drew near, he was not begging for oxygen, free of bedsores, and shaved.

In short order, my dad shrank and my gratitude grew. I had fifty-two years with an exemplary dad.

Mother Teresa said, "Blessed are the sick."

Bill Stork says, "There is no force more debilitating than lack of purpose."

We can treat congestive heart failure, pneumonia, and sometimes cancer. We can support or replace failed kidneys. There is no injection, pill, or intervention for the broken spirit of a man whose identity was producing, protecting, and caring for his family and friends.

That's exactly what he did, until his last breath—and beyond.

He and my mom preached it forever. In his last year, I learned to understand, appreciate, and respect the selfless gestures of good people.

Now, I'll spend the rest of my days attempting to measure up. 🐾

Big Boys Don't Cry

One image I have stored on the hard drive is my daughter's first thunderstorm. From Zeloski's Hill to Wilkie's Oak View Farm, an ominous bank of thunderheads roiled coal-black, purple, and split-pea green. With Paige swaddled in her summer-weight footy PJs, restless from a missed nap or a burp that hadn't arrived, I stepped to the porch. As lightning flashed her face like Grandma's Instamatic, the tears stopped short of her chin. Her whole body perked at the thunder rumbling like a dump truck on a cattle path.

Sadness gave way to wonder. Her face softened as the raindrops pushed past the pines and filtered through the screen, landing on her cheeks.

Ah yes, the world as seen through the eyes of a child.

No less impactful—the world as perceived from the other end of a leash.

Donna Kopp asked, "Well, c'mon, Bill. Have you ever tried walking without a dog? What's the point?"

Diane and Larry Alward are Diesel's third and final home. Diesel weighed in last Friday at just over a hundred pounds. He can vaporize four cups of his special prescription hypoallergenic diet in seconds, but the three things the boy requires more than kibble are lovin', ice cubes, and walking.

Hours with Mittsy, and sixty milligrams of fluoxetine in the morning, have managed to assuage much of the accumulated anxiety that is surely the product of, or the reason for, his tortuous path to Lake Mills, Wisconsin.

What's left, Diane has opted to walk right out of him.

On Thursday morning last week, I had pulled to the curb in front of Lakers Athletic Club and Steve's Car and Truck Service (and preachin' parlor). As I texted my ETA to the Griswold farm, I looked up to see Diesel and Diane southbound, past the headlights of the flatbed as Jr. pulled out to make room in the service bay for the first oil change. Six blocks from home, they've walked the town from Lakeside Lutheran to Interstate 94 by way of the Sentry Store and Country Campers.

On Friday morning, the appointment jumped off the screen: Diesel Alward, ADR. Every profession has its abbreviations. "AGE" is Claire's conception for anal gland expression, the cure for the Boxer butt drag. "V and D" is vomiting and diarrhea, "DDLA" is dull-depressed-lethargic-anorexic. "PUPD" is short for polyuria/polydipsia; she's drinking the toilet dry.

ADR is an Illinois acronym for "Ain't Doin' Right."

Twenty-four hours ago, he was dragging Diane down Main Street in the home-stretch of a two-and-a-half-mile walk.

I was cautiously optimistic when Diesel came bustin' through the door like Clay Matthews, but experience has taught us that clients' concerns are always justified.

"So, Diane, what's he doing?"

"It's what he's not. On our walk this morning, he just sat down and quit after one-eighth of a mile. He barely wanted to move. When I got him home, I opened the freezer and cracked an ice cube tray. He didn't even lift his head. Then I called you."

Every dog has his prognostication prop. "Ice-cube negative" for Diesel Alward is a signalment as significant as vomiting, diarrhea, or a prolonged cough.

I checked his mucus membrane color, hydration, heart rate, respiration, temperature, lymph nodes, peripheral and central nervous reflexes, and did an ophtho exam. All normal. If the history and physical do not yield a definitive diagnosis, it's time to take some samples.

If there's dead-air while waiting on bloodwork, we'll try and make small talk. Diane broke the silence as I pondered my list of differentials.

  BILL STORK

"Kids just love him when we walk past the playground. What really strikes me is that little girls are quick to approach and ask if they can pet the hairy, black giant, but boys just stand back." And the gender divide is not age-dependent. "At the Farmer's Market on Wednesday evenings, women are quick to bend down and get a face washing. The guys are more interested in free samples of smoked cheddar cheese curds."

Her tone was that of curiosity, but her observation didn't sit right with me. The only answer I could muster at the time was, "Hmm…" At that moment, I was more concerned with getting Diesel back on the road and ice-cube positive.

It's taken a week, but Diesel is eating, drinking, and eliminating on schedule. His walks are still short.

I've been thinking about the men and boys too preoccupied to dignify Diesel with a butt scratchin'.

I recall Keith McFarlane stretching the width of the exam room, his 230 pounds heaving and sobbing as he stroked the legendary Taylor's ears. From pulling him laps around the frozen lake in fourth grade through his firstborn child, he'd never known life without the maniacal black Lab.

One of the most meaningful moments of my practice was Dan, the truck driver, and me in Carhartts and coveralls, hugging and crying in the shadow of the corn crib when we finally said goodbye to Buck. Years later, I fumbled for the exam room door handle, tears pooled in my glasses, when Jon Dotzler put his arm on his son's shoulder as he kissed Mikey on his little Beagle nose and whispered, "I love you, buddy."

Not so much in defense of my gender, but more an assurance to Diane: little boys on the playground may be paying too much attention to the little girls. Young men at the Farmer's Market might be obsessed with the salsa man's Ghost pepper salsa.

But, just before the Rainbow Bridge, there's no doubt. Grease stains, calluses, Little League Baseball caps—big men, tough guys, and little boys all cry. ☖

Say What?

Six o'clock already
I was just in the middle of a dream
I was kissin' Valentino
By a crystal blue Italian stream
But I can't be late
'Cause then I guess I just won't get paid
These are the days
When you wish your bed was already made
It's just another manic Monday

Since long before The Bangles, everybody from Garfield the cat to Jimmy Fallon have begrudged the lowly Monday. It is my nature to try and buck such trends. After all, Mondays are repeatable and required.

On Monday, November 6, the wheels fell off.

Some background.

After the untimely demise of Dr. Robert Anderson, the founding German of the Lake Mills Veterinary Clinic, I found myself flying solo. At one point, I was on call for five straight years. By the time salvation was delivered in the person of a pinch hitter in Pella green coveralls, I was ready for a break. I scheduled a high-mountain bike excursion through Colorado with my brother John Humphries. I handed off the pager, and the disconnection was complete by the end of the driveway. I pulled into the Kwik Trip for a cup of Cafe Karuba and a newspaper. I celebrated every sip from Kwik Trip to the Milwaukee airport.

In addition to fancy coffee, reading *The Wall Street Journal* was a pleasure on vacations. When the American Airlines gate agent

  BILL STORK

announced the expected ninety-minute delay, I just folded the rag flat to the Lifestyles section and became one with the Naugahyde. Fashion is crucial on the driveways of dairy barns of Southern Wisconsin. I'd see what I could glean from the 5th Avenue Collection.

Business ownership is self-induced manic depression. When the phone is ringing, and the door is swinging, you're fantasizing about early retirement and a new road bike. The minute you hit a cancellation and ten minutes of telephone silence, you're fearing the next call will be Mike down at the Bank of Lake Mills, looking to repossess.

The party-line bias of morning cable news had once been amusing. For fifteen minutes, the talking heads and blonde du jour on *Fox and Friends* on the TV at the health club would convince us that Barack Obama and Democrats were dumb as a box of rocks. Then Richard would march in, commandeer the remote, and flip next door to CNN where they try and convince you we're all headed to hell in a handbasket with the Bushes, Lindsey Graham, and Ron Johnson giving directions.

Looking to stabilize these excursions, I wanted to know what was really going on in the world. So, ten years ago, I realized that I didn't have to wait for my next relief vet and vacation out west, and I subscribed to *The Wall Street Journal*.

A decade into my subscription to the WSJ, here is what I've learned. On Mondays, Wednesdays, and Fridays, BlackRock, Morgan Stanley, and hedge fund managers all agree the sky is falling, and Warren Buffet makes billions. On Tuesdays, Thursdays, and Saturdays, the economy is flying high, and Warren Buffet makes billions. So if the market thrives on volatility, could the tail possibly be wagging the dog?

Attempting to get back to last Monday.

The approximate layout of the WSJ front page is as follows: along the spine will be a synopsis of the twenty-four most relevant stories within. A picture and lead-ins to stories of acquisitions, mergers, and who'd pissed in Donald's Cornflakes the previous day will dominate the body of the page. On November 8, 2016, the Electoral College elected Donald Trump, our forty-fifth president, rendering hard news and satire sadly indistinguishable. Nestled quietly along the bottom tray will be a lighter news story: "Try Serving a Neutered Chicken," "Make Room for the Olive Garden Diet," or "Turkey's Window Tinting Rules."

On Monday, November 6, I opened *The Wall Street Journal* to see the headline:

"What Do Fuzzywogs, Toad-Stranglers, and Devilstrips Have in Common? A Dying Dictionary."

The Seussical title belied the ominous implications of the news to follow.

The dictionary that has bitten the dust is *The Dictionary of American Regional English (DARE)*. The project was birthed by an ambitious lexicographer from the University of Wisconsin named Frederic Cassidy.

DARE was launched in 1962, intending to document words, phrases, syntax, and pronunciations that vary across the United States. Cassidy sent teams of researchers in pea-green Ford vans affectionately known as "word wagons" from Hawaii to Maine. Armed with reel-to-reel voice recorders and a list of 1,600 questions, they intended to document and record how people spoke.

The researchers found folks quickly wandering off into left field from the list of questions, but Cassidy instructed his army to not attempt to keep their subjects between the lines. Intent on learning how speech patterns, phrases, and grammar varied across the United States, they quickly found themselves documenting history.

Their plan was to publish by 1976, a goal that seemed reasonable, until the Tennessee team interviewed a precocious little hillbilly girl and her mother in a place thought to exist only in the lyrics of a Loretta Lynn song. Ten years later, the team emerged from Butcher Holler with heads spinning and ears ringing.

Finally, in 1986 they released A through C and charged on, full of piss and vinegar, chanting the nerdy battle cry, "On to Z!"

In 2012, DARE was released in six bound volumes and a digital version.

 BILL STORK

Funding to complete the original DARE came from individuals, institutions, and businesses. Thanks to the internet and a population that is both diverse and dynamic, language is evolving more rapidly than ever. Yet, somehow, it was more sexy to create DARE than update it. Financial support has dried up like NASCAR sponsorship. The *Dictionary of American Regional English* will officially go the way of the Walkman, relegated to some dusty table at a county fair flea market between a plastic pair of Air Jordans and a Zebco rod and reel. A dedicated crew of volunteers will attempt to update the digital version now and again.

DARE has been used by northern lawyers deciphering cases in Kentucky. Publishers and actors have used it to master dialects, and doctors have referenced it, hoping to communicate more effectively with patients. "So, how are you, sir?" asked the doctor.

"Not so good, Doc. I've lost my nature." Thanks to a quick consult with DARE, the doc was able to scribble a script for a dozen little blue pills and three refills. A follow-up visit found the old guy all shits and giggles.

So, what are you asking us to do, Dr. Bill? Can I get a copy from Walmart or Amazon? Actually, DARE is available on Amazon Prime.

More than anything else, my goal is awareness.

DARE is an academic documentation, validation, and explanation of the diversity within the beautiful instrument, which is the English language, that a team of academics could capture in fifty years of trying.

And they barely scratched the surface.

Lester Holt and Megyn Kelly speak the language according to Merriam-Webster. Call it colloquialism, vernacular, or slang. Spoken on job sites, auto shops, churches, and brewpubs lies the language of creativity, ethnicity, productivity, and humanity.

Last November, Tom Gallitz and Jon Bound ignored a stout north wind, imagining how our house will be situated so Sheila and I can sit on the porch sipping coffee, holding hands, and watching the sun set. "Well, Jon, I'll poke the drive right up that fence line on the east."

Turning, he pointed at the pile of fill left over from the machine shed. "I'll peel the trees off that nob with the hoe and shov'r down in the gully. The water already wants to wander off down the laneway, but we'll throw a swale in just south of the property line." He motions his right hand, palm down, "Just in case we get a real gullywarsher."

A couple of years back, on a Helly Hansen, chili-eatin', Scotch drinkin' day, snowflakes the size of a spoon flew horizontal, accelerating under my hood and down my neck. I had five more cow calls on the schedule when my headlamp panned an oil slick in the farm-drive rivulets under my truck.

"Hey, Junior, Bob. Doc's got a blown fuel line on that Dodge he drives. One of you start at the tank, the other at the motor. I don't want to see nothin' but elbows and assholes until that pile of scrap-iron is the hell out of my shop."

I mentioned I'd heard about a car driving through an old dairy barn off Stony Brook Road. "Oh yeah," said Junior, "he folded up the corn crib like a shoebox. Musta been snoozin' and cruisin', cuz the oh shit marks on the road were only ten feet long. The driver was missing in action, but he took the seat covers along for a diaper."

DARE had nothin'.

My grandma died a week after she'd cooked us Thanksgiving dinner in 1983, only after she'd finished her Christmas shopping and bowled in three leagues. I can't eat a ham and cheese sandwich, or sit on a davenport, without recalling the woman whose last diploma was from fifth grade, but who could butcher chickens, cipher any number preceded by a dollar sign faster than Hewlett Packard, and died with three chest freezers full of food and not a nickel's worth of debt.

 BILL STORK

I've lived in Wisconsin for twenty-five years. I've been called to the Strasburg, Fedkenheur, and Griswold farms to aid Holstein dairy cows (emphasis on the nice hard Northern European *c*). Some of the most common maladies took place in fresh cows before the stanchion barn gave way to free stalls. Sometimes they wouldn't clean, toss their calf beds, or flip their stomachs.

Just as I don't think I could find my way to a farrowing barn or tie a knot in a feed bag without a wad of chew between my incisors and my lip, talk to me about hawg farmin' and fishin'. The syllables get fewer, the vowels get muddy, and the *g*'s all get replaced by apostrophes.

As a tribute to those who have shaped us, we phrase, inflect, and drawl. We cling to their faith, aspire to their character, and remember.

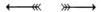

P.S. Dedicated followers of DARE lamented the loss. They cited the disappearance of the elusive New England *r*. Traditionally, New England's Mason-Dixon Line was the Green Mountains of Vermont. Over the last twenty years, those who drive their cahs to the bahs have migrated east, some think as far as the White Mountains of New Hamsha.

Not to worry, the *r*'s are well cared for in Central Illinois—every time we warsh our cars before taking the kids to our nation's capital, Warshington, D.C.

Put Me In, Coach

U.S. Bank Stadium in Minneapolis is turning out to be a house of horrors for Packers fans. The Vikings cordially invited us to their housewarming party in 2016, only to send us back across the Mississippi River with our tails tucked. On October 15, 2017, Aaron Rodgers rolled right and flicked a pass through the hands of Martellus Bennett, two steps before Anthony Barr arrived to crush the quarterback's right clavicle and Super Bowl aspirations of millions of Packers fans.

From Lake Superior to Galva, Illinois, and to Quinn's Packer Bar in Kailua-Kona, Hawaii, Packer Nation was consumed by a paralyzing depression. They lashed out at Olivia Munn. "If she hadn't made him go vegan." The optimists postulated that by way of titanium, super-human callous formation, and divine intervention, he'd be back in time to lead us to the Super Bowl. One particularly fatalistic mechanical engineer assumed the stance in the middle of a bar and demonstrated in detail how he'd never be able to make the throwing motion again and be forever banished to a broadcasting booth with Boomer Esiason.

On Wednesday, December 13, the *Wisconsin State Journal* splashed the biggest headline since Armistice Day—"Rodgers Cleared to Play!" The armchair experts started anew. In the pre-dawn of Thursday morning, between sets of tricep pushdowns, Ty Neupert panted, "He's nuts, man. There's no way we're going to the playoffs, and even if we do, our defense couldn't stop Kenny, and he's seventy years old." Ty presides over my debt at the Bank of Lake Mills and is built like a free safety. He oughta know.

About that time, a text message alerted me to a down cow. I pulled my coveralls over my Red Wings and headed from the sweaty old

BILL STORK

gym into the pre-dawn. I captured the low-res magenta glow of the hoarfrost sunrise and asked, "What would Ed Wollin do?"

My friend Scott Clewis is a medical malpractice attorney in Chicago. Hopefully, you never require surgery. If you do, it will likely go smoothly. If not, call Scott. Ed Wollin milks cows and farms with his two sons Erich and Kyle. A few years ago, both Scott and Ed had surgery to repair badly torn rotator cuffs.

Time out for a quick anatomy clarification. I've heard the rotator cuff referred to as rotator cup, rotor cup, rotary cup, or my damn aching shoulder. Understood only by a handful of orthopedic surgeons, it is an assembly of muscles and tendons designed to keep the head of the humerus seated firmly in the rather shallow acetabulum of the clavicle. It is either a poorly engineered piece of anatomy or the good Lord does not intend us to paint ceilings or play tennis because injuries, by way of repetitive motion or trauma, are very common.

Aaron Rodgers did not tear his rotator cuff. Scott and Ed did.

Ed's wife, Kathy, drove him down to Fort Atkinson Memorial.

Scott called his colleagues and searched malpractice documents to see who had repaired the shoulders of other elite athletes and been sued the least. He narrowed the list of Chicago's most reputable physical therapists to five and scheduled interviews with each (seriously). To remain productive, he downloaded voice recognition software that could translate opiate-influenced legalese and retained the services of a driver, assistant, and a nutritionist for six weeks post-operatively.

I asked Erich and Kyle how long Ed took off after his surgery. "Are you kidding? He took the whole week!"

"Yeah, but I finally got these knuckleheads to weld an extra handle on the tractor and figured how to shovel feed with one hand. Then, I was good to go." Ed defended his five days on the PUP list.

I've worked for Tim Claas for nigh on to twenty-five years. You may recall my reflexes have been kindly described as "glacial," yet so far, I've (mostly) avoided solid contact with flying feet. Then again, I only have to violate his cows long enough to palpate their ovaries and uterus. Tim has to milk them twice a day. Halfway through evening milking, he knelt to attach the unit to a fresh heifer who had yet to associate the claw and the soothing sensation of an oxytocin surge. She stomped on his right foot. His fourth metatarsal snapped like a sapling under a tractor tire and set him hopping around the barn ranting and cussing. Leaning on his cow-sorting cane, he hobbled over to the milk cart for his phone.

A-Rod had Brett Hundley to come off the bench. Tim did not have a backup. He'd have to finish milking, feed calves, and feed before he could go to the Fort Atkinson ER. They'd either put a cast or a boot on his foot, so he dispatched his wife, Lisa, to go to Farm and Fleet to pick up three pairs of Tingley's, sizes 12, 13, and 14. Keep the receipt, and we'll take back the ones we don't use.

From the time he was twelve, Wayne Kasten missed sixty milkings. Not bad for a guy who fought off two rounds of colon cancer and about half as long as the doctors ordered him to stay out of the barn after they'd removed several feet of intestines. Twenty years later, when his ostomy dehisced, he crawled half across the dooryard to the barn. He didn't go to the hospital until he'd milked the cows and fed the calves, pushing his intestines back in his abdomen each time he bent over. As they picked silage from his stoma, doctors and nurses speculated that another thirty minutes and he'd have been toxic and dead.

It's minutes until kickoff. Aaron Rodgers says he's not coming back to save the season; he's coming back to play quarterback.

What else is he gonna do? ⌕

Giselle and Louis

Like every business in the service industry, we try and schedule as accurately as possible and move with purpose. Some days, the wheels fall off. A cow with a prolapsed uterus or a Pit Bull versus trailer hitch will set you back like lightning at a Little League game.

It was ten o'clock on a Saturday morning. The parking lot was like a Taylor Swift concert, and the lobby was something out of Springer.

Giselle pushed through the crowded clinic with the look of a Victoria's Secret model slapped with rotten cow placenta, cleared her throat, and announced to no one eligible or inclined to listen, "Someone needs to see my dog—now."

Claire quick-glanced and extended a raised index finger of acknowledgment before finishing discharge instructions for Mary Daubert's cat, Ted. A registered nurse, mother, and mountain bike champion, Mary raised her eyebrows, "Good luck with this one."

Like a New York traffic cop, Claire turned with an open palm and politely put line three on hold.

The quarter-cock of Giselle's impeccably coiffed head and flare of her nose-job connoted her annoyance at Diesel, Chief, and Mutton Chop, who were all straining at their leashes and whining in her direction.

Receptionists at Hilton hotels are trained to promise what they can do and avoid what's obviously been overlooked. "How can I help you and your dog, ma'am?"

"Miss, my little Louis Vuitton has torn his dewclaw and is bleeding all over the pure Corinthian leather of my brand-new Mercedes."

Claire thought, "Grab a chill-pill from your Gucci, Giselle. Louis's dewclaw is a long way from his heart, and I've got a discount card for Hugo's Custom Car Detailing." Sarcasm would be throwing a Christmas tree on a tire fire.

She refrained.

"Well, that's serious, but not life-threatening. My doctors and technicians are working as hard as they can to care for other patients. My best guess is that it could be nearly an hour. I can give you directions to a dozen other veterinary clinics, the University of Wisconsin, or three accredited emergency hospitals."

I remember the day Harley ruptured an anal gland abscess. Scotty Roberts burst through the door with a look of horror on his face, "Doc, you gotta help my buddy. It's like something crawled up his butt and is eatin' its way out!"

Being the veterinarian is sometimes the easiest job in the building. We can concentrate on the patient in front of us, while the technicians collect and run blood, urine, and fecal samples, formulate estimates, and back up the front desk. We're often insulated from the war being waged against ringing telephone lines and the stream of humanity through the front door.

The day ended after double-overtime, but eventually, Louis went home with a Holstein-patterned boo-boo bandage and three days of anti-inflammatory drugs. Strict oversight by the DEA, and the necessity to maintain my licensure, overrode the temptation to send Giselle home with a fistful of fluoxetine and diazepam.

Ginny mopped the floors, technicians recovered the scene, and Dr. Clark and I wrote records. We had come to count on Claire to provide the color for the post-game wrap-up. Today she had plenty of fuel. Venting can be therapeutic. Internalizing charged emotions can bind you up like a bean burrito at a baptism. Airing our grievances, done well, can be so much more than a pop-off valve for our greater coronary artery.

Venting allows us to relive the event and search for how we may have better defused or avoided the situation. To achieve maximum benefit from a full-on rant, there is an onus on the recipient to give the ranter a hard body angle and full attention. The ranter is also obligated to not target the same victim repeatedly.

BILL STORK

A second useful tool in assimilating a frustrating encounter is awareness. Have I ever procrastinated, overreacted, or expected my (perceived) needs to be pushed to the front of the line? Whether in the moment or three weeks later, we might also ask ourselves, "Have I ever been Giselle?"

Remmi was the dog who never left your side. If she ever went missing, you simply went to the last room where you shut the door behind you, and she'd be waiting patiently. One evening I came home from work. Dad was up to visit and got home first. He let the dogs out minutes before I got home. Sheila followed fifteen minutes later. We all set about the business of doing chores and getting dinner. Token herded the cats and hunted groundhogs, and Sheila fed horses. Dad and I had a beer and outlined the job list for Saturday. Eventually, we noticed Remmi was not there. Without a thought, I went to the bedroom where I'd turned on the window air conditioner, the bathroom, the kitchen—no Remmi. I hobbled to the upper barn and back to the horse barn and searched every stall—still, no Remmi. The property was bordered by a highway, a county road, and a marsh. Remmi was thirteen at the time; her mobility and mentality were slipping. If she ventured off our seven acres, it was not going to turn out well.

I hopped on my mountain bike and started riding concentric circles, up and down Highway 18, through the trees, and both sides of the fence lines. My cries became increasingly urgent. As dark began to set, Sheila was beginning to break. With the last shred of collective composure, we phoned the humane society. By the grace of God, a kind woman on Highway G found an elderly yellow Lab staggering through the tall grass, bound for Sheila's farm. Evidently, she was not comfortable with Dad coming home first and headed to safety, seven miles away.

Fear and despair rushed out, and relief and gratitude rushed in— briefly. The humane society was twelve minutes away. We told the young lady we'd be there in ten. She explained that they were about to close, and we could pick Remmi up Saturday morning.

I lost my mind.

Over the years, the Lake Mills Veterinary Clinic had worked in cooperation with the humane society. I must have felt entitled to special treatment. There was an exchange having to do with long hours and overtime. The young woman was doing her job, as instructed. To recreate the diatribe I launched and how I treated that young woman would be to lay open a wound that has continued to seep for ten years. It was one of the least-prideful moments of my life and requires me to forever give the Giselles the benefit of the doubt.

For all we know, Giselle may have just discovered a wrinkle or learned her manicurist had been deported.

Worse yet, she may not have known a mother to show her to "Cast no stones 'til you've walked in the shoes of the messenger."

First impressions, give them a second chance.

Rack Out and Roll

The Amazing Dick Bass was a tenured professor of electrical engineering at Georgia Institute of Technology. I knew him as a graduate student at the University of Illinois. While sittin' on his front porch pickin' "Shady Grove" on his banjo, he was prone to leaping from his stool and chasing an occasional car down 4th Street. Toyota or Plymouth, he seemed to have little preference.

As nerds go, he was relatively fleet of foot, but without fail, the car would get away. Back on the porch, he'd situate the oft-maligned Sears and Roebuck bluegrass tool back on his lap. He'd catch his breath, shrug, and giggle, "You know, Billy Stork, some days they just ain't much to do down in Blackshear [Georgia]. Don't rightly know what I'd do if I ever caught one."

In a recent series of the comic strip *Pooch Café*, Poncho and Boomer were chasing a mail truck and caught it.

My daughter has found herself in a similar pickle.

Paige was in her last semester at the University of Vermont and about to graduate with a degree in environmental engineering. Burlington is bordered by Lake Champlain, Canada, and the Green Mountains to the east. On weekends, the gravitational pull of the mountains draws people to hike, camp, and ski. She had been teaching ski lessons to three-year-olds at Stowe Mountain. (A Vail Resorts property with free valet parking, a string quartet in the lodge, and chocolate chip cookies on the lifts.) She calls it paid birth control, and she was making good money. All of which Dad is fine with. I'm still in denial over astigmatism, statins, and child-bearing clients who weren't yet born when I palpated my first cow. Being called Grandpa would send me rolling down the embankment.

After delivering a defeatist pre-K from Jersey who'd spent the day rolling on his back with his skis in the air pounding the snow and crying back to his parents, she was looking to take a cleansing solo run down the mountain before returning to the land of Bernie. She hopped a lift beside a ski patrol.

Ski patrol is a noble fraternity. They are on the hill hours before first-lift, scouring the mountain for exposed rocks, outcrops, and downed trees. They'd close trails that would cost a skier plates, pins, and titanium screws in his tibia/fibula, and the resort a lawsuit. The iconic red down jacket, white cross on the chest, and two-way radio over their shoulder is a presence. Like the friendly neighborhood cop on snow skis, they police the hills to prevent "Yo dudes, check this out …" from being the last words of a GoPro snowboarder jacked up on Red Bull. In the event of the inevitable torqued knee or T-boned tree, they stabilize, mobilize, and calm the fallen skier until the toboggan arrives.

Ski patrol saved our friend Leann's life.

After making small talk, Paige asked the gentleman, "What's it take to earn one of those jackets?"

A seasoned patrol, he'd already seen her ski. Assuming she'd had basic mountain first aid, he responded with the classic volunteer firefighter's qualification, "A driver's license and a pulse. We're short-handed. Can you start tomorrow?"

She paused for an oh-shit moment.

Downhill daycare commences at ten when the lifts open. Ski patrol is on the hill at sunup, and the mountain is an hour away from Burlington.

Paige's text: *So, Dad, any tips on getting up at 4:30?*

Dad's response: *Does Clapton have any tips on how to strum a "G" chord?*

First of all, Paige, you've got forty-six chromosomes. Twenty-three of which will account for your intelligence and athleticism. The other set oughta get you out of bed well before sunup.

  BILL STORK

Your great-grandpa was a millwright at AE Staley and Company in Decatur, Illinois. He'd be out of bed by four thirty, which saved his life on July 19, 1974. He dropped Grandma off at Elmer's Tavern by six so she'd be ready to serve fried eggs, hash browns, and eight-ounce Schlitz drafts to the third-shifters. That'd give him enough time to catch and clean a basketful of crappie, shoot a handful of rats in the rip-rap, and on one occasion, piss off (literally) an early morning water skier who thought it'd be hilarious to buzz the old guy in the bib overalls.

Your grandpa was an operating engineer, Local 965. He's pushed dirt, set steel, and poured concrete on projects from sidewalks, gymnasiums, and libraries to a nuclear power plant.

"Son, if you're going to collect union wages and benefits, you (darn) well better show up a little earlier, work harder, work smarter, and build a better bridge. "

You just never know when you're gonna have a flat tire, get stuck, or blow a head gasket on the way to work. If starting time was eight in the morning, he'd be sitting in the parking lot drinking coffee and reading Louis L'Amour cowboy novels, waiting for nature to strike by six. Whether he was running a Bobcat or a five-hundred-ton Manitowoc tower crane, by the time the foreman and laborers showed up, his machine was oiled, greased, and full of fuel. The Detroit diesel would be warmed up and blowing clean. He'd have his left boot on the clutch ready to make the first pick.

So, Paige, if I recall, the college lifestyle challenges the "early to bed, early to rise" adage. In the event your a.m. alleles have been diluted, I've assembled some compensatory measures that could help you out.

Rick Schultz is the herdsman at the Tag Lane Dairy. He's elbow-deep installing straws of a bull named Broker in twenty-five synchronized heifers by five Monday morning. He shrugs, "You just get used to it."

To snooze or not to snooze.

The Khemani code dictates: "You gotta get up mighty early if you want to have time to take a nap."

Ryan Haack is a disciple of Kish. He racks out at four, hits the button on the coffee maker, then goes back to bed for a half-hour.

Dad says, "Hit the floor, not the snooze." Avoid the full bladder, blind, naked, zombie stagger, have your clothes laid out in the order you'll put them on. The night before, I'll recycle the advertisements and have *The Journal* exposed to the first article I want to read in the morning. I have a rotation of three hand-thrown bowls I eat my cereal from. It's like having breakfast with a friend.

Induction into the early-risers club can be by choice or necessity. What appears to be uniform is purpose. (I did see a Memphis businessman sprint into a Mississippi casino to play twenty minutes of Black Jack at 5 a.m., but that is an illness.) Rick Schultz is breeding cows. Steve Jr. Sterwald is either pulling a poor commuter out of a ditch or leaned over his Snap-on tool shed, scouring the internet researching a wiring issue on an SUV. Paul Kruse is walking Maddie (Rocky II) down Main Street. Steve Jensen is designing ductwork for a massive remodel on St. Coletta's, and Jon Laundrie has the Flavor of the Day on the Culver's marquis four hours before the first butter burger.

Open your eyes well before sunrise. Inputs and encounters are of your choosing. The thoughts in your head are your own, unswayed by cable news or images on a liquid crystal screen. Sunday morning you'll find clarity, where Saturday night there was confusion. Rest repairs rents in myofibrils and myocardium. You'll wake up stronger than when you laid down.

Dad had contracts to clear snow from businesses and parking lots with a road grader. I plowed fifteen driveways with a twelve-horse Wheel Horse lawn tractor. When we had to plow snow or go crappie fishing, Dad would crack open my bedroom door and sing, "Good morning, merry sunshine. Why are you here so soon? You chased away the little stars, and you chased away the moon."

If you're still having trouble, give me a call.

 BILL STORK

If you are my favorite associate, Dr. Deanna Clark, I offer a drastic approach. Pat Wynes's parents could sleep through the demolition of Yankee Stadium if they were using home plate as a pillow. They installed terra cotta tile under their dresser. On the bureau was a cast-iron skillet, hanging one-third over the edge.

Under the high side of the skillet was a small wedge, and in it was an old-time alarm clock. At 6 a.m., between the ticks would come a click as the mechanism tripped the release of the little brass hammer that would maniacally pound the pair of bells on top.

In doing so, the two-pound antique would skate to the bottom of the skillet and send it careening toward the tile. In time, Pat's dad became conditioned and could catch the cast-iron and the clock before they hit the ground.

And, finally, in the "you didn't hear it from me" file, my friends Ned and Sarah found a wristwatch that gives a jolt of electricity, so Mom doesn't have to go downstairs every morning with a pitcher of cold water. ᐅ

Temple's Stairway to Heaven

L et's just say that my admission to vet school was not a deadlock cinch. Were it not for a chain-smoking cardiologist with a sense of humor, a benevolent interview committee, and eight folks who turned down their admission, my books would have to be titled *In Stan's Shadow*.

Plan B was graduate work with a professor named Stanley Curtis. Dr. Curtis does not have a museum in his hometown or a television series like James Wight. He will never have the name recognition of Herriot, but the principles he set forth in his all-encompassing yet ultra-simple *Welfare Plateau* touch every facet of animal production and husbandry. Miraculously, accepted into vet school and grad school, I agonized over the decision. Dr. Curtis had a photographic memory, a motor that would not quit, and a generous physique. By obligation, he lived Newton's first law. He delivered his advice mid-stride. "Bill, just pick a direction, and go like hell."

Had I chosen a cube in the Animal Sciences Building, my labmate would have been a woman named Temple Grandin.

If you've never heard of Temple, you've likely not been close to a family affected by autism. Knowledge was scant, and understanding was minimal when Temple was born on the spectrum in 1947. Temple has lent insight, perspective, and hope to those affected by a disorder that touches one in sixty-eight children worldwide. In her first book, *Thinking in Pictures,* Temple explains how she translates words to images. In addition, she has literally written the book on *The Humane Handling of Livestock*. For someone who struggles with interpersonal communication and human emotions, few have contributed more to the comfort and well-being of farm animals.

BILL STORK

Her Stairway to Heaven system of catch pens, alleys, and chutes is designed from the cow's-eye view to minimize their stress during handling. Modifications of her system have been employed on thousand-cow Wyoming ranches, Colorado feedlots, and slaughterhouses nationwide.

Downsized modifications of Temple's principles are used on virtually every modern farm and ranch. On the other side of the hill from the Haack farm is the Russ Dahl farm. Behind the house, just past the three-bladed windmill wobbling in the breeze, under the corrugated tin lean-to scabbed onto the old dairy barn, Russ built his version to vaccinate, castrate, and pregnancy-check his hundred head of polled Red Angus beef cattle.

Some Mondays start with a forty-minute workout at the Lakers Athletic Club, a cup of coffee, and an article in *JAVMA* at the clinic before departing on a sunrise drive down I-94 to Kevin Griswold's dairy, tuned in to Jonathan and Kitty on WMMM-FM.

Others do not.

The phone pinged just as I was putting my Special K back in the cupboard. "Hello, this is Ritchie Behm. Can you help me out with a cow under the weather?" Token, the Wyoming Cattle Dog, is always between my feet when I put my boots on and waiting for me to open the truck door.

Tugger, the Louisiana mutt, perceives no urgency for off-feed cattle. He lays curled into Sheila until the last possible moment. After a half-dozen, "Come on, Tugs," he leaped into the back seat. Ritchie's under the weather cow was a mild case of mastitis. We spent more time lamenting the Packers' decision to trade Jordy Nelson to the Raiders than treating the cow.

As I scrubbed my rubbers and stowed the stainless bucket, the Samsung was blowing up again. With calculated disregard for the dangers of texting and driving, I hiked my glasses down and fumbled with the microscopic icon to download the message, while steering with my knees. Highway O in Waterloo, Wisconsin, is chalk-line straight. At 6 a.m., the hobby farmers are still feeding their backyard chickens, so I'm more likely to encounter a deer crossing the road than a commuter funneling toward Madison.

Tom and Sue Nelson had a fresh down cow. Milk fever is a routine malady, usually remedied in minutes with 750 mL of calcium gluconate. The plan worked beautifully until I encountered the first thing I had never seen in twenty-five years of practice. In the ninety seconds it took to retrieve two bottles of calcium and my halter from the truck, she decided to prolapse her uterus onto the barn floor. In keeping with the theme of the day, the surgery kit required to suture her up was sitting next to my desk, where I had tripped over it, cussed, and mumbled to myself, "Put the damn thing in the truck before you forget it," for two days.

A twenty-minute trip at posted legal limits, the Jefferson County sheriff's deputy was either sleeping or recognized the urgency in my travel. I was back to the farm, with the surgery box, in just under thirty-five minutes.

Thank goodness for stout young farmboys. Tom and Sue's son Dusty cradled the organ like an eighty-pound loaf of bread as I stuffed it through the pelvic canal. The cow danced in discomfort as we waltzed in unison until her calf bed was back home. I bent at the waist so Sue could hose the big chunks of blood and placenta off my back and shoulders. With no time to dry, I threw my shirts back on, thanked Dusty, and was eastbound, headed to what was supposed to be my first call of the day.

Thanks to a genetic obligation to rising early, the interstate highways, and tolerant State Patrol officers, I was only forty minutes late to the herd check at Tag Lane farm.

We were halfway through a list of a hundred pregnancy checks when Claire messaged a reminder that Russ Dahl was on the schedule to vaccinate and castrate thirty-five or forty calves. I pride myself on keeping my thumb on the pulse and eye on the schedule, but I am prone to lapses.

 BILL STORK

Rick could see the "oh shit" written across my brow. Rushing cattle is as futile as trying to hurry my wife through the bathroom on date night, but we scrubbed the sports and political banter and moved with purpose. When we whittled the list down to the last three, Rick let me off the hook. "Ahh, there are only two cows in the sick pen and one in pen nine. They'll wait until next week."

Dr. Clark was on vacation, so the technicians were holding down the fort back at the clinic. I'd been set back by a sick cow, prolapsed uterus, and missing surgery tools, yet the thought of re-scheduling Russ was not an option.

I assumed his son-in-law Dan had the day off school.

I covered the forty miles from the furthest eastern reach of Jefferson County to Russ's farm on the edge of Dane in just under forty-five minutes (thirty-five minutes of driving and a ten-minute roadside chat with Barney Fife). I slowed at the drive looking for Dan's grey Toyota pickup parked in front of the barn. There was none. At the sound of my truck tires on the gravel drive, Russ started from the machine shed to the barn. Nine months after his second spinal decompression surgery, he walked like a constipated robot. I glanced in front of the machine shed, by the grain bins, and in front of the garage—no pickup truck.

Russ's cattle are socialized but spirited. Two back surgeries ago, Russ was the guy you'd want on the end of the rope at the Labor Day tug of war. He'd cajole his cattle through the chute while his dad ran the headgate. Well into his eighties, Lester never missed a calf. I'd vaccinate and castrate as fast as I could. At the sound of my placing the two-by-four behind her butt, Lester would pull the lever. The heifer would bump the board and launch.

The surgeons assured Russ he'd be good as new in six months. Nine months out, and he can just feel his feet. So we have come to schedule our roundups on Dan's days off.

I thought.

Not a physically imposing lad, Dan has an outsized booming baritone. On the playground at Marshall Elementary, where he taught, I can't imagine the boys stepping far out of line, though I suspect he has a separate vocabulary. In the cattle pen, Dan applies his instrument to deliver a pent-up stream of artful expletives.

With some combination of youthful goomba, athleticism, and a whip*, he divides the animals from the large holding pens into the small jug and eventually through the chute. There comes an occasional *thwack, uuhh*, like the soundtrack from a bar room brawl in a John Wayne cowboy movie. As Dan calls into question the animal's parentage and suggests decidedly unbiblical acts, Russ and I talk elk hunting in Colorado and local politics.

Pressed for time and barely more agile than Russ, my left knee ached at the notion of pushing my own patients through the chute.

I confirmed with Russ there would be twenty or so to vaccinate and retreated to the warmth of my truck to preserve my hands and reconstitute five bottles of brucellosis vaccine. I lingered long enough to catch Jason Isbell's latest, threw one empty box in my lunch bag to capture the serial number, and stepped onto the running boards.

The Newberry knife is used to castrate bull calves. Google it. Though it looks imposing and pre-historic, the design helps ensure the castrator does not become the castrated or amputated. Every father should have one sitting on the counter when his daughter's prom date shows up. I extracted mine from under a couple of halters and stowed it in my boot.

From the passenger side of my truck came a spirited, "Good morning, Dr. Stork."

With her hair fresh out of curlers and covered by a shower cap tied in a bow beneath her chin, the top of her head was not quite the height of the taillight. As it turns out, the spirited little lady walking her Beagle I'd waved at en route to Haack's herd check was Russ's sister Nancy, our drover for the day. Her garden-soiled jeans were bunched atop the faux fur of a size five pair of Sorels. She had the demeanor of a recess monitor and weighed little more than a Red Angus calf at birth. In the crook of her left arm, she cradled the four-foot fiberglass cattle sorting tool.

BILL STORK

She hunched the eight-foot rough-sawn oak gate over the high spot in the bedding pack and waded in.

Like arranging anxious fourth graders for the school assembly, she spoke in the even tone of assumed compliance, "Okay, kids. All I want to see is heads and hinders. I'm gonna need the first three or four to show the rest of you'uns how it works."

Four heifers and two bull calves rushed the opening. Barely taller than their rumps, she stepped in front of the fifth and tapped the sixth on the noggin, reminding them, "Not yet, you two."

Dragging the gate back, she assured them she'd be back shortly.

By the time I laid my tagger, tattoo gun, and syringe on the makeshift table by the headgate, Russ pulled the lever on the first heifer.

I had the ice fishing report from Rock Lake, and the story about being detained by the town constable for doing eighty-one on the straightaway on highway A cued up. With Nancy cracking the whip, I didn't so much as have time to ask Russ, "How's your back?"

Once behind a five-hundred-pound bull, I reach for the Newberry. In one quick pull, I can have his most valuable possessions in my hands and restore the tool to my boot quick as a gunfighter. November through March, you'd like to take a couple of extra ticks to extract a healthy pair. Depending on his genetics, the organ can be the size of a Valencia orange and is ninety-eight degrees. The vet or cowboy who's been sinking hand heat to the cold steel levers on the cattle chute can recover a few joules from the bull's jewels by holding on a few seconds before plopping them into the pail.

Unless Nancy's pushing cattle.

With an ear and eye on the catch pen, I rest my hand on the latch for the back gate. Nancy negotiates with the pen full of six-hundred-pound kindergartners, "Okay, kids. I'll give you a lap around, and then I need someone to head down the hole."

And he does. When his hip clears the bar, I step to swing the gate in front of the eyes of the next heifer. In sync, Russ pulls the lever on the headgate.

Thirty-eight minutes later, the last steer melds into the herd. With whip in one hand, Nancy shuts the gate with the other. Dan would emerge from these sessions looking like he'd gone three rounds with Ronda Rousey in a manure spreader, and lost. Nancy brushed a little barn dust off her jeans and scraped her Sorels sideways through the snow to free up a chunk of manure caught in the treads. She could have gone straight to McDonald's for coffee with the ladies.

It would appear the extent to which stress is reduced when pushing cattle through Temple's Stairway to Heaven is operator dependent.

*Pause for PETA. Lest the reader conjure up an image of Indiana Jones and his eight-foot leather bull-whip, the "whip" of which we speak is a four-foot fiberglass rod, about the diameter of a putter. The proximal end is the rubber grip off a four-iron, and dangling off the distal end is four inches of nylon rope. In Dan's hands against a six-hundred-pound steer, it is the physical equivalent of a gnat on a dog's ass. We soon found that in other hands, it's a subtle but effective suggestion. "Would you mind heading this way?" ꕔ

BILL STORK

Bullshit

A wild-eyed young laborer finishing his ham and Swiss on rye lamented, "Me and my wife just bought a place out in the country. We've got a house and twenty acres, two cows, a chicken coop, and a well that's gone dry."

Brett was making over ten dollars an hour laying rebar the size of a meat cutter's forearm at the Clinton Nuclear Power Plant. Still, it was going to take several months of Sundays, at double time, to make $2,500 to drill a new one.

Next to him, Dad snapped back to consciousness after his trademark seven-minute nap. Thirty years of screamin' diesel engines had left his hearing selective at best. He caught up to the banter, hovering just outside the circle as men packed up their lunchboxes and commiserated about blown transmissions, bald tires, and child support.

As he settled his hard hat and safety goggles, Dad pried, "Just out of curiosity, Brett, where do you and your wife live?"

"Oh, 'bout eight miles east of Maroa," he responded.

"You know, Carl Eads is just about five miles or so north of you. We were out there cutting wood Saturday. We had the truck and trailer half loaded and were getting dry when my son noticed a pump handle and a windmill out in the corner of the pasture. I'll bet it didn't take four strokes, and that thing was gushin' the coldest, best-tasting water I've ever drunk. Tell him you're in a tough spot. I bet he'd sell it to you for a little a nothin'."

Carl Eads.

Carl was an ex-marine and cowboy. Lacking patience, or a lift, he once clean and jerked a Mopar 440 V-8 with a blown head gasket from under the hood of his farm truck to the workbench. He was also the union steward: middle management between the company building a nuclear generating station that would go nearly 1,000 percent (seriously) over budget and 1,200 heavy equipment operators who, at one point, worked seven twelves for a year.

Two days later, Brett tracked down Carl. Carl had shoulders wide as a Brahman bull that tapered to a waist like a splitting maul. His sunglasses, dark as welding goggles, hid the crease in his temple. Carl knew exactly where this line of BS had started. He shifted the half-bushel wad of Copenhagen he stored in his cheek and spat a brown bullet between the toes of the young man's Red Wings. "I reckon we don't need that well. Ain't had cows in ten years. Either me or my wife oughta be around all weekend. Stop and take a look at it."

For the Tuesday, March 20 edition of *The Wall Street Journal*, Elizabeth Bernstein wrote an article titled, "Fine-Tune Your BS Detector: You'll Need It." According to Bernstein, in the digital age, misinformation—from nonsense to lies—spreads faster than ever and is becoming an area of scientific research.

"A lie can travel halfway around the world before the truth gets its boots on," has been credited (inaccurately) to Ben Franklin, Mark Twain, and others.

Her article makes a number of inarguable points.

Ms. Bernstein cites studies published in the *Journal of Experimental Psychology* that show people are more likely to BS when they feel obligated to have an opinion on a topic they know nothing about or feel they aren't going to be challenged.

Without a doubt. The Smallmouth bass I caught up on the Flambeau Flowage is a good six inches longer at the Tyranena Brewing Company than at Easter when my brother-in-law, Tracy, is sitting at the table. He was in the boat.

 BILL STORK

Dr. John Petrocelli of Wake Forest University calls this the "ease of passing bullshit hypothesis." He also explains that BS will strengthen a weak argument. "I don't care what the research says," but weaken a strong argument.

Bernstein draws from the work of authors in journals at universities who rightfully contend that we are more likely to succumb to BS when we are tired or fail to think critically. Yup.

The fork in the road.

She mentions that, at the annual convention of the Society for Personality and Social Psychology (SPSP), scientists and researchers presented a paper titled "Bullshitting: Empirical and Experiential Examinations of a Pervasive Social Behavior."

The researchers go on to explain that BS is a form of persuasion that aims to impress the listener while employing a blatant disregard for the truth.

The SPSP's definition is consistent with the work of Princeton Professor Emeritus Harry Frankfurt, who (literally) wrote the book *On Bullshit*. Dr. Frankfurt claims that BS is different than lying. "Liars are aware of the truth and choose to push it aside."*

BSers don't necessarily care about the truth at all.

Well, Dr. Frankfurt, Ms. Bernstein, and members of SPSP, *my* BS meter is tuned up. The needle is pinned, and it's shooting sparks and blowing black smoke.

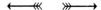

I was raised by, and work for, construction workers, farmers, machinists, firefighters, truck drivers, and teachers. In the business of BS, they are the best. On their behalf, I beg to differ.

The research.

The Wollin farm was leveled by a tornado in 1990. When a 111-mph derecho did it again in '95, Ed called his son who was completing his ag degree at UW–River Falls. "I think God's trying to tell me something. If you're coming back to farm, we'll build it again; if not,

I'll get a job in town."

The notion of a nine to five is torture for farm folks. Today, Ed and his two boys run a 150-cow robotic farm. Standing in the office, I asked their take on BS. Erich is stout as a stump and polite as an altar boy. He is not prone to disagree with authority, "Oh, I think there's a thread of truth in every line of BS Charlie Untz told us he sold his corn for five bucks a bushel. Translated: a lady gave him a five-dollar bill for a bushel to feed her deer and refused the change." You always consider the source.

Rick Schultz is the herdsman on Kevin Griswold's two-thousand-cow dairy. He was the valedictorian of his high school class and graduated with honors from the University of Wisconsin. Keeping his herd healthy and productive involves coordination between non-English-speaking milking crew, maintenance, and ownership. He knows his cows like a kindergarten teacher knows her kids. We were walking the quarter-mile (uphill, into a fifty-mph wind) from the heifer barn back to HQ.

Rick said, "Bullshit can be used as a stall tactic."

A skill taught to me by my good friend Arlin Rodgers, DVM, PhD: "Yeah, Willy. If you don't know why the dog is coughing, limping, and ataxic, just crease your brow and take an ear swab. Tell the client you're going to look at it under the microscope. Then you can run to your office and research the case in a book or call somebody."

Bernie Williams is a scientist for the Wisconsin Department of Natural Resources. "My boss asked me how it was going. I waved a lax hand and assured him everything was under control."

She was staring at a hundred new emails and a million-dollar grant.

I filled in, "But you knew you'd have it handled by the time it mattered."

"Exactly."

The oft-repeated idiom goes: "You can't bullshit a bullshitter."

The Stork caveat says, "Unless you're better."

My dad went to Bull Shoals, Arkansas, twice a year with a handful of buddies to crappie fish. They had a ringer. Their friend Jay Smith had retired from Illinois Bell. After thirty years, he traded his bucket truck for a bass boat and called himself a fishing guide, A.K.A. professional BSer.

Dad and Smitty were paired up the first morning of the trip. Smitty was a little nervous. His cardiologist had found an occlusion in his greater coronary artery. After their fishing trip, he was going in for stent placements. Dad dropped a chartreuse jig next to a stump and paused to wait for a bump.

"Ahh, Smitty, it ain't no big deal. They just make a little cut down there by your business and run it up there like a boring machine. Just don't let 'em charge you full price."

Smitty was silent until the cleaning table. The men were carving filets big as a bread slice from twelve-inch crappies. He took a swig from his PBR. "Bill, what the hell do you mean don't let them charge me full price?"

"If you ask the doctor ahead of time, you can get used stents. Hell, Smitty, we're darn-near seventy years old. We're never going to wear them out anyway."

There is unspoken BS.

It was that first day of spring when the ditches and alfalfa are blinding green, and Strasburgs had a calving. I excused myself past three waiting clients while Claire put the third phone line on hold. Dr. Clark was already double-booked. An hour later, I had blood splattered on my forehead and manure and straw stuck to the afterbirth on my coveralls. A heifer calf was bawling in the straw. Dave offered the milkhouse hose to knock the chunks. I waved him off. Don't want the techs to think we're leaning on the tailgate telling stories.

Lies, damn lies, and statistics.

Jamie Lauderdale works two jobs to make payments on a single-wide mobile home and support her son, Buddy. Buddy has Asperger's. He is plenty bright but struggles with a world that does not always go his way. The only one who understands is his Shepherd-Chow cross, inaptly named Sugar. We hadn't seen Sugar in six years when she presented panting and pale, with abdomen engorged. The very fact that she didn't rip our faces off dropped the prognosis from poor to grave. The basketball-sized tumor on her spleen was inoperable.

When they picked up Sugar's ashes, we carved out a corner in the lobby to share fresh tears and a hug. Fighting for composure, Jamie conjured a smile, attempting to manage Buddy's emotions. "Dr. Stork, if we had been able to afford more regular care, is there anything we could have done to prevent the tumor?"

There have been the Hannah and Mowgli miracles. The McFarlanes and Howells presented the girls to us at the first sign of illness. After bloodwork and radiographs, we found the tumors and referred them to Veterinary Specialty Services for ultrasound, radiographs, surgery, and chemotherapy. All for the cost of a good used Mercedes.

It is equally true—and the version I shared with Jamie and Buddy—that more than sixty percent of splenic and liver masses are malignant.

"Jamie, the majority of these tumors are nasty. By the time we discover them, they've already spread."

We didn't invent the truth; we just manage it.

Dear Dr. Frankfurt, Ms. Bernstein, and members of SPSP, your research and writing are enlightening.

After reading a number of your articles and listening to lectures, I've learned that a philosopher can lose me in lingo faster than a lawyer. As for these BSers who will speak to inflate their position, I know them well. I'm usually saddened by the suspicion they never had a family sitting across the dinner table from them. We'll leave that for the psychologist.

Wikipedia and Webster fully support your definition of bullshit. The Dictionary of American Regional English doesn't even have a definition. I may be going rogue, but I've got an army behind me. With all due respect, I call bullshit.

Contributors to my stories include machinists, veterans, farmers, construction workers, PhDs, electricians, teachers, poets, potters, and

Sylvia Sippel. Every one of us agrees that our brand of bullshit is not a disregard, but rather an active dance with the truth.

Do not tell us we're not bullshitters.

Tom Frederick had been living with Parkinson's ten years before my mom. When she was diagnosed, Dad called Tom. He was holding my mother's hand forty minutes later, helping her understand what to expect next.

Tom bought a new fishing boat. Dad had built an adaptation for his boat so that two guys could fish up front. Tom didn't even get the words out. Dad was in his drive, measuring the bow and making a template. A week later, he, Dave Oldham, and Dick Rentschler laughed until they wet themselves as my dad paced, panted, and ranted. For the first time in his life, the adaptation he built for Tom's boat did not fit. Then the salesman for East Side Marine pulled around the corner with the real boat. They'd pulled a bait-and-switch.

Dick and Dave drove four hours, once a month, to take Dad to fish fry after his stroke.

Jackie Schroeder was on the verge of tears when I returned from reading the cytology. The lump on the inside of Peyton's back leg was a benign fat tumor. I knew the fastest way to shatter her anxiety was to tell her Peyton had—astonishingly—grown a third testicle. I also knew Kelly was looking over my shoulder to shake her head, smile, and blow my cover.

No one gets hurt.

If Brett is going to get his feelings hurt over trying to buy a used well off a retired rodeo hand, his lifespan in construction is finite. Jay Smith had a week of playing cards and fishing with his buddies, more concerned with getting a good deal on a gently used cardiac stent than dying on the operating table. His wife is a nurse and set him straight before he made a fool of himself to the doctor. Dad knew that.

There is a class of people who take pride in being known as bullshitters. Timing, target, and intent are all integral to the art, as is integrity. If they sell you a boat or a car, it'll float, it'll start, and the oil has been changed every three thousand miles.

*From *On Bullshit*: "It is impossible for someone to lie unless he thinks he knows the truth. Producing bullshit requires no such conviction. A person who lies is thereby responding to the truth, and he is, to that extent, respectful of it. When an honest man speaks, he says only what he believes to be true; and for the liar, it is correspondingly indispensable that he considers his statements to be false. For the bullshitter, however, all these bets are off: he is neither on the side of the true nor on the side of the false. His eye is not on the facts at all, as the eyes of the honest man and of the liar are, except insofar as they may be pertinent to his interest in getting away with what he says. He does not care whether the things he says describe reality correctly. He just picks them out, or makes them up, to suit his purpose." 🐾

Little House on the Prairie

Storkfest '17 was Dad's last stop on his farewell tour—our wedding day, a family reunion in the most inclusive sense; and the introduction of honky-tonk queen Sarah Gayle Meech to central Wisconsin.

There were a hundred Kodak moments that scorching September day. In addition to the "I dos" and our first dance, there is an image I've burned to the hard drive.

Sheila's army had converted the barn into a reception hall with early-fall wildflowers in mason jars on six-foot folding tables and a chandelier fashioned from icicle lights and hula hoops. In the feeding frenzy that preceded the hoedown, Kaleb Walker searched for three empty seats. He parked his Rocky's Revenge and three-ply Chinet bending with brisket in a suitable spot and pulled a chair. Without conscious thought or concern, he dropped his head and silently gave thanks.

I've known Kaleb's dad, Jay, for thirty-five years; he's like a brother. As a husband and father, Jay is the high bar.

He'd stand a touch over six feet, were it not for the scoliosis that drops his left shoulder. Just out of high school, he could have been a pitchman for a pre-Walmart discount store on the east side of Urbana called Huey's. His drawl was from somewhere south of his native Effingham, Illinois, and his diction straight out of the Foxfire Books. "Man, Bill, we're shittin' in the high cotton now." He had a jump shot like Meadowlark Lemon. We'd call next game on the first court at the Intramural Physical Education Building. The Pi Beta Phis would look at us like the Duke Blue Devils would look at Lakeside Lutheran, laughing whether to guard the six-foot Indian, a David Letterman doppelganger, or the country boy Mick Jagger in Chucky Ts.

When the defense collapsed under the hoop, we'd just kick it out to the happy cherub patrolling the three-point line. Jay would launch a bomb over the melee, and we'd head to the other end of the court. After the third swish, the frat boys would start to grumble, "Is somebody going to guard that kid?" But no one ever did.

In the spring of '85, a classmate introduced Jay to the fresh-faced daughter of Erv and Leona R., from Cissna Park, Illinois, population eight hundred. One particular tequila-soaked misadventure that has forever been blamed on me did little to deter them. In August of the dust bowl summer of '88, with the congregation wedged into an un-air-conditioned church in Champaign, they forever became Jay-n-Joy Lou.

I was studying gastrointestinal physiology in my third year of vet school when the touchtone on the wall rang. "Hey, Bill. I've got some news," as he held the receiver to Tom Petty singing, "Nothin' Says Lovin' Like a Bun in the Oven." Seven months later, Kaleb Cole Walker arrived.

They bought a small two-story in the last subdivision before the cornfields. Micah and Hannah would follow in the next few years, and 1305 Alpine Drive was becoming tight quarters. Well into their seventies, Erv and Leona came up from Cissna. While Leona helped cook and take care of the kids, Jay and Erv set every truss and rafter and built every stick of furniture as the Little House on the Prairie grew to accommodate three kids, two in-laws, a dog, a cat, and an occasional visitor from Wisconsin.

Priorities well placed.

Erv drove his last nail at ninety-two years old. When Leona was no longer able to live on her own, she came to the Walkers. I once asked Jay to join me on an out West cycling adventure, oblivious to their obligation, "Nah, Bill. That sounds great, but we've got our hands full here at home."

Joy Lou did the heavy lifting, but the three Walker kids would all take their turn, with Hannah's future husband stopping by to play euchre with Grandma once a week.

"Kids these days" are awesome. Hannah was the first to get married on Memorial Day 2018. A merciful breeze ruffled the knee-high corn as the sun set over Hudson farm, just west of Urbana, Illinois. The best man regaled the three-hundred guests with how he and Jake were drawn together by their faith and competitiveness. Jake being more so, often resulting in a lost bet and a naked lap around the Alpha Gamma Rho house at the University of Illinois. The DJ breezed through the dollar dance and tossing of the garters. By nine o'clock, the concrete dance floor was a mass of humanity pulsing to hip-hop and pop-country.

Above it all sat Leona, a corsage tied around her right wrist, pink dress, and hair freshly blue, she watched without expression. I prayed she could appreciate the beauty of the event. Just then, Kaleb emerged from the throng. He set her walker to the side. With his tie dangling and collar loose, he hauled her to her feet. Toe-to-toe they stood, with hands steady, he bobbed his head and rolled his shoulders and shared a dance with his grandma.

The day after, I thanked Jay for an amazing day. I congratulated my friend on his kids and shared the image of Leona's smile dancing with Kaleb.

"Aw, Bill. As we all know, things have a way of working out."

Jay's father was a pipeliner. Summers in college, he'd drive to Alaska to spend time with him. Jay rides his bike eleven miles to work. He coached his kids in basketball and was a fixture on the sidelines at every soccer match. Friday nights at the Walker household, Jay-n-Joy Lou and all three kids watched movies, played games, and slept together in the living room until the day they left the house.

Happy Father's Day. Ɋ

The Dropsies

After thirteen years, we were sad to lose our Dr. Clark to the allure of love in the Buckeye State. When she gave notice on January 8, 2018, her departure date was to be determined. I had pitched our open position for an associate on every online and printed publication in Wisconsin, and in the *Journal of the American Veterinary Medical Association*. By the time snow receded to green grass, Dr. Clark was packing her bags, and we had received applications from three fine new graduates and an airplane mechanic from Kansas City. (Whom I offered to fly in for an interview, stipulating that he bring five pounds of Arthur Bryant's ribs.)

I was starting to fidget like a congressman in a confessional.

On the morning of Wednesday, April 18, I was absently flipping through offers from Orbitz, Ticketmaster, and The Barrymore Theater, with my index finger paused a centimeter above the delete key.

As an affirmation of faith and proof that things can be both good and true, came an email:

Hello, my name is Beth Wilder. I am a 2010 graduate of the University of Wisconsin Veterinary School. I have special interests and extensive experience in soft tissue surgery, dentistry, pain management, and client communication.

We interviewed her at eight the next morning and made an offer over lunch. A month into her tenure, I would add another asset to her skill set: she is a really good BSer.

I think.

Exhibit A: Ingrid and Dave adopted Colby as a geriatric. In the years they've had him, he's progressed through the laundry list of obligatory ailments that will befall an eighty-pound "Bully Dog." His back legs continue to atrophy in the face of non-steroidal inflammatory drugs, glucosamine, turmeric, fish oil, and a mile stroll down Stoney Brook Road every day. He struggles with smooth floors and developed urinary incontinence a year ago. That, we can medicate. Last Friday at two in the afternoon, the notation read, "Colby Nelson, dropping stool throughout the house, one-week duration." Fecal incontinence is largely the result of progressive denervation of the rectal sphincter. There's no direct treatment for the dropsies.

Sheila fed Colby three pounds of freeze-dried goodness as I collected the history. I wrung my brow, parked my pen, knelt to pet his bowling ball noggin, and commenced my physical exam. His conscious proprioception was better than I expected. I found no abdominal masses on palpation or pelvic exam. The Nelsons have been clients since they were in high school. There was no need for the Arlin Rodgers swab and scope ruse.

"Dave, give me a minute. I'm gonna go make sure there's nothing new for treating fecal incontinence."

I dispatched Sheila to ask Dr. Wilder, who was extracting molars from Molly Dettman in surgery.

The 2018 version of looking it up or calling someone on the phone is the Veterinary Information Network. It's a massive database staffed by board-certified specialists, all of whom have more letters after their name than I have in my name, teach at universities, and moonlight on VIN for beer money.

Dave was texting Ingrid when I returned with a scratch pad and drug doses for dexamethasone and loperamide. The disclaimer sounded like the latest erectile dysfunction drug commercial on Fox morning news.

"Well, Dave, here's what I found. The side effects are increased water consumption, appetite, and mental agitation. Patients on these drugs should not be allowed to operate heavy equipment and should refrain from consuming alcohol. Response to treatment will vary."

I stepped into the pharmacy, wrestling the squeaky pocket door shut behind me. About that time, Sheila returned from surgery. She wore a smirk in her smile and a question on her brow. "Beth asked if we had tickled his penis."

Being the old guy on staff, I'm anxious to learn. She went on, "If his rectum winks while you massage his business, the defect is not lower motor neuron in origin."

I'm also obligated to not act surprised when I'm hearing something for the first time in twenty-six years.

Anatomically and intuitively, it made sense. Several thoughts flashed:

- Sheila has artificial knees, so we have to budget her time on the floor. How do I get her to orchestrate this diagnostic?

- Exactly where, how, and for how long does one massage this old dog before we call the test positive or negative?

- If you've spent any time watching, rectums have a tendency to spasm. When the front end sees a cabinet door open and a technician reach for a thermometer, it tells the back end a violation is imminent.

- Is a wink as good as a pucker?

- Thank God the client is Dave.

- Thank God the patient is Colby.

More than anything, I wondered, "Is this woman yankin' my chain?"

More small favors. As Sheila entered prescriptions, Dave was still buried in his iPhone. Colby was positioned under the table with his tail erect. I could execute Dr. Wilder's penile rectal axis neuro exam in stealth mode.

The outcome of the test was more academic. It did not actually affect treatment, so we ordered drugs, advised they keep Colby on flooring that's easy to clean, and promised to call the minute the delivery truck pulled into the parking lot.

I went back to VIN. Not a word. I clenched my jaw and broadened my search to Google, fully expecting that searching "tickling penis and winking rectum" could land me on some porn site that would infect our system with a fatal virus.

BILL STORK

Still not willing to expose my ignorance or that I'd potentially been duped, I consulted the authorities by way of group text.

Dr. Gregg was not familiar but volunteered to be a test patient.

Dr. Ruth Clark felt, "I think this is more of a beer discussion."

The closest I came was my classmate Dr. Rand Gustafson. "Yeah, Willie, I got one neuron firing that remembers something to that effect." (Recall the central tenets of BS. "One is more likely to BS when asked an opinion on something they have no knowledge of.")

I walked back to surgery, still not willing to own ignorance or gullibility. With my best poker face, I asked Dr. Wilder the particulars of this highly sophisticated diagnostic with the intention of searching for a response in her face. I looked to the corner of her mouth for a twitch and her temple for a crease, both of which were hidden behind a surgical mask and safety goggles.

Colby will have been on meds for three days when we make the callback on Monday. We're hoping for improvement.

Meanwhile, I have no clue whether I fell asleep in a lecture, missed a journal article, or have been BSed by a thirty-something veterinarian who looks like the high school cheerleader at the top of the pyramid. ꆰ

Le Tour de Flora

We all know Tom Bodett as the bone-dry pitchman for Motel 6, "We'll leave the light on for you." He is also an author and philosopher. *The End of the Road* is his heartwarming account of life from Homer, Alaska. Early in the endearing little paperback, he waxes on the enormity of Alaska and a measure of superiority that comes from living in the Land of the Midnight Sun.

"Standing on the rim of a gaping fjord, I realized that if you were to dump every one of the billions and billions of hamburgers McDonald's ever sold into the bottom, you could barely see them."

I grew up in the flatlands of Illinois. After twenty-five years north of the Cheddar Curtain, I might reply to Mr. Bodett. Dear Tom, Wisconsin ain't bad either. We may not have gullies deep enough to hide hamburgers, but from Father's Day to well past Labor Day, our ditches, hillsides, prairies, and the edges of our woods are a feast for the senses.

There have been lows. In 2008, The New York Giants won the Super Bowl, the stock market crashed, and garlic mustard weed was thriving.

From west to east, it spread like disco and bell bottoms, obliterating nearly everything of beauty and taste in its path. If you looked hard, you could find an occasional daylily or purple phlox. The venerable chicory held her ground. Imported from Europe in the late 1800s, garlic mustard grew to be four feet tall and smelled like an Italian sous-chef's dirty laundry.

Either repulsed by our current political environment, or it's simply run its course, the noxious weed seems to be in retreat, once again rendering a trip through Wisconsin's blue highways a digitally-detached feast of the senses.*

BILL STORK

On July 15, we saddled up to celebrate my brother Glenn's sixty-first birthday with a Sunday morning tour around western Jefferson County. As a kid, Glenn was doing CrossFit in Kalamazoo, Michigan, twenty years before Reebok made their first shoe. His knees and shoulders have out-performed several limited lifetime warranties. Still, he looks ten years my junior.

Old guys on bikes.

Each ride is preceded by a half-ass hamstring stretch and dueling claims of futility.

"Well, Glenn, by the time we get to Haack's farm, I will have doubled my miles for the year."

"I'm with you. I had one too many mugs of BTQ at Tyranena last night, and my knee is on fire."

We agreed this would be an easy social ride.

Then we clipped in and tried to rip each other's legs off.

We kicked off from the parking lot at the Lake Mills Veterinary Clinic, the morning so still, the fog barely stirred over Rock Lake, flat as a mirror. The ground clouds hovered just above the canopy of flowers hunkered beneath in fallow fields and roadsides. We passed under the interstate. Condos gave way to cornfields. The morning smelled like mist over a marsh.

They were once speed bumps.

Now, we're off our saddles and panting hard, refusing to succumb to the rolling hills of Airport Road, two miles into our tour. The highway symphony fades, a breeze picks up, and suddenly it occurs—the fields are alive. The canvas upon which the mid-summer masterpiece is painted is the Queen Anne's lace and Golden Alexander. Like tiny wispy white and yellow umbrellas, every ditch not mowed, waterway, and hillside shimmers like the Milky Way over a Colorado midnight.

As Glenn opens the gap, my head drops to where blacktop meets roadbed. There grows the indefatigable chicory, decorating the ditches, camouflaging a thousand empty Miller Lite cans and cigarette butts tossed from jacked-up four-by-fours. Prized by health food nuts and hippies, her bittersweet roots sink deep in the hardpan. With tortuous barbed wire stems, she is unfazed by drought and tar. Pretty like the weathered farm wife with arms tanned on a tractor seat and shoulders hardened by a thousand bales of alfalfa. The dusty fronds of the flower, blue as her eyes, and the bandana that tends her hair, concealing the concern on her brow and resolve in her temple.

Clustered like sorority girls and happy as Pachelbel's *Canon* dancing in the west wind are the black-eyed Susans. You'll find them on the high-side of ditch banks, strewn across meadows and bordering woodlands. A few purple coneflowers hang around like gangly wannabees. Their tenacious presence from just after fireworks through the first hard frost is better than Prozac.

The daylilies—burnt orange, yellow, red, maroon, and hybrids. You'd never know they were there until the mid-morning sun climbs the sky and burns through the corn fog. Not until the heat waves begin to blur the blacktop do they yawn to greet the day. The ditch-weed divas, not showing their beauty until after coffee and croissants, and only days when the sun shines brightly.

Thirty miles in, we paused at the corner of West Medina Road and State Highway 73 to ensure the ping in my pocket was not a veterinary emergency and to catch my breath. I took a pull from my water bottle, gnawed a corner off a Cliff Bar, and gazed down the valley to Interstate 94 all aflow with outta-state SUVs, hybrids, and half-tons. They only get to pass through. Between gusts of the west breeze came a crescendo of the hum of radials on concrete and the thrum of a dozing driver jolted awake by the white-line rumble strip.

Between the river of weekenders and our country road cornice rolled a thousand acres of silage corn, spike leaves jutting skyward to announce the coming tassel and curling to escort any drop of dew straight to its roots. Just beyond, farmer Dave half emerges from the bowels of his machine shed, only his face is in the sun. He absently pulls a faded red shop towel from his back pocket to wipe the axle grease and mumbles a Hail Mary. He hopes for a market break to drive prices closer to break-even. One nostril draw directed my eyes to twenty acres of second-crop alfalfa laying in windrows before the baler gathers it, binds it, and throws it into the wagon behind. The next waft was eighty Holsteins just over the hill.

I finished off our rest stop with a water bottle baptism and a swig. As the lukewarm Gatorade dripped off my chin, I wadded half the Cliff brick into my jersey pocket. I shuffled my left shoe in the gawd-awful pea gravel and clicked my right into the pedal. Glenn issued disclaimer number two: "I'm starting to see stars. We'll really have to take it easy." In two miles, he dropped me like a landline.

The red columbine. She's a delicate flower hanging forlornly from a tiny stem, like the outcast who ate lunch by herself. Before the garlic mustard coup, she grew in abundance near the trestle over Rock Lake. The ten-year cloud lifted as I spied her in the scrabble beneath the stop sign at the corner of Medina and Ridge. She'd be the only one we'd see all day.

The phlox open up the summer flower festival by the first week in June, like an a cappella gospel group warming up a crowd for a country band. I always prayed they'd show up before Mother's Day. As dementia slowly consumed my mom's kindly mind, we'd delay the celebration until the ditches were alive with purple and white and say it was all for her. The purists call them dame's rocket and invasive, but they are a fragrant and spectacular intruder. They'll hide in the ditches among the cattails and grasses for June, July, and August, only to come back for a pre-fall curtain call.

We rolled into Cambridge on County Road O. I chuckled. Flags, banners, and signs beckoned families to check out The Vineyards at Cambridge, a host site for the 2018 Madison Builders Parade of Homes, on the south side of a hedgerow. On the north side is forty acres of summer wheat, recently combined, and spread with manure.

If the notion of another tariff, tweet, or headline makes your stomach turn like Sacha Baron Cohen in tighty-whities, ditch the device and take a hike, bike, or a drive.

*Wishful thinking back in 2018. As of July 2020, garlic mustard is as strong as ever. ꝙ

The Art of Roughhousing

It makes you wonder what happened in the back seat of the SUV on the way to the clinic.

Matt and Brooke White are the parents who flip the script so that we codgers can say, "You know what's right with kids these days."

In a recent article on the front page of the *Wisconsin State Journal*, authors cite an enormous body of research that echoes what common sense has known for millennia: playing is really good for kids. Experts from the Harvard School of Medicine, the American Academy of Pediatrics, and a group of researchers with multi-syllabic and hyphenated last names who are interviewed on NPR all feel that every conceivable real-life skill can be learned in the process of child-driven free play.

On playgrounds, in backyards and treehouses with their neighbors, friends, and their parents, kids learn language, connection, conflict resolution, resilience, confidence, empathy, and imagination. In *The Art of Roughhousing*, co-author Dr. Anthony DeBenedet cites the three modern impediments to physical play: screen time, an obsession with safety, and hyper academics (which I proudly could not even spell).

"Parents are more worried about a skinned knee or bruised feelings than life's real dangers of apathy and stifled creativity," says Dr. DeBenedet in one of his riveting Ted Talks.

Three-year-old Gabe White helped ensure his oldest brother would not suffer such a fate.

When there's a GMC Traverse with license plate HATRIX sitting on the curb, the first shift at Lakers Athletic Club is no longer a coffee clutch with treadmills. Matt White and several of his brothers played hockey all over the state of Wisconsin for over twenty years. Then came his wife, Brooke, and three boys. While I'm grunting out a rep with a pair of sixty-five-pound dumbbells, you'll find him under a 250-pound bar doing one-legged squats on a wobble ball with surgical precision and control. I imagine him as a projectile missile with pads and a stick flying around the rinks of the Fox Valley.

During a water break, he wiped the sweat from his face, while I caught my breath from racking the dumbbells.

"You're a vet, right?"

I'd tried, "No, but I did stay at a Holiday Inn Express last night," on a handful of millennials; not one ever got it.

"You bet," I assured him. He and his wife had adopted an eight-week-old Goldendoodle and were in need of care and guidance. I gave him an abbreviated guys-in-the-gym version of our pitch and encouraged him to give us a call.

Brooke is fresh-faced, doe-eyed, and every bit as fit as her husband. With right hand through the leash handle and toddler on her left hip, she reached for the door. Reggie, the puppy, sauntered through with the urgency of a Sunday morning, ahead of the rest of the White crew.

Like herding cats through a flock of sheep, Brooke made her way to the counter and greeted Claire with a smile and expression that said, "Just another day in the life."

We like to take at least forty minutes with first puppy visits to go over potty training, socialization, and proper health care. Not to mention, we really like puppy breath. Owing to the attention span of youth, Chuck Berry never wrote a song over two minutes, thirty seconds long. I adjust the tempo of my delivery in accordance with the energy of the kids.

Seven-year-old Griffin and five-year-old Sully were solid gold, gentle with Reggie, and attentive. Which means they're probably about to blow. Having covered potty training and socialization, I picked up my pace through vaccine protocols and parasite prevention.

As Brooke was asking about his fits of puppy piranha mode, I made a patient note to the effect, "beautiful coat, excellent body condition, no bite abnormalities, hernias, both testes descended, curiously calm." However, I suspected that sometimes he's the eye of the storm, and sometimes he is the hurricane. Using parent-friendly metaphors, I described games like puppy freeze tag (to inhibit mouthing on children) and appropriate use of timeouts with chew toys.

Little Gabe rested on Brooke's lap like a happy cherub.

Reggie was only eight weeks old, so I figured we'd breeze through the topic of neutering with a casual mention.

Gabe decided he'd demonstrate.

Without a hint to project his intention, Gabe slid from Brooke's lap, carefully ducked under the exam table, positioned himself squarely before his oldest brother, and delivered a thunderous soccer kick to the exact anatomic neighborhood we'd been discussing. Griffin crumpled to the floor like a wet towel, crying so hard that not a decibel of sound came out.

Brooke gave a quick glance at her second-grader writhing on the floor and focused on the conversation.

Following Mom's lead of non-reaction, I quickly offered that she and Matt make sure they use us as a resource. "Most things don't go exactly as you'd hope."

As she gathered up the puppy kit and clipped Reggie's leash, she rounded up her flock, "Come on, Griffin, it's time to go, and the floor is dirty."

I wondered what took place in the back seat on the way over. I also realized I was once Griffin. At about the same age, near the galvanized steel monkey bars at Brush College Elementary School, I used an abhorrent racial slur toward the only Asian boy in my class. In response, he delivered an emphatic lesson in empathy. And there began my departure from the narrow-mindedness that would piggyback a cracked exhaust manifold or blown carburetor into Dad's garage. Not from the mouths of bad people—simply folks who never had an opportunity to know better. ꧁

Grandpa's Walnuts

If there is a prion I'd attempt to implant on anyone who reads these ramblings, it would be awareness. Let us not get so wrapped up in whom our president has offended, whether Aaron Rodgers' knee will be good to go against the Vikings, or—God forbid—the next tweet or Facebook post to fail to absorb the splendor of a sunrise, sunset, or a random Tuesday afternoon.

One year ago, I was plucking black-eyed Susans to decorate our barn and rehearsing my wedding vows along the paths in Korth Park. Seventy-two hours after we said our "I dos" and "'til death do us parts," Dad was in the hospital. The end is inevitable, and when it was nigh, I made a conscious effort to absorb every emotion and nuance. As I sat vigil by my dad's bedside, wetting his lips with single malt and roiling over his eulogy, the CNAs and nurses cared as if he were their father, though they'd never known him close to his best.

Fond memories shouldn't require a wedding or a funeral.

Last Thursday, I met the Wollins for donuts, coffee, and commentary on sports, politics, and world news. We also palpated a baker's dozen cows for pregnancy. Routine, it would seem—as I watched the robot attach the claw to a Holstein—until I recalled the scene twenty-five years ago. Kyle was in high school, Erich at UW–River Falls, and Ed driven to the unthinkable brink of a job in town on the morning he bolted from bed to see the family farm leveled, for the second time in ten years, by a 111-mph derecho.

I try hard to never miss a moment of contrast.

The next stop was three miles south and fifty years back in time. Ellen Messmer milks her dozen cows into Surge buckets and carries them back to the bulk tank. Her dooryard is a drive-through dairy museum. Under the gravity-fed fuel tank is an open-faced lubricant shed, where hang a half-dozen grease guns and oil cans with bent snouts and brazed handles. Log chains, tire chains, turnbuckles, and clevises hang from the angle braces. A small anvil, to hammer old railroad spikes into gate hooks, stands atop a repurposed truck axle, welded onto an empty tire rim in front of the corn crib.

The circle drive arcs gradually enough for a tractor and hay rack between the dormant lilac bush and the farmhouse. The gravel is packed tight and rutted to puddle the rain and cradle the newly fallen fruit of the black walnut tree that stands near the clothesline pole. All pungent and green, they pop and roll beneath my tires. And with that smell and sound, I find myself in a moment back in Decatur, Illinois, 1972.

Mrs. Haynes lived kitty-corner from us on Nickey Avenue. She had pet parrots that flew around her kitchen while she made oil paintings of barns, schools, and churches, and baked cinnamon bread. An upright piano sat silently next to the wall by the stairs. Porcelain teapots with plastic daisies sat atop a doily. The sheet music for "When the Saints Go Marching In" rested dog-eared and yellowed on the piano. Her driveway was cobbled like an abandoned factory, her lawn like a chisel-plowed field seeded with crabgrass. At the top of her yard, half in the ditch, stood a walnut tree. I shoveled her snow and mowed her lawn from the day I was tall enough to reach the handle on the self-propelled Toro for seven dollars and a fresh loaf of her cinnamon bread. (Only now do I question the public health implications of the parrots flying around the kitchen.)

This time of year, the walnut tree would rain down two tons of their god-awful green fruit. Not only did they make mowing even more of a challenge, but my grandpa loved those damned walnuts. I'd collect them by the milk crate, box, and five-gallon bucket. Grandpa would go fishing while Dad and I were at work and school. He'd call after supper. "If you were going to be in the neighborhood, don't forget your filet knife, and did little Bill happen to pick any walnuts?" Dad and Grandpa would clean crappie, and Grandma would make me a quart-and-a-half milkshake I'd suck through a red-striped cardboard straw.

Grandpa would spread the nuts in the ruts of the cinder drive and run over them three or four times with his green Plymouth station wagon to get the flesh off and crack the shells. He sat for hours with a red plastic cup of near-beer on ice and a gnarly-jawed cracker. Straining over his horn-rimmed glasses, he teased the meat from the shells with pickers that looked like engraved dental instruments. The intact meat, bivalved like a butterfly, would get covered in caramel and chocolate in time for Christmas. The fractures and fragments were dropped in mason jars for cookies and banana bread.

I have precious few memories of my grandpa. The last was the gravel flying as my dad tore out of the parking lot at the baseball field in his 1968 Chevy when Grandpa had his heart attack. I was nine years old.

To this day, I can't stand the taste, texture, or smell of walnuts. It defies me why anyone would defile a perfectly good cake, cookie, or brownie with nuts of any sort. What I do recall is Grandma's milkshakes and how proud I was when we dropped the tailgate, and Grandpa would shake his head and woo at my haul. ◊

ADB

Saturday mornings, I listen to the Del McCoury Band, Doyle Lawson, or Rhonda Vincent. For breakfast, I eat a glazed blueberry donut and drink a carton of chocolate milk.

Some people come into our lives at a time of need or bring an energy, perspective, or spirit that affects our every breath. Whether by character or chronology, they become part of our DNA. I am blessed to know many, but I work to live my life in homage to the mazing Dick Bass.

If I speak kindly or extend a hand, it is in hopes that when I'm glory bound, I've earned the words said, and the tears shed the morning of Sunday, April 25, 1999, at the Cobb Creek Baptist Church in Atlanta, Georgia.

I came to know the Amazing Dick Bass at the University of Illinois. He was in pursuit of his PhD in electrical engineering, and I was in vet school. In order to step outside the haughty realm of academia and ensure happy hour Friday night did not segue into hangover Saturday morning, Dick and I would meet a block off campus at the Ye Olde Donut Shoppe at six o'clock.

Dick would have a blueberry glazed and a chocolate milk. He'd celebrate the first chug like a quart of Perrier in Death Valley, "Aww, so delicious, jes feel it coat your throat, all the way down to your belly." I'd have a white Long John in memory of Sunday mornings on the way to church with Dad.

We'd talk to Porter Kaise about the finer points of finishing asphalt and courting women from a front porch, with a pitcher of sweet tea. Porter drove a Lincoln Town Car and wore dress slacks to the donut shop. To this day, I don't speak his name without hanging on to the *aise* for a half-note and a nod.

One Saturday, we found ourselves in defense of *The Andy Griffith Show.* Bernie, the plumber, thought the rural references denigrating; Dick and I found the show romantic.

One nasty Saturday in December, staring down the barrel of finals week, I turned to Dick in numb resignation, "You know, this place does not have the best donuts ever."

"Naw, Billy Stork, I can't really argue with you there," as if Dick Bass would argue about anything. "Not to mention the coffee. This pond water in porcelain tastes like they've been using the same filter since Watergate."

We agreed it was all about the folks, put $2.50 on the counter, and wished our blue-collar brothers a good week. I pitched a dozen stalls, watered and fed four sick calves at the vet school, and had my head buried in clinical pathology notes when the library opened at nine.

I was oblivious to Dick's absence for the rest of that Saturday. Eight o'clock Sunday night, the door tapped open, and in walked a four-foot-tall stack of Krispy Kreme donuts. A bent pair of wire-rim glasses peeking over the top, he was grinnin' with his whole head.

Dick didn't know siccum about the mechanism of macrolide antibiotics, but his antidote for my anxiety over the pending exam was to drive to Louisville, Kentucky, and retrieve a truckload of the gold-standard pastries decades before they could be found at every corner gas station in the Corn Belt.

On fall Saturdays, Champaign–Urbanites would use the influx of football fans to empty their garages and basements—hippy Christmas for college students. We paused at a table that had prolapsed onto the sidewalk. It was piled with an ironing board, ab-rollers, a coffee pot, and a coda phone. By the garage, Dick moved a blender aside and held up the broken neck of a flat-black mandolin, the bridge and body hanging from four rusty strings. You'd have thought he'd just found Barbara Eden's bottle. "How much for the mandolin?" (pronounced man-a-lin)

Without bargaining, he handed the lady a five and thanked her.

He tucked the sad little instrument under his arm like it was Bill Monroe's '23 F-5, and we walked the three blocks home without a word. Dick Bass was one of those guys. If initially, he isn't making sense, he will. In time, my curiosity trumped my patience. I'd heard him play banjo, guitar, and piano.

"Dick Bass, you know anything about the mandolin?"

"No, Billy Stork, but it seems when folks down home get together to play, we're always missing a mandolin player."

For weeks the lonely instrument hung like a barn coat in the breezeway. Week by week, the strings were off, the neck was clamped, the bridge was glued, and she was strung again. Suspecting the spray paint was holding it together, he never tried to refinish.

The pursuit of a PhD is like the frog who jumps halfway to the wall. Writing a thesis is tedious, with lots of formulas, numbers, and collaboration. Labmates, instructors, and if you're Dick Bass, strangers on the street become family. He'd host Thursday and Sunday dinners. He'd cook fried chicken, meatloaf, turkey with all the fixin's, come one, come all. We'd stack the dirty dishes and retire to the front porch where he'd pass around a black three-ring binder with Big Square Grey House Book of Songs slipped into the cover, and we'd have a sing-along.

I'd request "Please Don't Bury Me," and Dick would twangle a banjo intro and deliver us to the first verse:

Woke up this morning,
put on my slippers,
walked into the kitchen and died.

I'd mumble and mouth the refrain until my favorite verse:

Throw my brain in a hurricane,
and the blind can have my eyes...

And so we'd spend Thursday evenings. If there was a break between songs, and a slow-moving Toyota crept past, Dick Bass would put down his banjo and chase it to the stoplight on Lincoln Avenue.

A newbie asked him why he chased cars. "I had an old dog that used to, down on the farm. He always had a big ole grin on his face when he was trottin' back up the driveway, so I thought I'd give it a try. Dog was right."

Dick Bass was a county fair caricature of an engineer. He spoke the learned diction of Jimmy Carter, with an occasional colloquialism sprinkled in. He was slightly built, with shoulders a bit sloped, disheveled red hair, freckles, and spectacles the size of a saucer. He'd take an elbow to the nose on the basketball court, and for weeks his gold wire-rims would be taped in the middle until he could get back to a soldering iron in the lab.

Compared to electrical engineers, veterinary students are a little more diverse. We were a gumbo of farmboys, army vets, Cajuns, rednecks, and a street musician, prone to half-barrel, backyard bonfire stress management. I asked Dick if he'd like to go along one Saturday night. "Sure, Billy Stork. I'd love to meet some of your friends."

We arrived in a forty-degree drizzle, a pair of old Pioneers in the window distorting Lynyrd Skynyrd:

Old Curt was a black man
with white, curly hair.
When he had a fifth of wine,
he did not have a care.

Lou, Lou, and Harry (Jon, Tom, and Hal) were proselytizing on education, fishing, and religion. Their faces glowing red, sitting on minivan back seats around a blazing pile of pallets. I parked Dick next to the fence while I went to fetch a couple of red Solo cups. En route, I found myself locked into a conversation about waterskiing and etouffee with Elizabeth Clyde. Self-conscious, but only mildly concerned I'd left my friend for over thirty minutes, he was right where I'd left him, semi-circled and slapping knees with Matt, Chris, and Paul.

His PhD thesis was titled "Large-Signal Tools for Power Electronics: State-Space Analysis and Averaging Theory." He had worked to advance adaptive and mobility devices for the disabled. His defense drew interest from the IEEE staff, the Veterans Administration, and

General Electric. The auditorium was packed. Several hours into his defense, he paused. "Man, I'm getting a little tarred in the head." At which point, he passed out boxes of donuts, gallons of chocolate milk, and laid acetate copies of Dr. Seuss on the overhead. And he read:
"Sam-I-am,
I do not like green eggs and ham."

Research says the downest day of the week is Tuesday afternoon, which is when Dick Bass would lead students, faculty, and administrators of the University of Illinois Electrical Engineering Department, high stepping and singing through the dank marble caverns of Everitt Hall, "I'm a Pepper, she's a Pepper, we're all Peppers. Wouldn't you like to be a Pepper too?"

They'd convene at the soda machine for a few moments of camaraderie, then get back to research.

I've previously written of how he aspired to Kermit the Frog, until the day we found him serenading a flotilla of pontoon boat partiers on Lake Shelbyville, kicked back on an inner tube, picking his banjo. "Billy Stork, Kermit the Frog ain't got nothing on me today," the closest I'd ever hear him get to bravado.

Dick received his PhD in 1990. He returned to his native Georgia to teach at the Georgia Institute of Technology and live four hours from his Uncle Johnny, who raised Vidalia sweet onions on his farm near Blackshear. At GT, he quickly ascended to associate professor and accumulated several awards for excellence in teaching. At Uncle Johnny's, they picked bluegrass on the front porch until a train came by so they could play countin' and guessin'.

I graduated in 1992 and migrated across the Cheddar Curtain, but the Amazing Dick Bass is the friend from whom you never stray. He and Johnny Bass would record ninety-second pickin'-and-grinnin' comedy skits, then play them into our answering machine while we were at work. And he'd send letters.

Dear Billy Stork,

Things are great down here in Georgia. Cathy and I joined the choir at our Baptist Church. They were fine with our singing, but had to teach us all about rhythm.

Just got back from a week with Cathy's family in France. They heard Americans like Coke and potato chips. After a week, I was ready for a little something different. The French don't get up too early in the morning, 'cept Cathy's brother. Since he didn't speak a lick of English, and I only know a few words of French, the only thing we could do is play Scrabble.

Regards, Dick

There are moments. The birth of my daughter. Hugging and holding my friend Ned when the plane flew into the second tower. And the call from our friend Bernie to deliver the news that the Amazing Dick Bass was dead. I tried to twist the cordless phone like an empty water bottle, then pressed it to my forehead until it started to crack. He was en route to the hospital to be with his dad when he rear-ended a semi.

Kish had introduced me to Dick Bass in the beginning; he was my first call. We decided we'd find flights to Atlanta and rendezvous when we got to town. A moment after we'd hung up, I walked to the screened porch and hit redial. "Kish, we're celebrating the legacy of a man who made every minute of every day and every mile of highway special—"

He finished my sentence. "Road trip."

Kish and his wife, Anita, and Gary and I met at the foot of the alma mater statue on campus at the U of I. I told of the time we helped move the dilapidated upright piano in the back of Dick's truck. Since I could handle a clutch, I got to drive. Moving day was gridlock on Green Street, so Dick Bass, the bluegrass man, started banging out pop tunes sitting on the fender well of the brown S-10, fielding requests from pedestrians and delivery trucks stuck in the jam.

We paused before the Big Square Grey House and Everitt Hall. Before we headed south on Route 55, we had burgers at Murphy's. Kish launched himself off his bar stool. Dick was known to spontaneously fall off his chair into the middle of a bar, spewing papers from his backpack.

We made the iconic Bluebird Café in Nashville by Saturday night for songwriters in the round. As the night drew to a close, Hayden Nicholas brought the house to its feet with "A Better Man," which he co-wrote with Clint Black. Only to be trumped by George Terry doing a little song he wrote with Eric Clapton called "Lay Down Sally."

A lesser-known and slightly-built writer named Jason Blum sat at the end of our table. When his turn came, he humbly leaned his lips to the microphone. "Well, I've never written for Clint Black or Garth Brooks, but I did write a song for the victims of the Paducah, Kentucky, school shootings." He sang in a whisper and barely touched the strings. "I asked for strength, and you gave me mountains. I asked for love, you gave me strangers in need."

He dropped his head and strummed the last chord. The respect in Bluebird was broken only by a golf clap and the scuff of boots and Birkenstocks, as folks filed toward the door. The four of us streaming tears, he turned and nodded, wishing us strength on our journey.

He had no idea of our pilgrimage. We had no idea our journey would be twenty years and counting.

We were pulling onto Interstate 24 Sunday morning as the sun rose over the Smokies. Under the fog, on the horizon rolled a cloud of gravel dust. Kish speculated construction. I pointed out the time and day. He hit the hazards. We arrived just as a Suzuki Samurai was making its final barrel roll. Still rocking on its roof, the door was buried in the number four road pack. Kish, Gary, and I were able to rock the little roller skate to the point we could tear the door from its hinges. Windshield cracked like a spider's web, and blood dripping from gashes on his forehead, the driver called for his buddy. A few more motorists must have stopped. I recall Anita directing them down the ditch for a manhunt. He was able to hold his head up, so I deduced he had not broken his neck. His pupils were appropriate and responsive, and he knew his name (or a name), so I figured it was safe to attempt an extraction. With his full weight hanging against the button, I could not free him from his seat belt. I stuck my hand behind me, and Gary laid his pocketknife in my palm like a relay baton with a razor's edge. I crawled my body under his and sawed the belt free.

If I were a fiction writer or didn't have three witnesses, I'd have us diving in the ditches as the car burst into flames.

A Tennessee State Trooper arrived in time to sympathize. "Ah, I wouldn't worry about his so-called buddy; he's just drunk." The ambulance arrived in minutes. We briefed them, they thanked us, and we were once again southbound.

We found a filling station at Route 102. Evidently, blood-covered Yanks at six o'clock on a Sunday morning are nothing new to Gomer Pyle. When I asked for the bathroom to scrub the blood and change, he just nodded and threw me the key—a dog chain through an inch-and-a-quarter socket to ensure I didn't accidentally put it in my pocket and head to Atlanta.

Kish drove tangents and tapped the brakes through the Monteagle Grade. I searched for the symbolism as we sunk into the clouds that hovered in the treetops.

We were fourth in line at the Krispy Kreme in Chattanooga, slightly nauseous, yet salivating like Pavlov's dogs, as the fried dough rose from the bubbling grease vat and crept down the conveyor to be sprayed with white icing, like Matchboxes through a car wash. The dozen glazed gut bombs were down to six before we were back on the interstate, ten minutes before they were rightfully cool enough to eat.

We made the dusty parking lot at the Cobb Creek Baptist Church as the first few mourners trickled in.

Strangers bound by kinship. When words failed, we'd nod and extend a hand. We found a bathroom in the basement to tie our ties and unruffle our suit coats. We nodded at the church ladies sorting silverware, tending casseroles and ham loaf.

Minus the only two white faces, the Cobb Creek Gospel Choir spread across the altar left to right. They swung slowly in their white flowing robes, singing "Down to the River to Pray" and "I Can't Even Walk" on low. Only a few polite decibels, their voices like a hug, filling every space not otherwise occupied by a person, pew, or Bible.

Dick had told me about his bluegrass gospel outfit. "You know, Billy Stork. It don't matter— Catholic, Baptist, Lutheran; we just like to liven up the service a little bit."

Around no microphone, the bass, fiddle, guitar, and banjo players gathered. At the bottom of their U, in missing man formation, a chrome stand featured a two-tone Sunburst Gibson A-12 mandolin, with the stem of one white rose wedged under the tuning pegs. They struggled through "I'll Fly Away" and "Old Rugged Cross," then fell silent. The guitar player crossed his hands over his instrument and made no attempt to catch the tears.

"Not only did we lose one of the finest man-a-lin pickers and tenor singers I've ever heard, we've lost a friend. Dick Bass had a spirit. I can't tell you if it was a pause, an inflection, or a single bent note, but the minute that man stepped into our circle—and every time since—it was like songs we'd been singing for the last twenty years were brand new."

The stained glass windows propped wide, the parking lot filled with Cadillac sedans, Mercedes SUVs, and farm trucks. Inside, the congregation swelled. The cavernous house of worship was filled with joy faculty, graduate students, kinfolks, and friends until we all stood shoulder-to-shoulder. I made small talk with the Dean of the College of Electrical Engineering who stood to my right. The choir decrescendoed, and the minister shuffled the ribbons in his Bible.

The silence was broken by a few coughs, several sobs, and then the screech of the brakes of three city buses.

With their eyes to the floor and wrists together like prisoners of war, in filed the residents of the Atlanta YMCA, group homes, men's shelters, soup kitchens … and the street. Dressed in the throwaways of the well-to-dos in the pews and Goodwill, the men, homeless and destitute, crowded the vestibule and the back of the church. After only a moment's thought, the minister spread his arms and motioned for them to sit among us. In the likeness of the man whose life we'd gathered to celebrate, loss knows no education, status, or fortune.

Looking to stifle the back-of-the-hand murmurs and crinkled noses, I leaned to the dean. "Have you ever asked what Dr. Bass does before he commences his research and teaching each day?"

He quarter-cocked his head and raised his eyes.

"He feeds them breakfast."

  BILL STORK

Just Dial

Claire will text when I'm in the middle of a herd check if she has client questions, new calls, or when she senses the technicians are staging a coup. My wife is the queen of concise and very respectful of business hours. She'll only message if she's spotted a broken-down farm sink by the side of the road, a she shed, or a homeless monkey. When the Samsung pings more than three times, it's either Uncle Scott on a political rant or a message from a client. It could be a vomiting dog, down cow, or a seven-gram turtle who's passed an eighteen-inch tapeworm (zero exaggeration).

Our phone service converts voice messages into text … kinda.

"Hi, Sue Nelson Alba first time effort and she had been milking really good, but she's dropped way off and can feed him the last day or two time, just would really like a check. So I don't know if she's got pneumonia Christie at that maybe da but when she did Coop this morning. So 608-555-1212 thanks."

Thank goodness for technology?

I migrated north of the Cheddar Curtain in 1992 to care for dogs, cats, cows, and horses, and for love (four out of five is eighty percent). Thanks to a Herculean family effort, I graduated from eight years of college debt-free. My starting salary was not chump change, but I was looking to live lean. A perk to the love deal was a farmhouse in Johnson Creek for $300/month.

My friend Jack Stachnik is a retired Air Force fighter pilot. He now flies freight for Federal Express. Whether a CEO, truck driver, or pilot, every new Federal Express employee starts on the line, sorting, loading trucks, and delivering packages. After weeks of working from the bottom up, they get to their corner office or cockpit.

The initiation process at Lake Mills Veterinary Clinic was less structured. A Wisconsin graduate named Dr. Myron Kebus and I started on June 15. Joyce Kuhl had been the receptionist at LMVC since the State Farm office was a blacksmith's shop. She's aged like Dick Clark. Several years ago, she moved to Trinity Pines Retirement Center. I'm pretty sure she mows their grass and shovels snow.

Day one, she sat behind the desk fielding phone calls. She covered the receiver with her left hand and glanced at the appointment book, "Good morning, men. Richard Maahs and Joe Spoke have cows off feed, and Jim Flood has a milk fever. Dr. Anderson says everything you need should be in the basement."

We fumbled in the dark for thermometers, fluids, IV sets, and syringes and threw them into our Craftsman toolboxes with the stickers still on. In 1992, a Garmin GPS cost $2,500 and couldn't find the Sears Tower on a sunny day. We had plat books and Joyce:

"Turn left out of the clinic, wrap around the north end of the lake, veer right at Dick Tarnutzer's place, go under the interstate. Keep trending left until you get to the barn with the Redbird mural on it, turn left, go back under the interstate, past St. John's Lutheran Church. He's the first farm on your left, at the end of the long drive. Joe can tell you how to get to Richard's."

Dr. Kebus and I stumbled through a half-dozen dairy barns armed with clipboards, stethoscopes, and shoulder-length latex gloves. With the collective confidence of a Lab pup in a lion's den and the efficiency of a government subcontractor, we generated our list of differential diagnoses, contemplated treatment options, and eventually managed to medicate two cows for ketosis and a displaced abomasum and amuse the heck out of a handful of dairy farmers.

Myron and I had questioned whether Dr. Anderson's hiring two greenhorns to commence on the same day was predicated on demand or desperation. The answers came quickly. The two-way radio wired to the whip antenna on his rear fender mysteriously quit the very day we started. Well into his sixties, Dr. Anderson resorted to cafeteria-style practice. He'd arrive first, put his initials next to a configuration of calls that painted the corners of our practice radius and route past Zwieg's Diner on Tuesdays for their meatloaf special.

🐕 BILL STORK

Dr. Anderson did not like pickup trucks or work boots. He drove a slow ark into the parking lot in his late aunt's Oldsmobile Delta 88 diesel, squatting like a Catholic family to Easter service. He'd removed the back seat to carry fluids, foot trimming equipment, and a block and tackle for pulling calves. Dr. Anderson kicked the Tingley rubber overshoes off his Allen Edmonds and offered us a shot of plastic bottle Scotch. Continuing the baptism-by-fire initiation process, he offered to take care of overnight emergencies, but he'd be at a meeting for the rest of the week. "The two of you can handle things just fine," he said with misguided faith in the Universities of Illinois and Wisconsin.

There were questions I should have asked.

He asked for our telephone numbers so Joyce could call-forward. I only made it to 6-9-9 when he looked at me like I'd just farted in his daughter's face on our first date. "Well, that's a Johnson Creek telephone number," he growled.

Looking to appeal to the Scotsman's tendency to pinch a penny into copper wire, "Yes, sir, it's a local call, and I'm eleven minutes from the clinic by interstate."

The other half of Dr. Anderson's Northern European family tree was German. "It is assumed that an employee of the Lake Mills Veterinary Clinic will have a local address *and* telephone number."

Compromise was not a component of Dr. Anderson's negotiating style, so Myron and I found a room in an old-folks home near the Catholic church for the nights and weekends we were on call.

When Dr. Anderson was on call, so was his wife, Mary Lee. If Bob was pulling a calf for the Wollins when the Schultzes called in with a down cow, she took the message and waited for him to find a barn phone and call in.

For my weekends and nights on call, I had no Mary Lee or equivalent. (For the record, Mary Lee Anderson was a force of nature; there was no replacement.) I had an answering machine. When I had to mow the grass, I'd make four rounds, then idle the tractor and run inside, across the newspapers on the floor to check for a blinking green light.

I spent the extra fifty bucks at Best Buy to get an answering machine with remote access. If I had a midnight calving, I could call the machine and retrieve new messages, if the farm had a touchtone barn phone. Then I'd hope no one called during the thirty minutes it took to scrub my boots and drive home.

I heard from clients that in the event Mary Lee was gone to a Michigan football game or NASCAR race, Dr. Anderson had a battery-powered squawk box. For the majority of the barns that still had rotary phones, he could hold the little device to the receiver, and it'd mimic the security code for his answering machine.

After a year of prolapsed uterus calls and keyhole cat spays, Dr. Kebus gathered the courage to pursue his passion. He became the state's first and only dedicated fish vet and opened Wisconsin Aquatic Veterinary Service (WAVS). German persistence being as it may, Dr. Anderson's only option to not be on call was the flat-topped, flannel-wearing flatlander. I politely explained that I'd be pulling my alarm clock and answering machine out of the nursing home on College Avenue that Myron and I had been hunkering in.

Dr. Kebus's departure was coincident with an advance of technology. Google says the first mobile phone was around 1973. It took another twenty years to make it to Jefferson County, Wisconsin. My father-in-law helped hard-wire a Motorola car phone into the dash of my powder blue half-ton Chevy WT.*

By the mid-1990s, my phone detached from the dashboard and into a bag the size of my grandma's purse, which would not pass for carry-on luggage, but I'd challenge any TSA agent to take it from her. From the dooryard, or near a window, on a sunny day, when I could visualize the tower, and if a flock of birds didn't fly past, I could get ahold of HQ. I think I had one brick phone. It was approximately the size of the Panasonic AM radio I listened to baseball games on as a kid. They did not float, were not particularly water-resistant, and the battery lasted about one short story.

Which was just fine, because in short order came the flip phone.

Flip phones were compact, durable, and had superior reception, but the best part was the move. Us rednecks would use the side of

 BILL STORK

our thumb while it was still down low. The white-shirt types would retrieve it from their breast pocket, step aside, cock their elbow and flick it open just before arriving at the ear. Dallas Cowboys owner Jerry Jones is worth three billion dollars. He, Warren Buffett, Scarlett Johansson, and Ryan Haack still use them.

Then came the pager. As fashionable as khakis and Crocs, the little black box on our belt would vibrate or ping, alerting us there was a message to be checked. They were also a valuable prop. If there were three baptisms tacked onto the end of eight o'clock Mass or windbag Jim was droning on during a Rock Lake Improvement meeting, I'd grab the pager from my belt, hit the button, stare at the display, crease my brow, cross myself, and hit the door.

We were liberated while on call. We could ride our bikes, go to the beach, or split firewood. If there was an emergency, the service would call.

For a while, the service was a real-live person who answered for the clinic, took a message, and called us—when they could stay awake. Jim Erb called with a dystocia at midnight. The service pinged my pager. When I attempted to retrieve the message, the phone rang to nowhere for four hours. When Spicolli finally answered, "Yo, sorry, dude. It was a slow night, and I was hangin' hard. I must-a fell asleep." (Yes, seriously.)

The next day, Doreen was in the market for an automated system. For the next several years, we used the Woody. Jim Woodward installed a system the likes of Air Traffic Control at O'Hare International. He was the only man on the planet who (kinda) understood it. The Woody worked well unless there was a thunderstorm over Kansas or a moped hit a power pole down by the Culver's. Well into the era of Facebook, Amazon, and the smartphone, to switch messages or recipients required traveling to the clinic. When it came to romance, it was the functional equivalent of taking the babysitter home. If I wanted to be off long enough to take Sheila to Norm's Hideaway for fish for our anniversary, I had to drive to Lake Mills and hit three buttons.

Confession. Nearly as soon as car phones became cell phones, they could ring, vibrate, repeat, and had their own voice mail. Why do we insist on using Spicolli, Woody, and Hal? Because clients in need will leave messages. Folks calling to find our hours, make appointments for a nail trim on Thursday, or find out how much a thirteen-pound bag of Urinary SO is, will not.

Which brings us up to 2018. Mittsy found a new system by Nextiva. She spent enough time in teleconferences with their programmers to be common-law married, but we can modulate the system from our cell phones. Hal has yet to miss a message. The system translates the client's perceived voice message to text. It captures their telephone number electronically and never misses. While I can almost always pluck a key word like, vomit, diarrhea, or bleeding out of the message, the context is usually really entertaining.

I received a call Saturday afternoon. The text translation read: "Hi, my name is James Brown. I see my daughter Casey Tuesday or shepherds are paid and ask for the last few days of mutton. He's been really itch, and Adam Popper on detail the end of a sale towards of anal area, and he's pretty much screwed up all the hair, and it looks kind of quasi. I'm not real sure what to do. I did put a call 921 keep irritating that please call me at 608-867-5309 at 608-867-5309. Thank you."

Hal also sends the voice recording. What the above caller actually said:

"Hi, my name is Jessica Baratti. I have a six-month-old Shar Pei-Shepherd cross. For the last several days, he's been itching at the base of his tail, kind of near his anal area. He has the hair in the area nearly chewed off. I put his cone on him, and I really don't know what to do. If you could give me a call, I'd really appreciate it. Thank you."

---

*My father-in-law was nothing, if not thorough. That dash-mounted Motorola withstood a full-on assault from a hallucinogenic Blue Heeler in full-on attack and shit mode. ⌕

Just Stop by Our Home

Sheila wasn't supposed to ride her pony until her folks got out of bed on Saturday morning. After thirty years of milking cows, Butch and Judy Barnes sold the herd and took up over-the-road trucking. When they were home on weekends, they didn't always see dawn. The little red-headed cherub would con her oldest brother, Ty, into helping her saddle her pony, Cheyenne. She rode through the dooryard, down the laneway to the marsh and back. She'd unsaddle, dry him off, feed him a flake of hay and a scoop of sweet feed and be back in the house before Mom and Dad stirred. Before Butch could pry his lids open, she'd beg him to help her saddle the tired little Shetland so she could ride again.

I was first welcomed to Wisconsin by Ned and Sarah Healy. Sarah was a technician at the Jefferson Veterinary Clinic, where I'd learned to palpate cows in my senior year of vet school, riding with the legendary Dr. Ed Dettmers. He also introduced me to the best pie joints and lunch specials in the county. In support of an iconic lineup of vets, Jefferson was blessed with an all-star lineup of technicians. In addition to Sarah, they had Linda "B," Jody Dudek, and Sheila on the payroll. Sheila has shoulder-length auburn hair and eyes that fade from blue, through green, to grey. She looks nearly as good in blue Dickies coveralls treating a down cow on a dairy farm as in her best pair of Wranglers, but the traits that define Sheila Barnes ride her RNA. Every tailgate conversation where she was a subject would conclude, "You know, there's just something about Sheila."

After fifteen years of admiration from afar, it took ten miles in the passenger seat of my Subaru to know exactly what that "just something" was all about.

I'd stopped at Tyranena for a set of neo-honky-tonk tunes from the Dang-Its, a Rocky's Revenge, and a pearl of wisdom from the flatland philosopher Charlie Roy. My final destination was the Harmony Bar in Madison, but Joel Paterson didn't play a note before ten at night. Ned and Sarah showed up, and Sheila followed shortly. I'm convinced it was not happenstance. The Healys had been in the barn since four in the morning and were catching a train to Chicago the next morning. Tyranena was to be one "now we're on vacation" beer. Swing dancing in Madison was their last intent, but they knew Sheila would bail if they didn't come, so they took one for their bachelor buddy, Bill. Sheila was tepid at best, content to head home or ride with the Healys. In his second good turn of the night, Ned kicked her out of their van, into my car.

I thank him daily.

On the drive, she spoke of her grandma, their garden, and the farm. It took eight miles, by the Deerfield exit, and I was smitten.

We called our first several months "not dating." When conversation turned to the farm, her tone would settle into calm. By the spring of 2010, I'd earned an invitation. We walked her three Labs Gunner, Matrix, and Remmi, a hundred yards south of the barn. Just past the grove of volunteer box elders growing on the spoil pile and up the hill from the dump was a brush pile old enough to show up on Google Earth. Like a little girl at a dollhouse, she pointed, "That's where I want to build my tiny house" (with two lofts and a wrap-around porch).

Each time she passed that sacred sight, her temple went soft, and her eyes shone. She'd rather live in a toolshed on that pasture than a mansion on the lake with staff to serve her. Seven years later, in a spitting March rain, I planted a flat stone where I thought our rocking chairs would be, knelt in the mud, and asked to join her family.

Jon Bound is the Jefferson Township builder of choice. He is also Sheila's cousin by marriage. A skilled and brilliant man, he took leave of his sanity and agreed to build our home—a lapse he'd surely regret at times. Our lot had been plotted in 1996 when Sheila's brother built his house. Detailed as watchmakers, Ty and Tina had sat on every board in the township and county. In order to pull all the permits, they could tell us where to dot every "i," cross every "t," and file every sheet of paper. Still, it took six months of meetings with the highway commission, town board, county board, school board, surveyors, Wisconsin Energies, and the second past president of the Fort Atkinson FFA to get final permission to build.

Jon referred us to the Design Alliance in Fort Atkinson. He felt Pete and Jason would be best suited to accommodate Sheila's preferences. They were gracious enough to accommodate our work schedules; we met mornings at six-thirty. Over cups of coffee, we convened in Pete's parlor and wrestled with the position of the fireplace, height of the ceilings, placement of the dining room, and the bathroom sinks. We deemed the kitchen, dining, and living room "the great space" and debated how big it needed to be.

I asked Pete about Christmas. My family was 250 miles south, and I could hold a reunion in a phone booth. I cherished holidays at Butch and Judy's farmhouse. When it was our turn to host, I wanted to ensure there was plenty of room for the aunts, uncles, nieces, nephews, grandkids, and in-laws. He massaged his chin and twirled his draftsman's pencil on his knuckle as he surveyed the blueprint.

"Bill, the most awesome concert you've ever been to, was it in a stadium or a bar?" He knew my answer. "The best part of holidays is being piled on top of one another around a folding table, eating ham, scalloped corn, and cheesy potatoes. Besides, the rest of the year, it's just the two of you."*

I smiled and we shrunk the space by several feet in both dimensions.

Finally, on December 16, 2017, Jeff and Nick from Gallitz Grading pulled on with a Cat D6 and a track hoe. Jeff dug two holes out back. One was big enough for our thirty-five-year-old Quarter Horse Stormy and our old goat Percy.**

The other was the foundation for our home.

They back-filled the foundation on January 16, a date by which many builders are going to trade shows in Florida, taking indoor golf lessons, or vacationing in the Dominican Republic. JB Construction built our home. Buffeted by coastal velocity winds, a month of snow, and single-digit highs, Jon, Brad, Garret, and Colton never broke stride. They had the deck on and the walls up in a week, a propane heater blowing in a pressboard corner, their pickups facing south at lunch, and perpetual productivity their only source of heat.

I had this notion of having winter 2017–18 free to ride my bike trainer and write my masterpiece. All we had to do was pick out the tile, wall colors, a few light fixtures, and cabinets. We could walk through on Sunday afternoon, take pictures, and marvel at the progress. Jon would let us know when to move in.

Not so much.

It started with a pile of barn beams Dave Behling had sitting by Kroghville Road a decade ago:

$80.00
OBO

My first thought was to build them into a mantle and a king-sized bed. I saved images on Pinterest and scratched out designs on scraps of paper, but for ten years, they were benches for Storkfest one day a year. The other 364 days, they were twenty-foot stumbling blocks. I fetched them out of the burning pile on three different occasions. I've got two prolapsed disks and a scrotal hernia owing to my indecision and ineptitude.

Sheila said, "You think we could frame the doorway to the sunroom with them?" Hewn from native oaks, they were drawknife scarred and broadaxe pegged. They'd represent a reverence for the hard-handed Europeans who had settled this state 130 years ago. They were also eight inches wide and thick. To avoid obscuring our view of the horse pasture beyond that door, we'd have to widen the doorway or rip the beams in half. My idea of fine-finished carpentry is a big hammer and a small chainsaw, which would surely challenge Jon's penchant for precision.

We needed Uncle Jerry.

Milford, Wisconsin, is a two-blink town—one on each side of the Crawfish River. What it lacks in population, it doubles in character. Steve Drevlow lives in the old cheese factory. He's an Army vet, ER nurse, carpenter, mechanic, artist, sculptor, and classical pianist, who grew up on the periphery of an Indian reservation in North Dakota. Across Highway Q is Jerry Sawyer, an artist, sculptor, and musician. Vandre's Riverside Inn has been boarded up for a decade or more, but across the river, you can get the fish fry voted Best in Madison 2015 at Crawfish Junction.

If you approach from the Wollin side of town, you'll pass a sign:

Jerry's Stump Removal
920-648-5000

There wasn't room for Jerry and Deb's stump removal, log sawing, massive flag repairing, blood drive volunteering, and trucking. The Milford Topels happen to be two of the nicest folks you'll ever meet. On my way back from Griswold's farm, I saw Jerry's trucks out back and the garage door open.

So, I stopped by.

I described my job. Jerry's sawmill has more horsepower than a Toyota Prius. It can render a sixteen-foot-long tree, four feet in diameter, into fencing boards in half an hour. He could hemisection a pair of barn beams like a Skilsaw through a paint stick.

Jerry drives truck for Roundy's four days a week. When he's on the road, he leaves by three in the morning. He was free Tuesday after work. It had rained for nearly forty days and nights, so I had the beams in the horse trailer. I checked my mirrors, swung wide, and snaked the truck and trailer six inches past their mailbox and down the drive, in one go. I was feeling a little proud when Jerry boomed, "Dang, man, if this whole vet thing doesn't work out, you'd make a pretty decent truck driver."

It took fifteen minutes to set, square, and level the beams on the sawmill. In his protective gear, Jerry guided the four-cylinder bandsaw with the focus of a urologist performing a robotic prostatectomy. I know about nails. Mike Perry's neighbor Tom has a sawmill. He declines to cut yard trees, pointing at the teeth, seven dollars apiece. I promised Jerry I'd look as close as I could. He thanked me and pointed to a stack of blades, "I bought a machine, sharpen my own."

I followed along the blade with my flashlight. Behind his safety goggles and earmuffs, Jerry watched my left hand for a big "ho" if I saw a nail coming. We missed two by millimeters.

I'd wrestled those sixteen-foot stumbling blocks so many times, and I was actually looking forward to them weighing half as much. Jerry insisted on helping me put them back on the trailer. A trucker never turns a wheel until his load is secure, so I double-checked the latch and pinned the end gate on the trailer.

I was pretty sure I'd have better luck pulling a dozen red roses out of a bale of straw than getting Jerry to give me a price. I squared up to give the old, "Well, Jerry, how much you reckon I owe ya?"

He cut me short. With his working-man forearms across his barrel chest, looking through his safety glasses, he looked to a couple of rows of tarps lined up neatly under the pine trees and rubbed his chin, "You know, Bill, I think a guy brought me some black walnut once upon a time. You want to see what that looks like?"

I did not hesitate. "What in the hell kinda question is that, Jerry?"

I hadn't seen my wife since five in the morning and hadn't eaten in eight hours. Sheila would understand, and I've developed some deposits of caloric reserve.

We pulled a blue tarp off to reveal a stack of slabs six feet long and four inches thick, with a live edge. The grains ranged from black to mahogany, tobacco, and chocolate. In years of drought, the rings were dollar bill thin and thick as a crepe when rains fell amply. A nut that had fallen at the edge of a cornfield near the start of World War II was now a work of art laying on a decommissioned trailer, a product of the sun and earth, fertilized by overthrow from a ground-driven manure spreader.

"So, Bill, what'd you think?"

We loaded all seven pieces on the trailer. Before I could ask him the question I already knew the answer to, he retreated to the bowels of

his shop. Behind a wall of one-by-twelve cedar, he pulled out one last hunk of six-feet-long walnut with two live edges and a knot at the end.

"This one's kind of a mutt. You might as well throw this one on top. Maybe you'll just chunk it up and use it for firewood."

Price haggling with Jerry is the inverse of used car shopping, "Oh, Bill, why don't you take it home to Sheila. She may not like it. See if you're even gonna be able to use any of it. Making you and Sheila happy is the most important part."

Builder Jon had a handful of fine cabinetmakers he had worked with in the past, and there were a half-dozen "custom cabinet showrooms" lined up down the Beltline in Madison. I'm confident they all do beautiful work, but I've ridden bikes with John Spaude for years. He's built benches for us at the clinic that have endured the weight of humanity for fifteen years without so much as a wobble or turn of a screw.

He lives just around the bend from Tim Claas on West Road. So, one day in January, after I'd treated a down cow, I stopped by.

On a Wednesday night bike ride in a Peloton doing twenty-two miles an hour, John will sit on your wheel through a crossing headwind, then attack you on a hill. He will bust your head fifty meters before the parking lot in a sprint finish. He qualifies for the American Birkebeiner every year. A magician with a router, plane, and table saw, John applies considerably less urgency to his art. Drying on racks and laying on benches were cabinet faces and drawers of three projects in various stages of completion. Jon the builder is famous for his critical path and adherence to timelines, so I asked if John the cabinetmaker thought mid-April was realistic. His Gabe Kaplan mustache rose, his head tilted, and shoulders shrugged, "That should be no problem." I told Jon to expect cabinets by late-May.

Thirty-five years of building kitchens for women is not lost on John Spaude. Before we could even think about oak, maple, or alder, he needed to know what time we get home from work, whether we cook from scratch, and how often we go to the market. Are we often in the kitchen together? How often were we likely to entertain, and who would we have over?

To capture John's skills as an artist, and test the suspension of his van and his wife Terri's back, we decided on hickory. It took Michelangelo four years to paint the most famous ceiling in the world, and the Sistine Chapel never flooded with ice water. Mid-January 2018, seven inches of rain fell on top of a healthy snowpack. The flood undermined the ice dams, which plowed through John's shop and heaved his floor. After John rebuilt his shop, mid-April became early June, but if it had taken until August, the wait would have been rewarded. The grain in the drawer faces under the liquor cabinet line up to look like an Arizona desert sunset. The row next to the stove—a Mojave sand glass art box. The face of the baking cabinet looks like a slice of two-hundred-year-old monument hickory. It's assembled from five different pieces.

In good times and in bad, I try and build multiple small celebrations, and art, into every day. I drink my Sunday coffee from a hand-thrown mug from my friends Brad Wells, Mark Skudlarek, or Bruce Johnson. My "world's best chili" is heavy on the cumin. The meniscus of the smoky red brew complements the chocolate-green glaze of a favorite bowl Mark left at our house ten years ago.

Mark had made the bathroom sinks in our old home. The realtor discouraged me from taking them when we moved. Mark built his wood-fired kiln the size of a two-car garage and his studio—surely he could make a farmhouse sink.

Mark lives at the end of Tranquil Lane, halfway between Cambridge and Rockdale, Wisconsin.

I stopped by.

A slightly built man, with hands of stone, Mark brought his shoulders halfway to his ears and massaged his chin when I proposed the homemade farmhouse sink idea. "Well, ya know, Bill, I'm afraid a square sink would just fly off the wheel," his horn-rimmed breakaway

cheaters hanging from his neck, the crinkle in his temple suggesting his humor was not an all-out rejection.

I asked if I were to build a box in the configuration of the sink, factoring shrinkage, if he could press clay into the walls and meld the corners. He stood straight again like he was coming up for air. "By God, we gotta give that a try."

When he asked our preference for a glaze, I sent a picture of my chili bowl.

Google "custom farmhouse sink." You will find white porcelain, stainless steel, and a gold one from a company called Rocky Mountain Hardware. At $19,700 (free shipping), it must be made from repurposed Super Bowl rings.

Tom Schuman is a retired roofer. He loves to hunt, fish, cook, and listen to Outlaw country music. He'll bust into the gym with a bowl of kale soup at six o'clock in the morning to tell me Dick Dale is playing the High Noon Saloon next week. We think Tom may have fallen off a roof (or two) and hit his head, but he and his wife, Donna, have exquisite tile and brick in their new kitchen addition.

So, we stopped by.

"When it comes time to build your fireplace, you have to call Jimmy Brock the bricklayer; he's the best."

We met with Jimmy. We showed him our fireplace. Pretty standard. He was busy as the proverbial one-legged man, but Jon had kept him busy when times were slow, so he'd get it done. He gave us an armload of catalogs and a couple of websites. We could pick cultured natural-looking rocks of all shapes and colors, simulated fieldstone, or Wisconsin Weatheredge Veneer. Jimmy seemed like a can-do kinda dude, but when I told him we had a rock guy, he was very concerned.

"Well, Bill, I need the rocks to have nice flat faces and consistent thickness. If they get too heavy, they could fall off, or fall through the floor." (Jon builds houses the way my dad built trailer hitches. I'm pretty sure the floor would hold a Cadillac Coupe DeVille.)

"Jimmy, you give me the dimensions and the day, and I'll have the trailer full of stones backed up to the front door ready to go."

To say Mark is my rock guy would be short-sided and possessive. He and his wife, Deb, and their Yorkshire Terrier, Tinker, work craft markets and trade shows all over the Midwest. He cuts crosses from stone, carves names and memorials, and gives three rocks away for every one he sells. Mark is *the* rock guy. When asked how he came to be a rock farmer, "God told me to," he'll answer. And how do you argue? Mark is built like a bundle of number nine wire with a blacksmith's handshake.

Sheila and I showed up Sunday morning after church. He handed us each a chisel and hammer and showed us where to strike the stone to split them in half if they were too pretty to pass up and too heavy for the fireplace. "As soon as you get a pallet full, I'll start pressure washing." The big Milwaukee shop radio parked in the middle of the gravel blasted gospel over the groans of the fifteen-horse pressure washer. By noon, the eighteen-foot trailer was squatting on the overload springs, and Mark was darting from pile to pile, throwing on a dozen. "Just one more pretty one."

We moved in on August 15. In my youth and ignorance, I'd once wondered out loud, "What's the fun in building a new house? There's nothing to do once you move in."

I was looking forward to sitting on the porch with a beer, watching the sunset. So far, we've installed hangers and shelves in the closet, sowed three acres of grass, built two retaining walls, a chain-link and tarp redneck cat shelter, and hung pictures.

Next spring, we'll have fences to mend, wildflowers to plant, and gardens to build.

At nearly eighty years old, Sheila's parents are still trucking. They haul everything from bread to Budweiser from Wisconsin to Ohio, Illinois, Missouri, Oklahoma, Arkansas, and Texas. Except when they'd rather be camping or four-wheeling up north, and when the snow flies. After eighty Wisconsin winters, they've taken a fancy to the pool deck behind their timeshare condo in Florida. Each winter, their departure gets earlier, and the return gets delayed. This year they planned to leave the day after Christmas.

"Would you and Bill mind hosting Christmas this year? We're leaving for Florida on the 26th."

I smiled as Sheila read me the text request. "Why in the hell you think we built this joint?"

We debated the menu. We'd all had enough turkey and ham to sprout feathers and oink. So, we declared 2018 a cowboy Christmas. We decided to eat at one, knowing fully that time is arbitrary with the Barnes family. I had a mountain microwave laden with ribs and another with cornbread, stoked on the Weber when folks started to cycle through at ten-thirty. Given the longest commute was just over the hill, Tracy and Deb and Sheila's folks brought the food first, then went back home to clean up.

By noon, Token had retreated to the dog bed in the garage.

Little Cooper got a new toy truck from Santa that had brushes on it to pick up dog treats and stuffing off the floor. Kinley got a sparkly new dress and ran around casting spells with her wand. Tracy was interviewing for a new job working maintenance at a factory in Whitewater. It's third shift, but he no longer had to travel. Junior finally figured out what caused the abscesses on Ollie and Paws. Uncle Bill and I hunkered in the corner and swapped Willie Nelson lyrics. Ty and I debated whether to have Bryce weld the bracket on the snowplow or take it to Steve's for an inspection and overhaul. Dahlin committed to UW–Eau Claire after graduation, never letting go of his girlfriend's right hand. Micaela works hospitality at Camp Randall Stadium. According to her Fitbit, she walked over fourteen miles on parents' weekend. Butch bitched about Aaron Rodgers' lack of fire on the sideline.

Paige bought Sheila a bathroom guest book. Visitors can blog and log their experiences, including time spent looking in the mirror, overall cleanliness, activity, and ambiance, and select the song that best describes their bathroom visit:

"More Than a Feeling"
"Push It"

"The Sound of Silence"
"Hurts so Good"
"Blowin' in the Wind"
"Good Vibrations"
"Ring of Fire"

As if this family needed prompting, that led to stories about Cousin Chris crapping in the hood of his hunting coat, Uncle Jim picking a rotten log to hang his hinder off, and the great Alaskan coffee heist.

You may recall the muttly piece of walnut Uncle Jerry threw on top of the pile. "Ah, might as well take this one too, probably chunk it up and burn it." While Sheila was in New York on business, I sanded it down to 220 grit and varnished it until it shined like a bowling alley. I rigged four pieces of three-quarter-inch rebar for legs to match the spindles on our stairway. It stands behind our couch with pictures of our honeymoon.

We were proud to tell Sheila's cousins about the scrapwood sourcing of our mantle, fireplace and porch, and handmade sinks. Yet, we could have been in a tiny house or a double-wide. What made Christmas 2018 the best was seeing our brother Glenn talking seventies muscle cars with my father-in-law and having our home filled with folks who routinely give without taking and love without judging. They also helped us move without asking.

*Pete was spot-on about being in close quarters at holidays, but there was one factor I withheld from the meeting for the sake of decorum. The only thing stronger than loyalty and lack of judgment in my adopted family is their constitution. When the jalapeno poppers and sweet potatoes make the transverse colon, a back deck and attached garage would be popular destinations.

**I've long said, "If my wife takes half as good care of me as her least-favorite horse, I'm a kept man." At this writing, the grave dug for Stormy and Percy is still empty. ⚑

BILL STORK

Alone and Acoustic

It was half past New Year's and a quarter 'til St. Patrick's Day. Outside Tyranena Brewing Company, it was dark as a suit closet and colder than the front door of a Catholic church at a January confession. Inside, it was the middle of the second set and hotter than Kingston Mines 1969. The Cash Box Kings were all lathered up.

I turned the fourth bar stool to face the band and rested mug thirty-eight on a coaster at the polished patch on the rail.

My standing request at those mid-winter gigs when the temperature struggles to see a single digit is Sonny Boy Williamson's "Nine Below Zero." White-ass Joe Nosek kicked off the classic with ten bars of half-hour whole notes, fatter than the bottom half of a bari sax. Mark Haines and C.B. Boeger, the world's most dangerous rhythm section, were hanging off the back end of every beat, while Joel Paterson feathered in a flurry on Joe's every inhale.

Out front, eyes closed, Oscar "the king of 43rd Street" Wilson cradled the microphone and swayed. The barroom banter faded to a murmur when the big man raised his hand.

Yeah, ain't that a pity
People ain't that a cryin' shame
Ain't that a pity
I declare it's a cryin' shame

Oscar gave Joel a dozen bars for a guitar break, then raised his hand and howled:

She wait till it got
Nine below zero
And put me down for another man

Music starts at seven, with the intention of ending near ten. The early evening start is a remnant of the mid-2000s, when Rob was the CEO, CFO, brewer, bottler, and bartender at Tyranena Brewing Company.

Best laid plans.

Joe usually kicks off "I Ain't Gonna Love That Woman" by ten. After a bar-walking harp solo and a dozen improvised verses...

I ain't gonna love that woman if it's been ten long, lonely years.
I ain't gonna love that woman if she says come on over Daddy.
I got a big ole filet mignon with a twice-baked potato, hot melted butter,
and a ten-year-old cognac.
I ain't gonna love that woman if she says Daddy-Daddy-Daddy.
I'm gonna rub your back just on that spot you love sooo much.

Ned and Sarah had finally made it out of the barn and wormed their way through the throng of bearded hipsters, lake-dwelling flatlanders, and retired teachers. Princess Diana could have arrived by white horse and carriage, and I'd be clueless.

Sarah wrested her right hand, farmer strong and warm as a new mom, under my collar and squeezed to introduce me to a friend.

I could have melted through the grains in the grout.

The blues is feeling good about feelin' bad.

It had been half a decade since I'd known affection in any physical form.

From that moment, I fully understood the simple power of touch.

In the likeness of my mom, I've made it a mission to capture my own experiences to understand better the struggles that others face.

I'm blessed with two wonderful kids, a hundred fine friends, a cohesive staff, and a thousand clients in my practice. Since that day at the brewery in '08, I've met and married a wife and family I thank God for hourly. I'll never forget the hellacious stretches—the emptiness of returning to a cold, dark house after a twelve-hour day to find every light switch and sugar dish exactly where I'd left it.

I use those times and that snapshot from the brewery to try and appreciate the plight of the aged, widowed, and perpetually alone.

  BILL STORK

Loneliness: the distress caused by a lack of satisfactory relationships. A hermit may not be lonely if a cabin in the woods is truly of his choosing. Another might be lonely in the middle of Times Square if no one knows his name.

Every kiss begins with Kay.

My ass.

Anyone who's ever spent their birthday, Christmas, New Year's Eve, or Valentine's Day alone despite their best efforts knows the very sight of a jewelry commercial or a Victoria's Secret catalog can trigger a brick-through-the-TV moment or the urge to put a serious hurtin' on a fifth of brown liquor.

Experts equate the physiological effects of loneliness to obesity, a sedentary lifestyle, smoking fifteen cigarettes, having six drinks a day, or worse. We can only surmise that all of the above tend to compound. In a review of 148 independent studies on loneliness, covering more than 300,000 participants, Julianne Holt-Lunstad of Brigham Young University and colleagues found that greater social connection was associated with a fifty percent lower risk of early death.*

Research suggests that those who are isolated are at an increased risk of depression, cognitive decline, and dementia and that social relationships influence their blood pressure and immune function, as well as whether people take their medications.

My dad stopped taking his statins after his best friend, LeRoy Summers, passed. A year later, he had a catastrophic stroke.

The deleterious effects of loneliness are especially pronounced in the aging. Baby boomers prized their independence and were more likely to separate and divorce than previous generations. Mounting challenges like mobility and balance make it difficult for folks to put themselves in social situations. Hearing and cognition loss can further cause people to pull away.

There was a day when I could introduce Dad to my friends Anita, May, and Charlie Roy. I'd make the rounds and listen to music while they talked on old cars and farmwork. When his hearing failed, and things got fuzzy, he'd lean against the door frame and stare in the band's direction. In his day, he would have been cuttin' an East Coast Swing or a Cha-Cha. His toe never left the tile.

Experts say the key to diminishing the crisis is wisdom and awareness. If Troy Aikman and Joe Buck can talk about erectile dysfunction during a Dallas Cowboys game, we oughta be able to talk about isolation.

President Trump is working to establish faith-based cooperatives. Great Britain has appointed a Minister of Loneliness. The majority of Meals on Wheels' 2.4 million annual recipients live alone and unsupported. Volunteers are being trained to recognize signs of distress. In Boston, a cluster of seniors in 2002 banded together to form a village so they could lean on each other for household services, social activities, and old-age planning. (Insert your favorite pickleball and Viagra joke.) That's spawned 350 chapters of what is now known as the Village to Village Network.

Senior apartments, over-fifty condominium complexes, assisted living centers, and clubs are forming in cities and towns of every demographic. A farm widow views moving to town as defeat. A husband thinks that reaching out for assistance with his demented wife of fifty years is abandonment or indignity.

Huddled in her full-length pea-green wool coat half fastened with bobby pins and baler twine, a shower cap tied under her chin, Elizabeth Poulsen brought Allen, her three-year-old uber charming Cocker Spaniel to the clinic for a once-over and a distemper-lepto vaccine. By the time I had listened to Allen's heart, looked in his ears, and done his ophtho exam, Mrs. Poulsen had launched into the third verse of her neighbor Harvey Spiegelhoff, the national champion track racer, and his neighbor Gene Kelley who was a Navy captain, and the German Shepherd she took to Dr. Smith, who told her to put the dog down, but then Dr. Stephan said, "Just give it time. She'll be okay."

The next appointment had canceled. There were four post-it prescription requests, two clients to call, and a pile of checks to sign on my desk. I stepped back and fumbled for the indentation in the pocket door. Twice I tried to get, "All right, Elizabeth. Danielle will take care of you up front," in edgewise, but she was on to the green Ford LTD station wagon that dropped off the litter of kittens in her dooryard in 1974.

Then I remembered Mittsy and Barb busting my dad out of his corner room at Lilac Springs Assisted Living to take him to their home for beef roast, beers, and to talk fishin'. Dad's buddies Dick and Dave drove four hours from Illinois to take him to a fish fry.

I slid the door shut, lowered my stool, and grabbed a handful of Charlee Bears for Allen. Elizabeth pointed a gnarled knuckle, "And when you see Dr. Stephan, you ask him about Stormie. Now that Dr. Merry, he was a real vet, but you'd better do just exactly what he said. He was twenty-five years younger than my dad, but he'd listen to him..."

*It was during my final read-through I realized the irony. Dr. Holt-Lunstad is studying loneliness at a university founded by the leader of a religion that embraced polygamy.

**The title of this chapter is borrowed (ripped-off) from one of the finest albums ever recorded. Buddy Guy on an acoustic twelve-string and Junior Wells on harp. ꝺ

Winfield Village

I had met my girlfriend early in my first year of veterinary school. She had invested a small inheritance in a two-bedroom bungalow three blocks from the world's second Jimmy John's and eight blocks from the vet school. It was a wonderful arrangement. JJ's sold their day-old bread for a nickel a loaf.

Academics came easier to her than to me. I let affairs of the heart supersede those of the head—a miscalculation that left me with a GPA that was not acceptable to the administration. I was presented with two options: seek employment in a different career or make a second attempt at the first year of vet school.

I chose B.

Three years later, I watched my classmates turn their tassels and launch their careers. I was left behind, but not alone. My friend Arlin Rodgers was sticking around to start his graduate work in parasitology, so we gathered our collection of pressboard furniture, cinder-block bookshelves, and four hundred CDs, and hunkered down for the home stretch in a government-assisted graduate housing commune called Winfield Village.

We called it Vet Village.

Green Street at the U of I wasn't exactly the French Quarter, but there was always temptation. You could find more entertainment at Murphy's, Mabel's, or the Rose Bowl than memorizing the volatile fatty acids produced in a cow's rumen and the Krebs cycle. Vet Village was four miles south, just enough separation from campus so that more mature students could focus on the business of their Master's, PhD, and professional degrees.

  BILL STORK

Each building was divided into four apartments with a three-by-three slab of concrete out front to fit a lawn chair and watch the kids tricycle down the sidewalk or admire the stars, take a leak, and replay the concert Arlin and I had just left at two in the morning. There were two bedrooms upstairs. The living room was spacious enough to accommodate a broken Naugahyde La-Z-Boy, a dog couch (that St. Vincent de Paul would eventually reject), a love seat, and a pair of Klipsch Forte speakers I'd used to DJ graduations and school socials to make a little book money. Out the sliding doors was the patio, just big enough for a hammock, Weber grill, recycling bin, and a quarter barrel. It was surrounded by a six-foot cedar-stained, staggered board fence, to separate us from our poor neighbors.

Our idea of interior decoration was the inside cover of ZZ Top's *Tres Hombres* album affixed to the kitchen wall by three push pins and a starving-artist variety velvet Elvis that Arlin had fetched from a dumpster, hanging cock-eyed over the dog couch.

The non-veterinary population of Winfield Village were engineering and computer-science PhDs, business students, and middle-aged aggies in work boots and pickups. Many were tuning up for their second careers and had already married and started families.

Winfield Unit Six, Apartment Three

The base population was Arlin and me, two cats inherited from my classmate Tom Shackelford, and three dogs: Cooder, Herschel, and Abby.

Cooder was born in a hollowed log next to Boneyard Creek, just off campus. He and his litter were surrendered to the shelter at weaning. The humane society brought the litter to the vet school to be spayed and neutered. It was a one-way ticket for Cooder.

He took his name and personality from blues guitar genius and historian Ry Cooder.

Cooder had two gears.

While I studied for my National Board Exams, he occupied the indent at the west end of the dog couch for fourteen boring days. At times, his big, brown eyes would be the only thing moving, for fear he'd disturb Tom's two cats sleeping on top of him as he took about four breaths a minute.

Our classmate Scott Waterman (who would go to bars as Jim Carrey in character) had a hunting dummy launcher. With a .38 shell, it could shoot the canvas decoy at 150 yards. Cooder was like a ghost. When we played fetch with all the dogs across the creek and into the bean field, you never actually saw him run, you never saw him take off with the pack, but he always returned with the dummy.

Abby was the Golden Retriever equivalent of a remarkably fertile, dumb blonde. Abby was calendar-girl gorgeous, had OFA certified excellent hips and elbows, and never barked. She learned to sit, stay, come, and shake on the first go. Her puppies had Westminster conformation, housetrained in a week, and never flinched on the sound of a twenty-gauge pheasant gun. For three hundred dollars a pup, Abby gave twenty-one families the dog of a lifetime, and Arlin a 1989 Chevy S-10 with an aftermarket CD player. That said, Abby was so dumb, she didn't know how to play with other dogs.

Then there was Herschel.

The first thing you'll notice is he gets his own introduction and his own paragraph. I stared at the screen for half an hour and finally messaged Arlin. "How would you describe Herschel?" The response came a day later:

In three words: Benji's evil twin.
Most people under 50 don't know Benji.
I'll explain later.

Herschel was a scruffy brown rat dog who never once could you say misbehaved. He would not come when you called him, but you never had to wait for him. He would not sit or stay or walk on a leash, but you never feared he'd run into traffic. Herschel conformed to nothing.

Our friend Rand had shoulders like a Brahman bull, a head like a dorm room beer fridge, and a voice like Wolfman Jack's Swedish big brother. For three and a half years, he cavorted around the U of I College of Veterinary Medicine in flannel shirts and work boots, portending to be the next James Herriot. One day into his first dairy internship, he examined a Holstein with bad feet, mastitis, and a displaced abomasum. Bessie's fate was the rendering plant. With a heart bigger than his head, Dr. Gus permanently became the world's biggest pet vet.

While Rand was in northern Wisconsin on his one-and-done large animal residency, Arlin and I watched his two dogs, Jarvis and Sam. Our herd of three was now at five.

Across Curtis Avenue from Vet Village was a farm field and miles of grass waterways. A dog park, before their time.

I'd often take the dogs to the field on my bike. I held Cooder's, Jarvis's, and Sam's leashes to my left and Abby's and Herschel's on the right. They were mushing me down the sidewalk at fifteen miles per hour when suddenly I could not help but notice I was lying face down on the blacktop with my legs tangled through the frame of the bike. I was jolted back to consciousness by Herschel licking the blood from my left eye.

He'd stopped to take a shit.

With five dogs at times and two cats, apartment three could sound like an animal shelter at feeding time. Having spent his high school years in Texas, Arlin was a hardcore Dallas Cowboys fan, a serviceable guitar player, and songwriter. When he wasn't yelling at Troy Aikman on Sunday afternoons, he'd be warbling an homage to his freshman anatomy dog Spotina, a waltz sung to the tune of Marty Robbins' country classic "El Paso."

Down in the Ill-nois town of Ur-bana,
I fell in love with a Labrador pup.

Arlin and I were disciples of the great Lone Star singer-songwriters Townes Van Zandt, Guy Clark, Joe Ely, Robert Earl Keen Jr., and Lyle Lovett. Though I was not blessed with Arlin's perfect pitch and golden throat, I'd sing along karaoke-style as he picked "The Front Porch Song."

Winfield Unit Six, Apartment Four

Our unfortunate neighbors, the Baptists.

Nearly thirty years on, I'm not proud, but that's all I knew of them. And even that is based on a supposition. They were a family of two parents and three uber-polite kids. Each Sunday morning they left the house properly dressed and in formation from Dad to the youngest boy. The ritual was repeated on both Sunday and Wednesday evenings, at precisely the same time. The only time we spoke was to borrow the symbolic cup of flour when I was desperate. Mrs. B gave freely and did not ask for so much as a moment of silence in return.

I'd like to think that Arlin and I weren't oblivious. There were two sheets of three-eighth-inch drywall and a two-by-four between their lives and ours. There was never so much as a thump-thump on the wall (that we heard) to criticize or mute our ninety-decibel existence.

Looking to practice on dairy cows, horses, dogs, and cats, my girlfriend had taken a job in Wisconsin at the Jefferson Veterinary Clinic. We tried to see one another as often as possible. I'd travel to Wisconsin and ride with her boss, the legendary Ed Detmers, learning how to palpate cows and locate the best meatloaf lunch specials. Long-distance love ain't easy working around emergencies, internships, and clinical schedules. We hadn't seen one another for a month.

She had been on call Friday night, which continued into a Saturday that featured every malady that can befall a periparturient dairy cow. After two calvings, three milk fevers, and a DA surgery, she made it to Winfield near midnight, exhausted.

We celebrated our reunion in a fashion frowned on by the Catholic church for a couple not yet wed and fell into blissful sleep, wrapped in one another's arms. I woke shortly after dawn, stretched, and dozed a half-dozen times. I delicately extracted from my lover's embrace so she could continue the restoration she so desperately needed. I squatted next to the bed to collect the *material* from our passionate reunion. Nothing. I dropped to my knees and swept an arc the length of my arm, which yielded three dirty socks and the early onset of panic. I looked down my arm to see Cooder.

BILL STORK

Standardly, he would have been stretched and standing at the door on the cue of the first wiggle of my toe. On that day, his muzzle was firmly fixed to the carpet, and his caramel-colored eyebrows dropped—first one, then the other. I mimed, C-o-o-d-e-r?! The brows twitched, and his eyes looked up so that all I saw was glistening white sclera and a half-moon sliver of deep brown iris.

His previous power-eating résumé included a half-crate of FFA fruit sale oranges with the rind, six pounds of Hills Maintenance Diet, and an entire Thanksgiving pumpkin pie.

As fate would have it, I was the student on call that weekend for small animal surgery. The resident who would supervise me was a phenomenal surgeon. Dr. James McKenna once corrected a patent ductus arteriosus on a one-kilogram Miniature Poodle puppy. The man had skills. Out of the OR, his favorite party trick was to pass a strand of cooked spaghetti in one nostril and out the other. A million-dollar surgical theater at a world-class veterinary teaching hospital would in no way spare the jabs, and we were weeks shy of Vetscapades, the annual all-school, no holds barred, student-faculty roast. I could only imagine the medical record would read:

"Nurse, the serosa and mucosa of the jejunum appear to be intact and healthy. We've managed to successfully extract the intestinal foreign body. It appears to be barely used."

Cooder was a veteran of induced emesis. I descended the stairs two at a time. As I rifled through the medicine cabinet for hydrogen peroxide, Cooder took his place on the Formica in the corner of the kitchen. I uncapped the brown bottle, straddled my friend, pointed his chocolate nose to the ceiling, and instructed him to chug like a frat boy. After three good glugs, his stomach started to churn.

We crossed the living room in two strides. I flung the front door open and pushed the reluctant little Lab onto the concrete pad. I stood in the open door, praying for puke, and contemplating my first phone call if he didn't, just as the Baptists emerged to begin their journey to Sunday's first worship.

I decided in a split second that it would be less scarring on the kids to see what Cooder was about to eject onto their path than a pasty white, six-four Sasquatch in tighty-whities trying to block their vision.

I shut the door to separate myself from the scene and peered through the split in the metal blinds.

As the Baptists made the turn from their step to the sidewalk, Cooder heaved three Kleenexes and a University Health Department-issued Trojan condom onto the sixth concrete square.

Mr. B lifted his chin just a tick, stepped on the ball of his left foot, and pivoted a perfect military turn for two counts, then planted his right and turned again.

His family marched a perfect square around the scene.

To this day, I wonder if the Baptists' Sunday prayers for the salvation of the heathens to the east are not the force that's kept me safe from serious harm. ⬙

BILL STORK

Put Yourself in My Shoes

From national news to your next-door neighbor, there is a great deal of discussion on the country's mental health crisis. Those in veterinary medicine are not immune, with one in six experiencing a significant psychological event. We are the fourth most likely profession to commit self-harm.

I'm blessed with a loving family, a phenomenal staff, and an amazing book of clients, but I've come close enough to hard times that when a workshop on workplace stress and well-being was offered by one of our drug reps, I signed up.

The meeting took place at Patterson HQ in Pewaukee, Wisconsin, which is in a strip mall, just past the McMansions, next door to a Mercedes-exclusive mechanic. I left my truck window open a crack for donations.

The moderator was skilled in matters of mental well-being, but her BS meter was out of batteries. We went around the room introducing ourselves, how long we'd been in practice, and what we were hoping to extract from the day.* I proclaimed that in over twenty-five years of practice, we've never known stress or conflict at our clinic. I was attending as prophylaxis, just in case.

She was in awe.

The first breakout session took place just after bagels and donuts. We were to identify sources of stress in veterinary practice. Half-invested in my small group, I cherry-picked the banter around the room.

Number one, two, or three on every list was walk-ins and calls just before closing. Often, the pets' conditions have been going on for days, at least.

I'd bet a year's beer money if I'd ask at Steve's Car and Truck Service, Calloway Electric, Jensen Plumbing, or Thelma's Thimble and Thread, they'd all nod and grumble.

"Hello, this is Geraldo Rivera. I need to get my dog in to see the vet, *this morning,*" will come the call just before noon on Saturday. Abbey pulls up the record. We haven't seen Scinto since the first Obama administration. Against a full day of wellness appointments, we were already working on a couple of same-day calls. The last ninety minutes of the schedule looked like a Jenga game just before it crashes.

"Well, Mr. Rivera, we'll help him if we can. What's going on with little Scinto?" Abbey tries to triage.

"Ah, he's just laying around, does not want to move. He's not interested in his food, he has been vomiting, and his poops are loose," will come the dire history.

Abbey asks how long the signs have been taking place.

"Since last Tuesday."

Little Scinto is a ten-year-old, twelve-pound Chihuahua, who should be eight pounds. He has mature cataracts, Grade III dental disease, and a heart murmur. One rogue tablespoon of chorizo could induce a life-threatening case of pancreatitis.

Abbey has only recently taken the reins at reception. She cracks the door of exam room two to ask me about it.

"Sure, just have him come on down, but warn him we'll be working him in, so there could be a wait."

Geraldo and Scinto must have been calling from Kwik Trip; they were there in minutes. Abbey escorted them to exam three (surgery), where Heather did a TPR. His temperature was two-tenths shy of our favorite radio station, and he was near ten percent dehydrated. The prognosis took a plunge when he didn't even try and bite Heather.

In exam two, the lidocaine gel was numbing the torn dewclaw of Rex, the 125-pound Rottweiler that post-holed through the crusted snow.

Patty Griffin was flipping through a year-old issue of *Cat Fancy* in exam one. She had woken up that morning to see her little Tortie

Frida straining in the litter box. Her urine sample looked like a hazy IPA in the syringe and still had three minutes to go in the centrifuge, which gave Heather and Francine time to get a blood sample from Scinto. Somehow, they got two cc's from the little prune whose vein was but twice the diameter of a horsehair.

As expected, Scinto had a white blood cell count like a Powerball jackpot and an ALP like Sammy Davis Jr. His chances were poor. In the absence of aggressive treatment, Scinto was not going to see Sunday. We set an IV catheter and got him started on fluids, antiemetics, and buprenorphine for his pain. After a weekend in ICU, he was once more eating, lunging, and biting anything he could get his four teeth on.

The dregs of winter. The holidays are in the rearview, the days are getting longer, but it's still dark at five in the evening, and the average daily temperature is still going down. I call it boat show season. From the weekend after the Super Bowl, until the grass turns green, the Alliant Energy Center in Madison does not rest. First is the Home and Garden Expo, followed by the Log Home and Cabin Show, New Home, Used Home, Trailer Home, Model Railroad, Fishing Expo, and finishes up with the Boat Show and Bike Show.

It was half past five on the second Thursday of February. The dental appointment from hell had gone into double overtime. Still a semester away from her certification as a technician, Francine was baptized by fire as she and I juggled two sets of appointments, while Dr. Wilder played catch-up. The surgery suite still looked like the set of a Civil War documentary when Hellen grumbled through the front door.

With the focus of a quarterback running the thirty-second drill, Danielle assuages lines one, two, and three before she settles her brow and addresses the tearful woman patiently waiting at the counter.

"Hello, my name is Hellen Heffernan, and not only do my first and last names start with *H*, but I really need to get my parents' dog in. I think *it's time*. I can't get ahold of their regular vet. The poor dog is twenty-five years old, can't get up, and he's messing all over himself."

I allow myself a string of thoughts that are less than professional before settling my head. If he can't get up, *his time* was at least a week ago. Had HH called an hour ago, we had an emergency slot open. Why can't your parents take their own dog, and who is this lazy-ass vet who won't answer his phone?

Under no circumstances would we let this poor dog suffer, but we were obligated with her final plea. "We used to see Dr. Stephan. He was so wonderful. I'm hoping you can help us out." Dr. Gregg Stephan is like Brett Favre with the New York Jets. He owned the Sun Prairie Animal Hospital for thirty years. After he sold to big corporate, he still had some gas left in his tank. We were a hundred yards beyond his non-compete clause and halfway to his mother's farm. He works for us and keeps the techs entertained between walleye tournaments and hunting trips.

"We'll do the best we can, ma'am. We're a bit busy at the moment," Danielle politely points out the obvious. "Where is he?"

"He's in the back seat of my car."

Twenty-five years ago, my parents leveraged their retirement to come up with a down payment, and I became the proud owner of a gently-used veterinary clinic. At that time, the clinic was well in excess of seventy-five percent farm business. Our practice radius covered Jefferson and swaths of Dodge, Dane, and Waukesha counties. We had a lot of time to get familiar with FM radio and our thoughts. Lake Mills did not have a stoplight. The nearest Ace Hardware and Culver's were in Watertown. So, when I was called north to Eugene Coughlin and Continental Grain for sick cows and sore feet, I'd stock up on carriage bolts and butter burgers.

I was sequestered in the Stihl department of Ace, fantasizing like a high school kid over Dad's *Playboys*, when a drawl crawled over my shoulder, "Dawcter Store-k, how'r ewe doin'?"

Stuart White migrated north from Oklahoma by covered wagon and began his veterinary career at the Jefferson Veterinary Clinic a decade or so before I did. Vets can be strong-minded and independent.

BILL STORK

He located an abandoned health club and moved fifteen miles up Highway 26 to establish The Rock River Veterinary Clinic. Stuart could outshoot Jethro and Jed Clampett. He loved to hunt trophy game and often traveled to Africa to stock his head room. A bit of a roughneck entrepreneur, his racquetball courts were jammed with equipment repurposed from military hospitals and area rugs from Persia, India, and Nepal.

"I was fixin' on giving you a call," he shrugged to catch the brown juice at the corner of his mouth. "I'm heading out on a little trip. Just in case we get any cattle calls, you mind if we send them down your way?"

I assured him we'd do our best to take care of business, "How long you gonna be gone?"

"Oh, 'bout a month or so. I'm on my way to the airport now." I have the image of Dr. White in line at TSA in his faded green coveralls and boots.

Cast no stones.

In my twenty-six years of practice, I've employed every conceivable on-call arrangement. In the early days, I was on one night and off two, and on every third weekend. I shared with some combination of Dr. Kebus (formerly Dr. Keebus), Dr. Anderson, Dr. Fred Lord**, Dr. Johnson, Dr. Clark, and myself.

Eventually, my comrades on call migrated to fish practice, the eternal bottle of Scotch in the sky, Green Bay, emergency practice, and Edgerton. I was the last man standing. At one point, I was on call for five straight years. I explained to my farm clients that if I am able, I will be there. If I am not, please call one of our neighbors at the Waterloo or Jefferson clinics.

In the fall of '18, Sheila and I took a bike trip through the magnificent Big Bend National Park with our buddy John Humphries and Lizard Head Cycling. It was eighty-six degrees on day three of our trip, and I was getting dehydrated and delirious, laboring into the last climb before the ghost town of Terlingua, Texas, when I thought, "I never did call Dr. Rob to tell him I'd be out of town."

Remmi was *the* yellow Lab. She was fourteen years old and could barely walk, even when you helped her up. We'd been cooking and hand-feeding her for six weeks. Her bloodwork pointed to her liver. I was powerfully suspicious of cancer, but the closest I could come on radiograph was, "Something doesn't look just right in her cranial abdomen."

We had catheterized her and run IV fluids three different times and had run fifty gallons of LRS through her subcutaneously over the last year. She was the last daughter of a legend named Gunner and the reincarnation of my old dog Cooder. We just couldn't let go.

Sheila was the COO at Wisconsin Equine Clinic and Hospital. It was all hands on deck season, and they were shorthanded. I could make room in the schedule from eight until ten. I'd wondered for weeks if we might be able to find something on ultrasound that we could either remove surgically or make the decision easier.

So, at four-thirty in the morning, we headed for Madison and waited in the parking lot until Dr. Wirth showed up.

We rationalize the behaviors in ourselves that frustrate us in others.

I allow myself to get crotchety with a client who calls at eleven on Saturday morning with a dog that's been limping for a week, but on the drive home, I recognize that for any grumble, cuss, and fist-clench moment, I've been them.

Around the dinner table, Dad and I would be blowin' off steam at coworkers and classmates. Mom would listen, then quietly offer up the benefit of the doubt.

Dr. White's son had taken his own life.

Hellen was en-route from her sister's funeral to her niece's chemotherapy treatment.

Geraldo simply did not know.

*A colleague and I recognized that no matter how many years past your silver anniversary, you are forever "over twenty-five years in practice."

**Not lacking in confidence, Dr. Lord would announce his arrival on a farm, "Never fear, the Lord is here." ⌕

A Peaceful Death

"Do you know any good tattoo artists?"

Sylvia Sippel's file at the Lake Mills Veterinary Clinic resembles the 1978 Encyclopedia Britannica in word count and weight. She brings CSA eggs from Kelly's High Meadow Farm for Sheila and knows Claire's last three boyfriends. She brings poems, books, and an occasional comeuppance when I deserve it. She's keenly aware that I'm not our staff expert on body art. "Sure, Sylvia. I can get you in with my guy down on LaSalle."

"Good, preferably this afternoon, I'm going to have *NO* tattooed in the middle of my forehead."

Out-performing her cohorts physically and certainly mentally, Sylvia has become the Jefferson County Collie respite center. She adopts aged animals surrendered by owners struggling with their own health issues. They then have the peace of knowing their friends' remaining days will be their best. She loves every one of them as if she bottle-fed them.

This time, she had become Rainbow Hospice.

Molly had been foisted upon Sylvia by a friend of a friend in failing health. "This is not a Collie," she deadpanned, pointing to the twelve-year-old German Shephard at the end of the slack leash as they made the twenty yards from her parking place under the pines to the porch. Molly's hocks dropped to the pavement, and her spine jutted like a knife, her epaxial muscles and every gram of fat having been burned in the ongoing effort to breathe. The corners of her mouth pulled back, neck stretched and base wide, she struggled to drive every molecule of oxygen across her alveoli. The gentle rise in the blacktop must have felt like Kilimanjaro.

BILL STORK

We revved the rotor on the x-ray machine, leaded up, and laid her on the table. I hit the throttle on the first inhale, and we returned her to the floor, already slightly purple from a few seconds in lateral recumbency.

It didn't take a boarded radiologist to make the diagnosis. Her thorax was full of fluid, drowning her heart and pushing her lungs toward her spine. I demonstrated the fluid line with the cursor. "It would be like you trying to breathe with me sitting on your chest."

I expected to be reaching for the Euthasol. Sylvia asked, "What can we do to make her feel better?"

I explained the fluid was likely blood, courtesy of a hemangiosarcoma, or equally heinous tumor, residing at the base of her heart. I could likely drain some of the fluid, but it would return relatively quickly.

"Well, then, get to work," she responded, fully understanding the long-term prognosis was grave.

We lowered the surgery table and covered it in rubber mats and a blanket. Sheila and Elisha propped her up. Consumed with the business of breathing, and kind by nature, she didn't flinch as I placed a lidocaine bleb and slipped an eighteen-gauge catheter through the intercostals behind her fifth rib, then attached a three-way stopcock.

In a half-hour and thirty rounds with a sixty-cc syringe, we had collected over a liter of fluid the color and consistency of a box of Merlot. Molly's temples softened, the corner of her mouth relaxed, and her breaths settled from a constant struggle to thirty or so a minute.

We snapped a radiograph to confirm the presence of the heart-based hemangiosarcoma that had been hiding behind the fluid.

"It could be hours. It could be days," I speculated as to how long it would take for her chest to refill.

That was not the point.

My heart sank the next morning as I turned into the parking lot to see the maroon minivan snugged up to the garage. "Damn, she decompensated overnight."

From the glaring morning sun off the faded blacktop, I poked my head into the darkness of her Korean canine transport vehicle. Molly was lying sternal, closed-mouth breathing, nuzzling an old tennis ball.

Sylvia was resolute. "Ok, *now* it's time to let her go."

The Greek translate euthanasia to "peaceful death." Merriam-Webster defines it:

"The act or practice of killing or permitting the death of hopelessly sick or injured individuals (such as persons or domestic animals) in a relatively painless way for reasons of mercy."

"This must be the worst part of your job. This is why I could never be a vet," says every grieving family between the Telazol we use to sedate their pet and the final injection. I have never started my day looking forward to putting an animal to sleep. Veterinarians place an extremely high value on guiding families as to an animal's quality of life.

In the hands of conscientious families who deeply love their pets, we have the opportunity to spare them their worst days. In those last moments, I have been exposed to the greatest acts of humanity and learned life-long lessons often from folks I would not expect.

Next time, I'll write on Corgi pups and fuzzy kittens, but today I tell this gloomy story. It is not so much for the family whose eighteen-year-old Lab can no longer stand or twenty-two-year-old cat in kidney failure who hasn't eaten in a week.

It is for the family whose eight-year-old Boxer has an inoperable squamous cell carcinoma the size of a ping-pong ball on his gums and spread to his lungs. It is for the H's with Konnor who's struggled with spondylosis for half of his twelve years and had finally decimated his anterior cruciate ligament. On his last day, Konnor was licking faces and drained an entire treat jar.

Possibly the most agonizing was the family who adopted the Hurricane Harvey dog from the streets of Houston. In spite of the full-on resources of our behavioral staff, the owner's relentless efforts

to counter-condition and socialize, and months of medications, the dog lashed out at anyone who came close—family or foe. If he was awake, he was scared.

There are times when they still eat, poop, and wag their tails. Much like Sylvia did for Molly; we seek to save them from their worst days. ꙮ

Mama's Boy

I'd been on a band trip to Disney, a fishing trip to Leech Lake, Minnesota, with a church youth group, and a couple of sleepovers, but for the majority of my first eighteen years, it was Mom, Dad, me, and a Collie named Sugar. I was the first of my family to attend college. Townsend Residence Hall at the University of Illinois was forty miles from Nickey Avenue in Decatur, Illinois. It may as well have been South Sulawesi, Indonesia. It was all one great big unknown.

Our dorm room assignments arrived in early August:
• Muson, Bill – Bement, Illinois
• Gerbasi, Joseph Aloysius – Vernon Hills, Illinois
• Clewis, Scott Richard – Chicago, Illinois

Presumption and the inaccuracy of the first impression.

With a name like Gerbasi, from the north suburbs of Chicago, Dad thought Joe's family must have mob connections. Bement was a small town just down the road from Decatur. He figured Bill would be a good ole farmboy. Clewis Scott, to Dad, sounded like a black guy from the South Side of Chicago.

Mom thought they all sounded like nice boys. She started buying Tato Skins, Ritz Crackers, and popcorn to put together care packages.

Bill Muson sat around in his tighty-whities, picking zits off his back, watching MTV. After six weeks of being short-sheeted and having his bed slammed, he petitioned the RA for a transfer. I haven't seen Gerbasi since graduation. I refer to Scott Clewis as Brother. It's been thirty years since graduation, and we talk five days a week.

Scott is gluten-, sugar-, and caffeine-free. He's got more energy than that bunny wired to a tractor battery. He met our friend Kish for a

  BILL STORK

cocktail after work one Friday. Kish asked, "What do you wanna do next?"

"We should go to Vegas," Scott answered. Just like that, the boys were bound for Sin City on a redeye. Forty-eight hours later, they were back at work, running on adrenaline and a cat nap in coach.

The abridged version of Scott's curriculum vitae would weigh like a hard-bound *Moby Dick*. In the thirty-six years I've known Scott, he's run residence halls, learning centers, and taught flunked-out inner-city kids English. While putting himself through law school, he ran the Cook County Juvenile Court, overseeing over a hundred employees and a multi-million dollar budget.

While Chicago-Kent College of Law does not appear on a search of the ten best schools in the country, and Scott was not the valedictorian, he could sell a block of ice to a used car salesman, and he will never be outworked. Diploma in hand, he researched the top three law firms in the city, made copies of his résumé, pressed his suit, and shined his shoes. He charmed his way past the receptionist and told the partners he was there to produce and learn. Patrick Salvi of Salvi, Schostok, & Pritchard took the bait. After a six-year apprenticeship, including a record-breaking jury verdict, they offered him a partnership. In short order, his ego and independence got the best of him, and he opened Clewis and Associates. Under his own shingle, he treated his clients like family. They treated him like a brother and son. They invited him to weddings, graduations, and funerals.

At this writing, Scott has been practicing medical malpractice and personal injury law in Chicago for almost twenty years. I'll pause as you conjure the image. If your vision is that of a Tom Cruise doppelganger driving a black BMW in a suit that costs more than a new set of tires for my pickup truck, two cases of Chateauneuf-du-Pape in his wine cellar, and a condo in the loop, you're three for three. He has a strict twenty-step daily skincare routine and a haberdasher, manicurist, and pedicurist on retainer.

Evoking Mom's rules about judging books, and my assault on the notion of first impressions, Scott Richard Clewis is not defined by cars and labels. He is a man of resilience and family because that's how Elaine Clewis raised him.

Scott is a mama's boy.

I met Mrs. Clewis at Thanksgiving break our freshman year of college. She stood in the doorway of our dorm room in a housecoat and headscarf with a purse the size of an airline carry-on over her shoulder. We were homesick, hungry, and nursing Old Style hangovers, which mattered not to Elaine Clewis. Our level of organization and housekeeping were not up to her standards. We spent the next three hours picking up, cleaning, and organizing as she dictated orders like a Northside drill sergeant at three recruits cleaning a latrine.

Scott's dad rose from the construction trades to become a state senator and an alderman. Though he seldom missed a supper, he was often gone to meetings. From the age of twelve, Scott was the little man of the house. When his dad died at fifty-six, Scott stepped up.

I'd visit Scott shortly after college. I have images of their breadbox bungalow at 5140 W. Warwick, just a short hop from Wrigley Field. Scott would sit on the couch in the parlor, kissing his mom on the temple, holding her hand, and telling her he loved her. Scott brought several girls home to his mother. They could be runway gorgeous and work with orphans, but if Elaine didn't give 'em the nod, there was no second date.

As a freshman lawyer at Salvi, Scott was in awe at their first employee appreciation banquet. The partners handed out praise along with bonuses in sealed envelopes. His colleagues slipped off to the restroom and snuck peeks under the table.

No less giddy than his mates, Scott slipped his into his breast pocket. When the evening adjourned, he called his mom and told her to stay up late. He drove an hour out of his way so his mom could open his first bonus check.

Scott is an engaging speaker, a champion debater, and a hound for details. Chicago-Kent taught him law, but he learned cardiac and neurologic anatomy and physiology on the job from textbooks and midnight calls to physician friends. In twenty years of practicing medical malpractice law, he has lost only twice.

He once explained practicing law. "Hick, you wake up every day going head-to-head with opponents. There's no hanging out at the water cooler talking about the Bears game." It is the ultimate adversarial profession. Going to work is going to war.

He's tired.

Like a virtual carpool, in the twelve minutes from the Lake Mills Veterinary Clinic to the hill on Highway G when I lose cell reception, I'll talk to Scott. I'll try and recreate the moonset over the marsh west of the farm and the cricket chorus around the pond. He'll break down the latest developments in trade talks with China, the Big Ten champion pole vaulter who guested at his gym, or a chat with Christie Hefner.

Scott will be the first guest on my podcast. I'll put down my microphone and go mow the grass.

Benevolence is essential to Scott, along with hair care and exfoliating. Uncle Scott tries to expose his nieces and nephews to things they'd otherwise never get to do. He has dinner with his parking attendant and befriended a locker room attendant from his club to show him life outside the housing development where he grew up.

After twenty-five years of practicing law, he is going pro—helping people.

Scott applied to the prestigious Masters of Positive Psychology program (MAPP) at the University of Pennsylvania in Philadelphia. Key players in the MAPP program include Dr. Angela Duckworth, who wrote the book *Grit: The Passion of Power and Perseverance* and taught it to West Point cadets, and Dr. Marty Seligman, who upended psychological doctrine. As the president of the American Psychological Association, he pushed to optimize what is right with us, rather than spin wheels attempting to fix what's wrong. The most basic premise of positive psychology is the scientific study of what makes life worth living.

The Masters of Positive Psychology is not a Disneyland degree.

Scott has graduated from two colleges and law school. He's prosecuted multi-million dollar medical malpractice cases and run businesses with hundreds of employees. He claims the MAPP program is the hardest thing he's ever attempted.

The program format requires almost a dozen three- or four-day weekends on campus and no fewer than forty hours per week of research, presentations, papers, and tests—a heavy load while balancing full-time work.

One exercise in the curriculum is to pick a test student, write an outline, give a lecture, and teach them a few of the most basic tenets of positive psychology. Identifying me as his friend in greatest need of a tune-up, I was his lab rat. The sessions were to be roughly an hour. With digressions, we routinely doubled our regulated time. I learned the components of resilience and character strengths that contribute to virtue. He taught me the effect of thinking traps on our perception of interactions, the value of sharing our victories with someone who cares, and the difference between optimistic and pessimistic decision making.

I loved it.

Scott's classmates, forty-eight in total, chosen from around the world, include Harvard and Yale MBAs, an Emmy Award-winning producer, a CEO from Sweden, and a former NFL cheerleader. They are in the home stretch.

At the very last onsite module, the faculty hosted their annual Quaker Dinner. Everyone was encouraged to reveal a piece of themselves that fellow MAPPsters had not yet seen. To that point, Scott had been the enigmatic attorney from Chicago who occasionally showed up in a lampshade or a Minnie Mouse dress for Halloween. He had every intention of keeping it that way until Henry the Australian Rinpoche laid his hand on Scott's shoulder. Like an encore at a rock concert, Scott made his way to the podium.

He began by thanking his parents. In grade school, Scott had floundered. He was more interested in getting to work like his dad and grandfather and convinced school was for the teacher's benefit. Whether the lessons were lectured or written in textbooks, he struggled to understand. When called upon in class, he'd do a soft-shoe and tell a story to hide that he could not long divide. Teachers in the Chicago Public School System in the seventies simply hoped to make it home alive. They had no desire to hold anyone back. He lived every day in fear he would disappoint his parents. When his scores on a high school entrance exam arrived in a manila envelope, a family summit was called at the dinner table.

Scott feared the worst. Instead, his dad assured Scott he believed in him. Elaine asked, "How can we help?" Buoyed by the unconditional support of his family, he crammed eight years of elementary school into the summer of 1979 and made a spot in the remedial classes at Gordon Tech High School. By May 1983, he graduated with distinction from a full curriculum of honors classes and was accepted to the University of Illinois.

The catharsis of Scott Richard Clewis before forty-eight classmates and the founders of Positive Psychology was purely spontaneous, and Henry's hand may have been a divine intervention. When he scanned the room, there were few dry eyes. His first hug was from a hotel employee who had been wiping the tables and collecting dirty dishes. With tears streaming across his brown cheeks, he explained that the struggles Scott had just shared from his childhood were note for note his son.

Thanks to Scott's three-minute confessional, that man would never give up on his son.

Ten months of academic boot camp, validated. ⃕

Fence Me In

I had dreamed of this moment for over ten years.

Joe and Sam tamped the gravel around the last post until it was rock-solid. They stepped back, and Austin Kind stepped in, drew his DeWALT, and sunk the last two screws on the final board. The origin of the fence was a quarter-mile north. The first post had been planted over a month ago.

It was eighty-eight in the shade. The crew gathered their tools and guzzled water. I had compromised the disk between L5 and L6 two days and fifty posts ago. I ratcheted my spine to a sixty-five-degree angle and thanked everyone.

There had been impediments.

We moved into our new house in August 2018. The first urgency was to plant grass before the burdocks took their pasture back, and the dogs tracked the yard into the living room. In two twelve-hour days, with the help of Sheila's nephew and niece, Dahlin and Micaela, we had our four-acre lot rock picked, graded, and seeded with two hundred pounds of Fort Special grass seed. By sunset Sunday, it was fertilized and spread with sixty bales of straw. The final fortuitous move was a dozen passes just before dark with Jon's cultimulcher, as forty-eight hours later came two days of near biblical rains. Five weeks later, we were mowing.

The second order of business was a retaining wall to keep the backyard out of our basement. The first Saturday in September, Builder Jon rolled in at six in the morning with his mini-excavator and Austin and Brendan Kind, Jon's left- and right-hand men; he refers to them as One and Two. Twelve hours later, Austin was leanin' hard on his hoe handle. His hands were like hamburger, but we turned six pallets

BILL STORK

of seventy-five-pound Sienna Brown bricks into a helluva start on a retaining wall. My best efforts to finish the wall by fall were thwarted by more apocalyptic rains. Snow flew before we were able to get the last courses set and backfilled. The project sat idle until Easter weekend, 2019.

Aldo Leopold I am not, but I get all geeked out by wildflowers. They show up early April and persist into late September along the walking paths at Dorothy Carnes and Korth Parks. Along Highways F and 73, landowners have seeded and tended acres of native prairie flowers, all for the benefit of the bees, butterflies, and those driving through not glued to their devices. I wanted a patch of my own. I envisioned our friends, Gary and Dianne, waking to the scent of purple phlox wafting through the window of the guest room when they came to visit. It takes minutes to mow a half an acre and days to water and weed two hundred square feet of flowers. Still, I stumbled in.

The uber-kind folks at Prairie Nursery in Dane walked me through their Wildflowers for Dummies website. The third Wednesday in May, I rolled up the drive to six boxes of plastic trays on the front porch. Like a kid on Christmas, I carved open the boxes. The labels read Brown-Eyed Susan, Prairie Coneflowers, and Big Bluestem on one side and genus and species on the other. I trembled.

I had five hundred square feet behind the retaining walls and two raised rock gardens to plant. The tiller bounced and lurched off the clumps of clay like Raggedy Andy on a rodeo bull. I raked, eyeballed, and graded the pulverized earth until the fallen rain would trickle from the house to the field. Sheila and I planted, plugged, and labeled the blue sage, fire pink, and golden groundsel according to height and when the little labels told us they would bloom. We call our neighbor Dave Stelse the mayor of Kiessling Road. He patrols the neighborhood on his Kawasaki Mule, disseminating the crop report and truth, as he sees it. Mayor Dave also drives the dump truck for Blodgett's Nursery. He delivered eight yards of cedar mulch, and we bedded our plants down like little green kids at a sleepover.

To this point, weekends had been dominated by *the list*. We'd rack out early and work. If there was daylight or energy left, we'd go for a bike ride or to the pub for music.

The abridged Honey* Do List:
Set up workbench
Unpack
Hang pictures
Build retaining wall
Plant flowers

There was one more entry before The Great Paradigm Shift.

Build fence

With a good crew, you could put T-posts and hotwires around Jefferson County in a weekend. This fence was to define our homestead. When the last post was set and board hung, we'd ride our bikes or go to the lake and do the work if there was time and daylight left.

A month, three trips to the chiropractor, four trips to John at Countryside Jewelry, and one trip to St. Gabriel, and we were done. Five bundles of cedar posts and six pallets of two-by-sixes had become 1,300 feet of high-low two-board horse fence.

Damn Pinterest. Thank God for my wife.

Sheila is my voice of reason, and governor. When the to-do list says to build a fence, my nature is to drop a straight line, dig some holes, hang some boards, and go. My wife starts every project with 1,300 images from Pinterest. She calls three different lumberyards for estimates and has the material delivered. Then we build a fence.

She's right.

Shelly Reichart of Paradigm Farms in Lake Mills has a pristine white three-board plastic fence around her herd of Olympic-class Grand Prix dressage horses. We have five Quarter Horses re-homed from Flying B Ranch in Wyoming and a broken Clydesdale that Sheila couldn't stand euthanizing. Stormie and Yukon are down in the assisted living pen. They've been on the farm since Sheila was in diapers. Our herd would look like Jethro Bodine at the Oscars behind such a structure.

We'd build wood.

It's the Blue Beetle Syndrome. When you're in the mode, you notice every fence in the country. Three-board follows wooden fence like

cornbread and beans. Sheila is not a follower, and our horses would stay on the other side of baler twine strung between T-posts. We decided two boards would be plenty. She accused me of preempting a future request for a miniature horse by building a fence he could walk right under. The truth is, my knees are well past their warranty. That low board would cost a goodly chunk-o-change and an extra 130 genuflections.

Google "treated lumber." Your first page of hits will be Home Depot and Menards. London Lumber has three employees, a landline, and one computer. They also have more straight boards in stock than every big-box store in the state of Wisconsin. Not to mention, John read my books and offers to drop stuff off on his way home. They always get the first call. He could get it in a week, but Pal Steel in Palmyra could deliver the next day.

I figured a post every ten feet. If ever there was a day I'd consider digging 130 posts by hand, it was not at fifty-four years old. Mid-State Equipment rents post hole augers for the front of a skid loader. Mayor Dave was pretty sure his grandson Cody had a three-point auger layin' behind the barn. I liked the idea of saving $120 a weekend, but I had two concerns. The last time I saw that auger in service was ten years ago when we built the pasture fence. It'd been laying in the weeds since. It would likely take a gallon of grease and a ten-pound sledge to get it on the PTO. The other reservation is preservation. If you've ever seen a post hole auger for a three-point, you'll understand. I can smash three fingers walking by the bastard. I thought about squeezing my left index finger in the vice, just to get it over with.

Part of me hoped Dave couldn't find it. Sure enough, it was in the weeds behind the old motor home and the corn head for the combine. I whacked the weeds and scooped it into the bucket tractor. I had it mounted and turning in under twenty minutes, leaking oil like a '65 Nash Rambler. My moment of pride was brief as the bit was too tall for the tractor, and it dragged the ground when I traveled. I'd never get lost, but that and a wonky clutch on the Allis 185 would make it pretty hard to get my holes started straight.**

Thomas Edison said: "I have never failed. I have an extensive list of things that don't work, but I have never failed."

I had that thing on and off a half-dozen times, trying to adjust the auger and the drawbar. Self-fulfilling prophecy? Absorbed in the throes of another failed attempt, I laid the thing behind the tractor, pinning my ring finger between the differential and the top arm. I lifted it off and climbed back on the tractor. Five minutes later, I noticed the pain persisted, and there was moisture in my glove. The sensation was similar to the time I cut my leg with a chainsaw, and I noticed my boot filling with blood. I pulled off my glove to find my wedding ring smashed flat on my rapidly swelling finger. I was just across the fence from the garage and my toolbox. I was able to squeeze the ring with a pair of channel locks, relieve the pressure, and scrub the grease off so I could get to work by 7:00 a.m.

By noon the swelling had not relented to the point I could slide the ring off. I imagined the throbbing waking me at midnight with my hand the size of a bratwurst, stumbling around the garage in my bare feet wrapped in a towel trying to wedge the tips of my tin snips between ring and finger. John Black at Countryside Jewelry built the ring. He had me come by after work.

Those who saw me driving down Highway B holding my hand high out the window will be less surprised when I show up in the memory care unit of Lilac Springs in a few months. We iced my hand and sprayed it with Windex. John came with a fine pair of jeweler's channel locks, but when he squeezed it wider dorsal and ventral, it would constrict medial and lateral. Heidi tactfully held her tongue as we wrenched on the band of gold. I held one side with my Leatherman while John cranked the other with the pliers to finally release my finger. If our marriage holds up as well as the ring that represents it, we're in it for good.

Fence building ain't brain surgery, but Sheila wanted to have the kinks worked out before we called in the troops. She found a spool of binder twine in the back of the shed. We tied the distal end to the last post in the old fence down by the road and sited the spot that would be the corner of the new fence parallel to the drive. We spray painted a dot every nine feet, ten inches. I backed through the pasture and pushed the tip of the auger top dead center on the first white dot, pushed the

BILL STORK

clutch to engage the PTO, and dropped the drawbar. Rattling and wobbling, she drilled the ditch like Grandma plugging a watermelon. Six inches into the third hole, I recalled the guys from We Energies scratching through a foot of frozen tundra with the frost tooth on their backhoe, trenching in our power line, which ran approximately **right between the wheels of the tractor I was sitting on**. I grabbed the drawbar and mashed the clutch. The image flashed of the crime scene outline of the guy who forgot to call Diggers Hotline.

We relocated operations to the back of the house until Diggers showed up.

Three days later, there were red flags heading up the hill. I crossed myself and looked skyward.

The spray paint wrapped around the spoiled dirt of the hole I'd pulled out of.

I had this vision of every post solid as a soldier and straight as a laser. That notion was shattered early on. We took the bolt cutters to the binders on the first bundle of treated cedar posts. You can't make a post straighter than the tree. On the third hole the auger hit rock, headed south, and the tractor started to buck like the bull at Billy Bob's. I was minimally amused when Sheila pointed out, "That's why this is a horse pasture and not a plowed field."

We had an idea where we wanted the fence; the fence had others.

Sheila had *the* idea of 2019. She suggested that instead of end to end, we stagger the boards in a high-low pattern. Not only could we get a bigger bite on the posts, but it would absorb the variance in our hole positions courtesy of the glaciers that delivered a quarry just beneath the topsoil of our lot—a stroke of brilliance and creativity, which held up for seven full posts. The gap to the eighth was ten feet, four inches. Our fence boards are ten feet, zero inches. John at London Lumber had plenty of twelve-footers.

We made it from the woods to the laneway at the north end of our lot in a Sunday afternoon. We had all the posts set and were four boards away from the corner when it started to rain. I don't recall Jim at the Lake Mills Ace Hardware saying the DeWALT 20V cordless drill was not waterproof, so we kept at it until the mud was caking two inches thick on the bottom of my boots.

Expanding on Edison's theory, we learned with confidence that the 185 with the auger hanging not quite vertical added an element of difficulty that we didn't have the skill set or patience to absorb. I called Mid-State Monday morning and rented the auger for the skid loader the following weekend. It was time to call in some youth and vigor.

Each spring, the Fort Atkinson High School FFA has a community service auction. When I was in band we went from door to door selling candles and cards. These kids offered to do anything from babysitting to baling hay in exchange for a donation to the FFA. We got a pulled pork dinner, a carton of chocolate milk, and four hours from a thirteen-year-old farmboy named Isaac and eight hours from a fifteen-year-old equestrian and volleyball player named Hailey, for under two hundred dollars. When we called to make arrangements, her mom quipped, "Oh, this will be fun; she's never done anything like that before."

Completing our crew was Braxton Walter. Chris and Christa Walter are two of my favorite folks. Christa runs a 10k and does an hour of yoga before her oatmeal every day. Chris grew up on a farm in Ohio and played fullback in college. He just celebrated fifty. He could still throw on pads and open a hole the size of a Ford Ranger. Their twins Braxton and Bennet are what's right with kids these days.

Ten-year-old Braxton was sipping a root beer at the end of the bar at Tyranena. He gave me a handshake and eye contact. He and Chris ran a Tough Mudder obstacle race down in Illinois last fall. I asked him how his training was going, and he assured me he was on track for a podium finish this year. The kid loves to run, and Chris had him doing bodyweight exercises. "Well, Brax, I've got just the exercise for your forearms and shoulders." I asked for his hand, turned it palm up, and rubbed it with my thumb. I nodded, "Yup, I have a tamper that would fit your hand just right." Chris's temple creased behind his cheaters.

Braxton asked, "Dad, what's a tamper?"

Chris has a laugh big as his shoulders, "Son, I'm sure Doc Bill would be happy to show you."

Saturday morning.

Sheila made five pounds of sloppy joes. She didn't have the crew showing up until eight, so we could get the first holes marked and dug. I glanced at the forecast and had Johnny Cash in my head:

How high's the water momma?
It's three feet high and risin'.

Sheila's phone started pinging at seven, "Are you guys still building fence?" AccuWeather had a near one hundred percent chance of rain predicted for Jefferson County, Wisconsin. The radar looked like a kindergartner spilled red, green, and yellow paint on a map and stirred it with a toothbrush.

The John Humphries credo reads: "There is no such thing as bad weather, just a poor choice of clothes."

The computer was correct. Christa drove through a downpour between Lake Mills and our place. Hailey's mom drove around two flooded intersections coming up from Whitewater. It would be a bit centric to suggest divine intervention, but there were multiple times I could see torrents of rain like a mountain monsoon falling on Tom Doeberlein's old place a quarter-mile to the west and the Andersons to the north. On three occasions, I had Braxton gather the tools in case we had to make a run for the machine shed. We got what Ritchie Behm calls a three-inch rain. It was three inches between the drops in the dust on the hood of the John Deere.

We gathered for a pre-game pep talk. I had everybody try and wiggle the last post Sheila and I had set. "That's how we want 'em all to feel."

I had a sixteen-pound monster maul I used for a tamper. The triangular head fit next to the post just right, but with a four-foot handle in a three-foot hole, I spent more time on my knees than a high school boy in confession. I scrounged a four-foot hunk of pipe from the barn and scabbed it on to the handle. I googled "stand-up tamper," and I got a hit for an espresso maker on Amazon and a political video of *Borat*.

I was thinking the monster tamper might get to be a bit much for Braxton pretty quickly. I thought it might get to be a bit much for Bill after lunch. I added a piece of PVC to a six-pound sledge. I may be the only guy you know with a mini and a monster stand-up tamper.

It didn't take long for us to find a system. I used a fender washer dangling from three feet of six-pound test for a plumb bob. Braxton and I would mark ten holes, and then I'd hop on the skid loader and drill 'em. I showed farmboy Isaac how to start backfilling every hole with a little gravel to wick water away from the butt of the post. Brax would site us straight-up north and south. We'd alternate dirt then gravel until each post was solid, then move to the next. Sheila and Hailey would rake up the spoil dirt, and Hailey would build a cairn out of the rocks too big to backfill.

The youth infusion of our crew kept my language PG, but every third hole, the clutch on the auger would bite and growl, and I'd be out of the seat beating and prying rocks out of the hole. We got fifteen posts ahead, and the girls broke off and started hanging boards. Hailey looked like she was headed to volleyball practice in black rubber barn boots. With arms big as hoe handles, she was totin' 2x6x10-foot boards two at a time. Sheila showed her once how to set the clutch on the drill, and in short order, she looked like Rosie the Riveter building bombers for WWII.

I'd catch Braxton leaning on a shovel and ask if he planned to work for the county when he grew up. At thirteen, Isaac looked like he'd been shaving since he was ten. He liked talking a little more than working, but a "Hey, farmboy" every now and then would keep him in the game.

Folks work a little bit better with a goal. "I know y'all want to keep going, but when we get to the corner of the house, let's go inside and have a bite of lunch."

Braxton and Team FFA got us twenty-two posts to the box elder by the driveway by Saturday evening. I was out of the house and on the job by five-thirty Sunday morning, which gave me two hours to waste setting nine posts, building a maze I'd seen at the Kettle Moraine to slow down bikers crossing the horse trails.

My idea was that we could walk or zig-zag our bikes through the maze, but the horses would just see wood. Sheila took one look. "Yukon will be grazing the backyard in ten minutes."

The second Sunday impediment.

At its completion, the fence would be a quarter-mile long, 130 fence posts, 260 boards, three gates, and four man-passes. There was ONE hole that had to be in A spot. As predictable as beer at a Badger game, the auger broke the topsoil, then just sat and spun. I rocked all eight thousand pounds of machine on the tip of the auger, to no effect. For the other two hundred rocks we'd found, the bit would bind, the rig would buck.

This was the Moby Dick of boulders. I pried with the breaker bar, beat on it with a sledgehammer, and drilled four holes around it. Tracy dropped off Micaela, who was home from college and cash-poor. "Holy shit, brother. I've got a demolition hammer at home." And so it went—two hours on one hole, three inches at a time.

Thanks to my maze to nowhere and Moby, we only made the end of the laneway by lunch on Sunday. Sheila and I were starting to fade.

Thank God for Micaela. As a kid, Mic was a bit of a daddy's girl. We'd wondered out loud how she'd fare in college. If fence building is a barometer, she'll win her first Nobel before she's thirty.

The next run was a straight shot, with nineteen posts next to Santana's paddock. Calling upon the definition of insanity, I switched from the twelve to the nine-inch auger. I wouldn't have a lot of room in the hole for the tamper, but we'd reduce our chances of hitting rock by twenty-five percent.

Well played.

I drilled and set posts, too dry to speak and too tired to think of something to say. Mic and Sheila followed, hauling with the golf cart, hanging boards, and babbling like a couple of school girls. Sheila reminded Micaela that she had been the most annoying of the nieces and nephews.

I had grand visions of getting the project to Highway J by lunch on the first day. The reality was that by the time the sun was grazing the treeline to the west Sunday evening, we'd made it to the bottom of the burial mound. We still had a bundle and a half of posts at the end of the drive. Eight hundred feet of fence built, five hundred left to go.

Life intervened, and the job sat for another two weeks.

Critical Sunday.

To this point in time, we'd been building at a rate of thirty-six posts a day, and once again, AccuWeather predicted rain.

It was time to call in the ringers.

Joe and Sam Pappa are Joe's Handyman Service. They've painted our house, the clinic, replaced garage doors, basement doors, and stained every inch of trim in our house. They are all about git 'er done.

Austin Kind has been Jon Bound's chief grunt for four years. Working for Jon is like playing for Lombardi; there are expectations. Micaela was home from college again. I'm convinced she could build the fence by herself in a few days.

My friend Glenn Fuller was down for the weekend.

Give Glenn Fuller a canvas, a photograph, and a week, and he'll paint a piece of history. Hand him a breaker bar and a shovel, and he'll give you all he's got, plus ten. He was all about pinch-gripping, dead-lifting, and farmer's walks before the term CrossFit was ever coined. He's got the joints to prove it.

Dad said, "You know, son, that Glenn always gets his end."

The ultimate endorsement of the workin' man.

In spite of my tamper innovation, eighty fence posts had not been kind to my lumbar spine. With eight hundred milligrams of Vitamin I onboard, I was still bent over like Quasimodo. At eight on the dot, the white Chevy pulled up the drive, followed by Austin's little grey Volkswagen.

Shit was about to get done.

The Blues was born as workers chanted field hollers in unison as they slogged across cotton fields. Austin and Mic bantered the plot lines of

Disney movies while they engineered the step-downs where the fence drops into the ravine by the old dump.

I backed down the chalk line in the skid loader, drilling holes then switching to the pallet forks to haul posts to keep Sam, Joe, and Glenn stocked. I grabbed one of Joe and Sam's posts—not a wiggle. I was amazed they could go in that fast. Joe caught me. "I'd do the same thing to you, Doc, and you know it!"

Joe's Handyman Service has taken over the jobs I used to do, and some I never could. It saves time but is a bit emasculating to call to replace a ballast or patch some drywall. I felt my blood testosterone nudge a nanogram or two, spending a few hours on the end of a shovel working with the guys for once.

They say good fences make good neighbors. Sheila's parents and brother live next door. We installed a remote-controlled gate so they could drive their golf cart up to supervise our progress on the deck or take Tugger for a ride.

Folks build fences to keep dogs, cattle, or kids in. They build them to keep rabbits, foxes, or neighbors out.

We built ours to say "this is our home."

Sometimes the journey can be so long and challenging that we forget to celebrate the destination. Not this time. When folks ask, I can puff up a bit and assure them that *we* built our fence. I valued working shoulder to shoulder with the FFA kids, Braxton, Micaela, Austin, Joe, and Sam. Now I'm gonna grab a beer and watch the horses graze and the sun set.

---

*Yes, plural. My wife is not one to delegate and sit. She'll be doing her part.

**After the fence was built, Mayor Dave stopped by on his Mule, making the rounds. "Oh ya, Cody mentioned something about the top arm on that auger bein' bent or something." Ɋ

No Bad Weather: The Inverse Corollary

I have written frequently about my friend, John Humphries. John is a cycling guide and a spirit. John and I have ridden our bikes across the top of the world, and he's helped me find strength I never knew I had. He has also introduced me to the Norwegian adage: "There is no such thing as bad weather, just a poor choice of clothes." Immersion has taken twenty years and been challenged, but that philosophy has enhanced my existence in ways I expected, and others I did not.

Recently, I stumbled upon the inverse of "no bad weather."

I may have mentioned that I enjoy listening to music. There are no fewer than fifty shows on my list of the five best concerts I've ever seen.

I've seen REM, The Black Crowes, and the Red Hot Chili Peppers in a dive bar in college. I was at the first Farm Aid in 1985. Five years later, I heard Stevie Ray Vaughan play his last note. Shows are added to the list with regularity, many featuring a Buddy Holly retro-looking guitar player named Joel Paterson.

JP was raised in Madison and moved to Chicago to shop his chops in the big town. He lives in a one-room apartment and drives a grey Honda with over 300k on the odometer. He's been described as the best guitar player in the city of Chicago, a freak, and a genius. Joel has been a part of a dozen or more of my five best (including the first non-date with my wife, Sheila).

A few stand out.

Wayne "The Train" Hancock calls himself the king of Juke Joint Swing. Wayne isn't but five and a half feet tall and doesn't weigh over a buck fifty, but I'm not arguing with him. Google Images has one shot of him with a semi-lighthearted smirk. Otherwise, he looks like a pissed-off Ernest T. Bass. He was born in Dallas, Texas, but his home is the road. He's famous for playing three-and-a-half-hour shows without a break. That way, he doesn't have to talk to anyone.

Wayne had just finished a show in Chicago, after which his lead guitar player and pedal steel man got into a knock-down-drag-out fight. One ended up in jail, the other in the hospital. Wayne was sipping a water at the bar, lamenting out loud that he'd have to cancel his show in Madison the next night. The bartender wrote Joel's number on the back of a coaster. "Call this guy."

Wayne looked up with his bulgy left eye. "Who the hell is Joel Paterson?" As if he had an option.

It was that middle Wednesday in January when the sun doesn't even come up. The snow was blowing sideways down Highway V in front of the clinic. I was flying solo. A down cow and two calvings backfilled the space created when my last two pet appointments of the day got stuck or couldn't get their cars started. Two hours later, I staggered back to the clinic. The legs of my insulated coveralls were saturated with blood and placenta and frozen into solid tubes.

Thank God for Terri.

I had pimped this show for weeks to anyone with ears, and my girlfriend at the time loved music and dancing as much as me. She met me at the door with clean, dry clothes and ordered me into the shower.

We paid the cover and wedged ourselves among every musician in the city of Madison who'd come out to see Wayne. I was bumped in the back of the leg by a guitar case. Joel asked, "Hey, Bill, do you know which one is Wayne?"

They shook hands by the foot of the stage. "You know my stuff?" Wayne asked, just a little bit uneasy.

"Western Swing, right?" Joel assured him, "We'll be fine."

The rest is written in the annals of Madison's music history. It could have snowed the doors shut, and we could have reelected Richard Nixon, and folks would tell you about the look Wayne gave the kid with the guitar as he picked on Chet Atkins, Merle Travis, and his own guitar gumbo. At one point, he walked off stage, handing the reins to Joel.

I've seen Joel blow away a room playing a bowling-ball acrylic lap steel he'd just bought at a pawnshop for ten bucks. He squatted between the tanks at Tyranena Brewing, strung it, tuned it, plugged in, and took a solo in the middle of "Honey Bee Blues."

One night at the Crystal, Oscar "the king of 43rd Street" Wilson called out "Purple Haze" for The Cash Box Kings' second encore. Joel leveled the joint. I asked him afterward if he'd ever played Hendrix. "No, but I've heard him a million times growin' up."

Aren't we talking about "no such thing as bad weather?" Yes, I'll get there, but I'm prone to digression.

Joel posts ninety-second videos of him picking the greatest riffs in history on Facebook nearly every day. Now in his forties, the lines have blurred. His style is all his own. I asked how in the hell he did it. "Bill, if I'm awake, I have a guitar hanging around my neck." He also books all his own gigs, writes, records with every ace musician in the city, and runs his own record label.

Check out his compilation of instrumental Beatle covers *Let it Be Guitar,* at www.joelpaterson.com. While you're there, click on his calendar.

Out of respect for Joel and the thousands of other amazing musicians I've known, I'll limit the superlatives to just one.

Joel Paterson is, without a doubt, the world's most elusive guitar player. The man plays as many as three gigs a day. Go to the calendar on his website, and you'll find it's empty. Joel is all over YouTube, but if you want to hear him live, go to Chicago and check him out on Facebook. About twenty minutes before the show, he'll post.

Alternately, be on the lookout for him to be playing with someone who does share where they might be playing. That list includes, but is in no way limited to Joel Paterson and the Modern Sounds, The Joel Paterson Trio, Devil in a Woodpile, Joel Paterson and Chris Foreman, The Cash Box Kings, The Western Elstons, and occasionally

JP McPherson, The Cactus Blossoms, JP and Oscar Wilson, and The State Line Americana Music Allstars.

An impediment to hearing JP play is geography. He plays a standing gig at Joe's Bar in Chicago every first and third Wednesday with a band called The Western Elstons. The Elstons are old-school country and rockabilly, the perfect vehicle for JP's country-jazz Chet Atkins/ Merle Travis mastery. The cover charge is ten dollars, but add in the cost of taking a half-day off work on Thursday morning, and it gets a bit pricey. He plays every Sunday at the legendary Green Mill jazz club in Chicago with ace organist Chris Foreman, but their second set gets started about ten minutes before my alarm goes off Monday morning.

So, when I ran across a Facebook post that Joel was playing with Mark Haynes (the world's greatest blues drummer), Jimmy Voegli (the world's best blues piano playing dairy farmer), and three guys I've never heard of, at a joint in Beloit, Wisconsin, I had to process, but not for long.

Mark, Jimmy, and Joel are worth the price of admission, and if Joel is driving to Beloit on a Sunday afternoon, it will be good.

We're there.

I told Sheila on Tuesday afternoon we were going to Beloit on Sunday afternoon. Sheila does not share my enthusiasm for music. My wife is a ninja opportunist. She knows how to phrase statements as questions, to which there is only one safe answer. "Would it be on the way to catch the (sadly) going-out-of-business sale at Roughing It In Style?"

Translated, "I'll go to Beloit to listen to music if you'll go shopping for area rugs and end tables."

I know when I've been beaten.

The show commenced at three in the afternoon. She asked me what time we needed to leave. I had not heard Joel in two years, and I didn't want to miss a note. Roughing It In Style is nearly straight west, and the Grand Avenue Pub is due south.

I bravely declared a one o'clock departure.

The day arrived.

You may recall that I had declared a paradigm shift. This summer, I vowed that once the fence was built (which became, after the deck was built, and then third-crop hay), if there was good entertainment, I was putting down the log splitter, leaf rake, or Sawzall, and by God, we were going.

It is relevant to note that the last three weekends had been full-on monsoons. It had been three weeks since we could step off the pavement at the farm.

Sunday, October 20, near half past six. The sun rising through airborne ice crystals washed the eastern horizon with a golden-red glow. A towering spire shot into the cloudless sky over neighbor Doug's chisel plowed bean field. Dawn was but the opening act. If this day were a Broadway show, it'd be *Hamilton*. The third of the leaves that had fallen did not move a centimeter. As if the ice showed only to treat us to a top-ten sunrise, the frost quickly retreated, and the thermometer shot to the mid-fifties by the time Ray threw the newspaper to the bottom of the drive. Uncle Erv always loved the woods to our south. I took him a half-dozen pictures on high-resolution. Technology has not invented enough pixels to do this day justice.

It was the most spectacular day in the history of weather. I was hoping to switch my mower over to leaf vac mode, dig three new fence posts, and install the cat flap into the pass door in the garage. Instead, I had resolved to go furniture shopping, then to a bar in Beloit with 180 minutes of daylight left on the clock.

My resolve was put to the test.

We arrived at Roughing It by half past one. We found an area rug for the sunroom for seventy percent off on the first lap of the store. The furniture had been marked up before it was marked down. The rustic wrought iron toilet paper holders were above our pay grade.

There's no straight shot from the furniture store to Beloit. Google Maps charted a course through the rolling hills of southern Wisconsin, and I believe we dropped into Iowa for a few miles. We were not going to make the first note. What my ears were missing, my eyes were feasting.

BILL STORK

Farmers had chopped most of their corn, and much of the soybeans were off. There was a blaze-red maple on the corner of Main Street in Clinton that would have been a rock star in Woodstock, Vermont.

The Grand Avenue Pub was two doors off the swollen Rock River. Slightly muted, the music poured into the street. My phone had pinged just as we found our parking spot. I tried to focus on Amy Hanson, whose cat had vomited a Nerf dart. I tapped my toe on the concrete and listened with one ear, while a chipmunk was swing-dancing with a grey squirrel by the bike rack.

The Grand Avenue Pub had tin-stamped ceilings, friendly bartenders, and the best walleye sandwich I've ever eaten on a Sunday in Wisconsin. And my hunch was quickly rewarded. The leader of the band was Gary McAdams. He wore workin' man's boots and a trucker hat and had a voice that could sing the red off an apple. They played Frank Sinatra to Fred Eaglesmith and owned it all. Joe, Pete, and Mark opened the second set with three instrumental jazz standards. The place felt like family. There were guys with ZZ Top beards, ponytails, and trucker wallets doing the old guy swing with their dates, elbow-to-elbow with the khaki and plaid professors from the college as Gary ripped through "Mack the Knife."

Folks'll be talking about Sunday, October 20, for a good long time around these parts. Putting down the post hole digger and going inside on a spectacular fall day was one of the hardest things I've done. The make-or-break was, "No such thing as bad weather."

We'd built fence in the rain, cut wood in a blizzard, and ridden mountain bikes across the top of the world in a monsoon. I figured we had four hours in the bank.

I found my people. Gary introduced "Silver Wings."

"This is a Merle Haggard song, but we're gonna do it different. This ain't paint-by-numbers folks; this is art."

Oh, yes, it was. ◌

Perspective

South Main Street in Lake Mills, Wisconsin, had deteriorated into a tree-lined cattle path. My preferred modes of transport are a three-quarter-ton pickup and a mountain bike, so it didn't bother me much. But when the Priuses and minivans started to bottom out and we lost a Smart car in a sinkhole, it was time to repave.

To make room for parking and bike lanes, and to secure state funding, it was dictated the trees along the boulevard had to come down. Smartly dressed, persuasive, and articulate, Charlie Roy and the whole town rallied, but the government won. Today, Main Street looks like Barneveld, Wisconsin, after the '84 tornado.

We can take some solace. Walter Cnare was an arborist for the city. He said if the Stihls hadn't gotten the ash trees, the Emerald Borer would have.

For two years, crews worked on replacing the underground utilities in increments.

Early spring of 2019, the barricades came up, and the A-1 Excavating army rolled in from the north. The boys from Bloomer had a dozen Cat, Case, and John Deere 'hoes, 'dozers, and end loaders hauled in by a fleet of lowboys. Some still had plastic on the seats and paint on the buckets.

Not for long.

The Lakers Athletic Club has anchored the one hundred block of South Main Street for over thirty years. For most of that time, three days a week, I'd idle down the hardwood-lined main drag, waving at the dog walkers and marveling at the seasons, en route to my workout. When the construction gates closed, I redirected to the Woodland Beach-

Ferry Road backdoor route. It upped my eighteen-minute commute to twenty-one and doubled the stop signs, but I was able to watch the daily progress on a couple of waterfront mansions under construction and wave at Diane Alward being walked by her German Shepherd pup, Quinn.

Stage One of deconstruction took place just outside the glass door. I get to the club by five forty-five. Sources reported the crew would do last call at Sporty's Saloon or TT's Tavern, but by the time I was done with crunches and sit-ups, the guys were oilin', greasing, and fueling their machines. By six-thirty, they were blowing black smoke and moving material. When they tore out the old road, the triple-axle Macs were lined up nose to end gate. The guy on the hoe swung steady as a metronome. Every stroke, he laid four yards of broken asphalt in the bed of the trucks gentle as a baby in a bassinette. When they hauled in breaker rock for the new base, every load of limestone was greeted with a dozer blade. It was like a choreographed, diesel-powered dance.

We get off at six when things go well at the clinic, seven on Mondays. More often than not, A-1 Excavating would just be sweeping the sidewalks and idling down. Early in my practicing years, I was whining to my dad after a long day at the clinic. "Son, it ain't the same twelve hours driving between calls and BS'n with the farmers as setting rebar and pouring concrete." I always roll through the job site slowly, raise my hand, and mouth a "thank you" through the windshield.

Summer evenings, I'd ride my bike through to see what they were up to. You could not find an empty tobacco tin, Mountain Dew can, or sandwich bag on the A-1 Excavating job site. Their equipment was lined up in formation. They were bound by contract to have the first phase done by Memorial Day for the sake of the small businesses in town. All spring it rained like Noah and the Ark, and they had to core down twenty-two feet in the three hundred block to reach solid base. Still, by mid-May, they were a month ahead of schedule and had to wait for school to get out when they got to Lakeview Terrace on the edge of campus.

The job foreman was a hard-handed young man named Cody. He looked like he could have won a state championship in wrestling at 180 pounds. Mid-June, his Brittany Spaniel ran through a barbed-wire fence. He apologized profusely for disrupting my Sunday. I explained the clinic he was standing in and my education were subsidized by a heavy-equipment operator working seven twelves setting steel; it was the least I could do.

For twelve years, we were entertained by an exuberant English Cocker Spaniel named Lilly who belonged to our friends Joe and Wanda Pleshek. If ever there was a dog that would live forever, it would have been her. Alas, we finally had to say goodbye, but the void would not last long. Joe found Buck, heir apparent to the legendary Lilly from a top-flight breeder in Vandalia, Illinois. I know the area well.

"Vandelly" is an hour south of Decatur and halfway to my Aunt Mary and Uncle Kelsey's farm in Greenville. My grandma and I would road-trip in her '74 Plymouth Valiant. Grandma drank iced tea dark as a Guinness stout by the gallon. We always took an obligatory bathroom break at a rest stop in clear view of the state penitentiary. She called it The Peanut Farm.

Joe is the CEO of a large biotech firm and looks the part. He spoke highly of his experience with the breeder Jay Lowry. The drive he could have done without. "Man, Dr. Stork. Once you get south of Rockford, there is nothin' to see."

Boredom is in the eye of the beholder.

Since Dad died, I make that drive every Thanksgiving. It's an hour to Rockford and another to LaSalle–Peru, then Bloomington, and finally Decatur. The road is straight as a snap line, and the land is flat as piss on a plate, but to me, there is plenty to see.

 BILL STORK

Unbeknownst to my wife, I plan our departure to have us just south of Rockford at sunrise. By mile marker 115, I feel a physiologic lack of encumbrance. As you climb out of the Kishwaukee River valley, you're greeted by red flashing lights atop the wind turbines. Ten years ago, I attempted to count them. I lost track at sixty-six. They've reproduced like the Haack family since. Each tower is three hundred feet tall. The blades are a hundred feet long. The concrete base is a hundred-foot cube, and the generator weighs fifty tons. On the windiest days, the blades look to be turning like a second hand on a Timex. I had Paige count the RPMs. Calvin was in geometry, so he remembered the formula to calculate circumference. We multiplied the length of the blades by two times pi. Knowing the distance traveled per revolution, we could multiply to conclude the tips of the blades are traveling 122 miles per hour! Last Christmas, my father-in-law asked about how the towers were constructed, so we watched a time-lapse video on YouTube.

Wisconsin farmers will talk about 2019 ad infinitum. One could counter that farmers talk about every year, forever. Touché. The same near-biblical rains that hampered the road crew in Lake Mills made it impossible to get crops in the ground. There was talk at the diner of planting corn by pontoon boat or floatplane. June and July felt like summer on San Francisco Bay. I'm not sure what a "degree day" is, but we begged for enough of them to even get the quickest-maturing corn to the finish line.

I had to see how the farmers in Illinois were faring.

Corn silage is a staple of a dairy cow's diet. The entire plant is cut and chopped at sixty-five to seventy percent moisture, then stored in those tall concrete silos you see next to barns or in a concrete bunker covered in plastic. Silage is usually cut mid-September, but there is a narrow window. Too wet, and it all runs out the bottom of the silo. Too dry and it won't ferment. Cows won't milk, breed-back, and get really sick. Even if the field it's standing in is a swamp, the corn will continue to dry down. In Wisconsin, a lot of big tractors got stuck, and fields got rutted trying to make good feed.

In Illinois, there are precious few dairy farms to feed silage, so six or eight weeks later, we hope corn and beans are below twenty percent moisture so we can harvest them for dry grain. Harvest too early and wet, and you're docked at the elevator to dry it down. Wait for the crops to dry in the field, and you risk Halloween 2019—it looked more like Christmas. Three late October snowstorms with winds thirty miles per hour resulted in thousands of acres of soybeans at five hundred dollars per, lying on the ground, black, brown, and moldy.

Now in late November, I thought for sure I'd be reporting a sob story to Rick at herd check Monday morning. "Oh yeah, the guys down in Illinois still can't get their beans off, and there's corn standing everywhere." I saw two sections of beans still standing just after the Paw Paw exit to confirm my suspicion. If I were Facebook or Fox News, I'd go to print with the story, but Sheila was sleeping, and I had another three hours to kill. I figured I'd put some numbers to it like Pam Jahnke, the Fabulous Farm Babe. I didn't see another bean field standing until LaSalle– Peru, so I'll report that they were doing pretty good on beans. Corn was a different story. It's not as easy as it looks to take inventory on both sides of the Interstate and drive at the same time. So, I did one side of the road, one section at a time. I concluded by my head-math there was a solid thirty percent of the corn still standing.

That made me wonder about fall tillage.

Once you get the crops off and the combine cleaned out and in the shed, it's tempting to go to town and have a beer. That works fine if you can count on next spring being warm and dry. Not likely. If '20 is anything like '19, there will be about eighteen hours in late-May to get crops planted. You'd better get the cornstalks chopped so they'll decompose under the snow and break up the ground.

I was noticing that in the Land of Lincoln, they pick up the chisel plow six rows before the waterways to avoid erosion. Then came a distraction that kept me entertained all the way to Clinton.

Ten feet wide, and a football field long, huge plastic bags were sitting at the far end of the fields. In Wisconsin, these would be full of corn silage. Cattle feed. The closest thing to a Holstein in Ogle County, Illinois, was a quart of chocolate milk at the Huck's store in Hillcrest. (I find Hillcrest, Illinois, comical in the same sense as subdivisions

  BILL STORK

with names like Oak Crest Village and Maple Bluff rising out of a cornfield.) These bags were a mile away from the nearest buildings, and I couldn't see or smell a trace of a ruminant of any magnitude.

By then we were slowing down for the suburbs of Clinton. I needed to take inventory, so I'd have to table the big-bag dilemma.

Altorfer Ag Products is a Claas-Lexion dealer out on Old Highway 51. I usually have to pull over and count. One trip, there were thirty-nine combine harvesters at half a million dollars a copy, on the lot. Thanksgiving Day 2019, there was one, and it was parked at the service bay. Translated, farmers are hopeful.

The speed limit dropped to forty-five, and Sheila stirred to consciousness at the first set of stoplights on the north side of town.

We try and arrive a little early. We only get to see the family once a year. Not to mention, Dad's cousin Jim is a retired machinist. His job was to take the most intricate parts and products from the engineer's CAD design to the assembly line. In retirement, he took up blacksmithing and coppersmithing. While the turkey is cooling, we'll step out back. Jim has a shop with mills, lathes, grinders, and a fridge full of Apple Pie hooch he brings up from his forge trips to Tennessee.

By the time the turkey gets carved, Sheila has talked Jim out of a hand-hammered copper vase, and my ears are warm from the moonshine. I'd ask him if he could make a couple of hooks to hang pots from the cow stanchion Sheila and I hung from the ceiling. His first answer to every job was, "Well, little Bill, I cain't really do that because…" "Don't worry about it, Jim. I've got a guy up home that'll handle it." A week later, it would show up UPS—stainless steel, spot-on, and polished.

For those of us who are concerned about kids these days, we're gonna be OK. As evidence, I present my dad's cousin's son and his family. Derek and Mandy live on four acres in central Illinois with their two kids, Colton and Maddie. They raise two steers for freezer beef, a handful of chickens, and a garden. They fish in the neighbor's pond and hunt. The kids know well, if you kill it, you eat it. Derek works for Mandy's dad on the farm.

He'd know about these damn bags at the edges of the fields I'd been eyeing on the way down.

He explained that with fluctuation in grain markets and the seasonal shortage of propane, farmers could store grain off the field for pennies a bushel—a lot like putting your paycheck in a savings account, waiting for the stock market to jump. If President Trump gets off Twitter long enough to cut a trade deal with China, producers just might be able to cover their costs.

The point of this all is perspective.

I ate dinner with a construction worker for my first eighteen years. I got six months of entertainment watching a road being built. I've worked for farmers for nigh on to twenty-five years. On the same piece of highway that Joe Pleshek saw nothing, I never nodded, without so much as a radio, iPad, or smartphone.

My friend Jennifer Rodriguez once shared a quote: "We come away from every human interaction forever changed."

Let's make damn sure we do. ↷

Hello Darkness, My Old Friend

Sweetie is the feline equivalent of that old lady who lost her filter. She's a sixteen-year-old Persian with an unruly mane. She has to be sedated for her *spa* appointments. Sweetie doesn't hold her liquor like she used to. The day after her most recent style and perm, she was still feeling a little low and slow. Her temperature was normal, and her heart was strong, but she was a tad dehydrated. Some subcutaneous fluids and an injectable anti-nausea medication would have her back to sassy in short order. (I'm glad I didn't have access to maropitant in college.)

Convinced she was going to be OK, I looked forward to the ten or so minutes it would take for the lactated Ringers to run under her skin. Sweetie's people are Margot and Peter. Margot is always smartly dressed and well put together. She exudes the elegance of an era past. She is a retired professor of English and a prolific author. Invariably, I learn something. She has complimented my writer's voice and taken the red pen to my grammar. Peter has a cautious demeanor and a measured manner of speech that piques my curiosity as to the things he knows and the places he's been. Peter is a devout homebody, but when he does leave College Street, he travels to destinations that I have to ask the spelling before I can look them up. At a time in life when many might be content to whittle away the days napping, reading, and waiting for cocktail hour, they've hit pause on the aging process.

Clint Eastwood said, "I don't let the old man in."

Margot and Peter acquired a three-month-old Shetland Sheepdog named Scout.

We returned Sweetie to her carrier and talked about house training, exercise, and engagement for the little Sheltie.

As we parted, I wished them a Merry Christmas and asked about their plans. Margot speaks with the diction of a silver-screen siren, "Oh, we're not much for Christmas. We celebrate the solstice."

In recent years I've developed an appreciation for the things we can do better in times of perpetual darkness. I was interested in their take. "Mostly, we just sit quietly and think."

Exactly.

In the thousands of years before Google Calendar and AccuWeather, people hunted, gathered, and grew. Their very survival was predicated on tracking and recording celestial and meteorological events. December 21 is the longest night of the year—the winter solstice. For the millennia prior to Alexander Graham Bell, we could not see past our noses for months on end. Lest we sleep eighteen hours a day, our thoughts turned inward. After six months of progressively less light, on the night we finally turn the corner, pagans and Christians alike celebrate the birth of the sun. Observers will start a raging fire, representing light and hope. On the heels of a period of introspection, folks recall aspects of their being they wish to shed. Whether it be judgment, insecurity, or forgiveness, they'll scribe their vices on a sheet of paper and chuck 'em in the flames.

We all revel in seventy-five degrees and sunny, but in the darkness and cold, we tend to grumble. "I can't stand this time of year. It's dark when I'm driving to work, and it's dark when I'm driving home."

It does not have to be that way.

The ground is frozen hard, and the grass won't grow. Interview your eldest kin, and write it down. Read a book, write a book, listen to *Astral Weeks* from start to finish, call a friend, or just sit and think like Margot and Peter.

A wrought David Letterman asked Warren Zevon how he dealt with terminal lung cancer, "Well, Dave, you enjoy every sandwich."

I have no clue how many days of good health and clear thought I've been granted. I try and make them count. If I can enjoy fourteen hours of darkness per day, I'm well on my way. ॐ

These Boots

Early in my vet school days, love, or some endocrine-fueled variant thereof, found me in the suburbs of Chicago known as The North Shore. The first measure of how far this fish had washed ashore was when I was asked to park my 1974 Plymouth Valiant on the curb, up the block. They either assumed it would leak oil or weren't quite ready to own an association with this flannel-clad ginger their daughter had drug home with his beard, boots, and down-state twang.

A second indication: it was a spectacular June afternoon, and we were inside, assembled around the dining room table to welcome a family friend. We'll call him Sheldon. I was raised to take my shoes and ball cap off when I enter someone's home. I tucked my Mudhens t-shirt into my Levi's. I was not up to the khaki, colored socks, and Oxford dress code I'd been led into. As the guest, Sheldon took the head of the table and spoke first. Comments were to follow in a clockwise rotation. There were more graduate degrees at this table than an Ivy League regatta (alt Hudson River regatta). My dad was a latter-day Lincoln who spoke the language of the workin' man. "Son, it's better to keep your mouth shut and let 'em think than to open your mouth and prove you're ignorant." I fully intended to keep quiet and sip my tea. (Yes, seriously.)

Sheldon was an engineer. He'd just returned from the Caterpillar Tractor Company in Peoria, Illinois. In the late-eighties, he designed in-line sensors that would measure viscosity, temperature, and the specific gravity of oil, coolant, and hydraulic fluid on Cat's bulldozers, excavators, and graders. His computers could objectively tell the operator the proper time to change filters, fluids, and lubricants to maximize the life of bearings, pumps, and pistons. The design team at Cat wasn't quite ready.

"Those idiots didn't listen to a thing I said. I could have saved them millions," vented Dr. Epstein. As conversation made it around, the physicist at the table queried the specifics of the technology, and the accountant calculated amortization of the additional expense. When my turn came, I was looking to take a pass.

I was not allowed the courtesy of silence.

My mom was a comfort food gourmet. She always set an extra place at the dinner table. Our neighbor, Bob, frequented that extra place. Bob spent thirty years on the assembly line making parts for Caterpillar Tractor Company. Dad could do a vasectomy with the fifty-ton backhoes Sheldon was looking to automate.

I measured my words for maximum diplomacy, but I would not compromise my heritage. "Dr. Epstein, that sounds like amazing technology, but I'm thinking that a skilled operator might be able to tell how hard he's pushing his machine based on the sound of the engine, the smell of the exhaust, and feel on the levers. I'd think they'd factor in soil type and temperature as well."

My comments cut and pasted from conversations over meatloaf and mashed potatoes back home were met with a PhD pee-shaw. "Yeah, right. Those guys are a bunch of trained apes. Where in the hell are you going to find operators who know what they're doing?"

Clearly, there is no correlation between class and the prefix and suffix that bracket your surname. Dad always said, "Son, do your work and shut your mouth. If you're worth a shit, they'll know."

Feeling a little like Jethro Bodine on his first day at Beverly Hills Elementary, I was relieved that the next stop in the redneck show-and-tell was at least outside. Loretta Hupman lived at the end of the cul-de-sac. She had white wicker patio furniture and classical music playing through a patio speaker. A Waterford Crystal pitcher of mimosa sat on a glass-top table surrounded by old fashion tumblers. Loretta had lived in the neighborhood since the tennis courts to the east were a cornfield, and the arborvitae was a hedgerow. As the neighborhood ladies greeted one another with North Shore mime-hugs, I took a seat on the retaining wall. Loretta hunched her chair to a forty-five, looking to pull me into the conversation, or excuse herself from it.

BILL STORK

As the ladies critiqued the Chicago philharmonic's performance at Ravinia and the latest on NPR, she conspicuously inspected me from the Red Wing 402s to my Connelly water ski hat. "I bet you always wear those boots when the goin's tough."

My dad went to his grave never knowing new car smell firsthand. He'd fetch broken lift straps and grinders out of dumpsters at job sites and stitch them back together and solder on new cords. He brazed broken blades on spades and shovels that still had solid handles. He would not skimp on shoes. "Son, you gotta make your living on your feet. Take care of 'em."

We went to Iverson's.

There was a brick wishing well with three goldfish at the front of the store. On the wall hung the iconic Red Wing neon sign and the Buster Brown boy and his dog. In retrospect, with his eyes wide and ears and lips pulled back tightly, the dog looks as if he's either rabid or tetanic and about to bite the boy with a mouth full of Grandma's false teeth. If he can close his mouth.

Earl Iverson was a Decatur, Illinois, dead-ringer for Mr. Rogers. I'd rest my right heel in the cool aluminum Brannock, and he'd measure length, width, and the position of my arch. I begged Mom for a pair of suede high-tops with pockets on the side, just like John Paul Snyder wore, or green canvas Converse like Wayne Dunning. I would sprint the sidewalk between stores and come back chest heaving, trying hard to breathe through my nose, strutting like I'd just done a four-five forty. I'd nod to Mom and Mr. Iverson, "These are the ones."

Until the cartilage in my left knee disintegrated into road pack rubble, I loved to play basketball. I had the vertical leap of Norm from *Cheers*. I couldn't clear a quarter at a dead run, but I always had a pair of leather high-tops. My roommate freshman year of college ran track in high school. He'd run two to four miles after classes. Looking for new experiences, I tried to keep up. I never entered a race or event, but I did string together three or four twenty-mile weeks at a seven-minute pace, and I did it in shoes that were fit by Mr. Rogers.

My cousin Tom got me a seasonal job doing farmwork when I was in eighth grade. You wouldn't take a crowbar to an Algebra test, and you don't walk beans or bale hay in basketball shoes. When you're working, you wear boots.

Years before Roundup and GMOs, crews would trudge through mile-long fields of waist-high soybeans six abreast, each of us responsible for three rows on each side. Wielding Gillette-sharp garden hoes, we'd hack down forests of velvetleaf milkweed and volunteer corn. The Jimsonweeds smelled like a basement full of rotting corpses once you cut them down. We started at sunrise. The morning dew would soak us to the skin in a hundred yards. Our breaks were a couple mile ride sprawled on the farm flatbed between fields. We'd pray for a box elder tree for shade and take twenty minutes for lunch. I learned to pace myself and hydrate. More than once, quitting time felt like a pair of channel lock pliers squeezing my temples, vision blurred and bent double, puking between my Red Wings.

After school and Saturday mornings, I cleaned cages at Brush College Animal Hospital and sold nightcrawlers and minnows at Dave's Tackle Box. In the summer, I mowed grass. The first nine yards were behind a self-propelled Toro. A union operating engineer, dad was all about safety. We picked up a good used mower at a yard sale one Saturday morning. The foot guard was cracked. Before he'd even let me start it, we cut a piece of plywood and made a new one. If my foot slipped in a hole or the mower rolled backward, the blade would have to shatter three-quarters of an inch of marine grade pressboard and slice through my Red Wings before it got to my metatarsals.

CT Taylor was my best friend in high school. The C was for his grandpa Carl who was an ex-Marine. CT called him Poppy. He was also a rodeo hand and construction worker. He had a farm just outside of town on the Sangamon River. CT and I would ride our bikes to the farm so we could ride motorcycles and fish along the river. Poppy's deal was that before we could ride, we had to clean out a winter's worth of bedding pack from the horse stalls. We'd take turns. One would bust off chunks of the organic glacier with a pickaxe, while the other pitched with a fork and shovel. Of all the barnyard species, horse manure is relatively innocuous, dry, and packs well. We'd end up with a mound just outside the barn the size of a VW microbus. We could launch off the pile on our motorcycles and get some big air.

BILL STORK

Our family friend Butch Sprau raised fifty head of Hereford cows in a mud lot farm museum. I'd wrestle newborn calves onto the overturned hood of a '50 Ford pickup, and he'd drag us back to the barn behind the tractor, the cow following along, bawling.

Every musician who's ever made it has a story. They play with the same passion for three people and the sound man, as they would for ten thousand. One of those three just might be *the guy*.

In undergrad, I cleaned rat cages three days a week. In a research lab buried in the caverns of Noyes Hall with rubber gloves, apron, and rubbers, I'd scrub and disinfect a hundred cages between my eight o'clock lecture and eleven o'clock chemistry lab. My boss was a diminutive Vietnamese immigrant named Boonton Syalavong. Boon didn't speak a hundred words the whole time I worked for him, but somehow you felt compelled to move with purpose. Legend has it he once knocked out a gang of four thugs who thought they'd snatch his wife's purse. He'd stroll through and make note of the mountain of sterile plastic enclosures, and nod. In my interview for admittance into vet school, the professor of cardiology, Dr. Dave Smetzer, scanned my resume over the top of his cheaters. Following the overgrown, tobacco-stained index finger, he cackled, "Mr. Stork, you worked for Boon."

I was in.

By my sophomore year in college, I had a PhD in small animal excrement, but farm experience was limited to building motorcycle ramps out of horse shit. I applied at the Swine Research Center. My interview was quick. I was six foot three and weighed two hundred pounds. They had shovels, scrapers, or rakes that fit my hands perfectly. And so began my experience feeding, cleaning, and weighing pigs for the likes of Temple Grandin and the other graduate students.

Reporters from the *Champaign News-Gazette* were looking to do a story on student summer jobs in July of 1988, so the boss man sent them to me. For those of us ancient enough to recall, it was a historic drought.

We were in the middle of fifteen straight days of hundred-degree highs. At night, it never made it below eighty-five. Maybe the heat had gotten to me, or I was just having what I thought was innocent fun. With an Oshkosh B'gosh do-rag sweated to my head and a Huey's t-shirt with sleeves removed for ventilation, I leaned on a barn scraper and told them my name was Dick Bass from Blackshear, Georgia. I gave them the life story of a banjo-strumming, onion-picking, electrical engineering graduate student. The reporter thought it strange that an EE PhD candidate was working a hog farm slopping stalls, "Aw, I thought I'd just do sumthin' a little dif-rnt," I drawled.

Complete with a picture, the story made the front page of the Sunday paper. The next week I got a talking to about journalistic integrity.

I first pitched the stalls, cleaned cages, and hauled a mountain of manure of any species I've ever injected, intubated, resuscitated, bled, spayed, neutered, pregnancy checked, been kicked by, headbutted, been bitten by, or stuck a fork into.

And every scoop was with a pair of Red Wings on my feet.

But all work and no play makes an old guy grey (and eventually bald). After three years on active daily duty, my Monday through Saturday 402s get promoted. They become Saturday night goin' to town boots. In a perfect world, their last act of service is mowing a half-dozen loads of hay. Nothing scours (pun incidental) the shit off and puts a patina on a pair of boots like tromping around slipping between a couple of hundred bales of second-crop alfalfa.

The flatted fifth and seventh played on a Fender Strat through a Super Reverb have brought me more solace, joy, and peace than Prozac and Budweiser ever have, or Viagra ever will. I was baptized in the blues, according to Coco Taylor, Jimmie Johnson, and Buddy Guy in the student union at the University of Illinois in November 1984. In the thirty-six years since, on dance floors from Champaign, Illinois, to Gruene, Texas, every love I've ever won, lost, or attempted has been in sync with twelve-bar blues and West Coast Swings, courtesy of outfits like The Cash Box Kings, Joel Paterson, and Little Charlie and the Nightcats.

BILL STORK

Try a duck-out, spin, or turn in a pair of Red Wings before four thousand farm hours on the farm. They'll grip, and you'll go tumbling like Pee-wee Herman in a plowed field. After a couple of years sliding in and out of your overshoes, the edges will round. A couple of thousand miles on barn floors and the pedals of a skid loader will rub off the logo and the tread, leaving just enough slide for the Cha-Chas and two-steps. I have repeatedly demonstrated, "There is no such thing as a woman who can't dance, just a man who can't lead." So when I lead the heel of a dance partner's boot onto my right toe, I'm grateful for the extra layer of leather.

It was on the dance floor of a live music mecca called Mabel's in Champaign, Illinois, in front of a band called The Mudhens that I first courted a girl from the big city. It was either my flatland swing, or the fact I had a car on campus, but I scored an invitation to spend the weekend with her family, boating on the Mississippi River in Wisconsin. With Barb sleeping on my lap, I snuck a wad of chew near Richmond, Illinois, to keep me awake while I crossed the blessed Cheddar Curtain for the first time. Three hours later, my back was soaked with plastic seat sweat, and we were close enough to smell Big Muddy and brats on the grill when we passed the gate of the LaCrosse Shoe Company. I did a U-turn and paused for a moment of silence. Buried in a box in the basement, I have a picture of the four-foot-tall black letters across the top floor: *Boots and Overshoes*. I explained to Barb that from this temple of productivity came the thirteen-inch-tall Vulcan rubber vessels that protected my Red Wing 402s. LaCrosse Shoe Company was the economic engine for the river city from 1897 to 2012, when it was sold to a Japanese conglomerate.

I've known I wanted to be a veterinarian since the third chapter of *All Creatures Great and Small* in 1979. Getting here was not easy for me. The old call logs are in three-ring binders mired in mildew in the basement, but my most conservative estimate has me at no fewer than 45,000 farm calls in the past twenty-eight years. I've never palpated a cow, pulled a calf, treated a milk fever, done a right DA surgery, or replaced a uterus with anything else on my feet.

I was not wearing a pair of Red Wings Thanksgiving Day 1993 when I proposed marriage to my first wife, but I sure as hell was while swinging Dad's homemade maul. I split a mountain of oak wheels into cordwood under the light of my headlamp, wondering if she'd be home before dawn. There were times my hands made it to my knees as I stared between the toes. It took all I had to not fall in the dirt and curl up like a fetus.

In my life, I've faced fourth and goal with no time on the clock a dozen times. My faith, family, and those Red Wing boots were the only thing that held me up.

I wore them to the Jefferson County Courthouse in June 2005, the day the judge dissolved my first union. The need to be accepted and respected required a rethink on my ironclad idea 'til death do us part. As flawed as that marriage was, there are two amazing, balanced young adults and a stronger, more resilient Bill Stork as a result.

Hellbent on finding mutual respect, unconditional love, and acceptance, I searched Fitsingles.com and Match.com, only to find a redheaded farm girl in the beer garden at Tyranena Brewing Company. With an assist from my best friends, she conceded to going to the Crystal Corner Bar to swing dance to Joel Paterson and the Modern Sounds.

In a driving rain in April 2017, I knelt on the spot in a horse pasture where our home now stands and asked her to tolerate me for the rest of my life. I wore my Red Wings the day we married and the night we danced. I wore them when we honeymooned in New York City, walked twenty-six miles in two days, and sat in the fourteenth row of the Walter Kerr Theater, as The Boss ripped his liver out of his throat on the intro to "Born in the USA."

I wore them to Decatur Memorial Hospital the day I got the call Dad had a stroke, the day I drove him from the only home he'd ever known, and I slept in them by his bedside sitting vigil in his last days.

I did not wear them to his funeral.

When Dad took his family out for a steak dinner, Mom out dancing, or to church, he tied his tie and polished his wingtips. His handshake said, working man. He never looked the part when he went to town.

Some three thousand words ago, I sat down to write a little piece on what my favorite boots feel like on my feet. Without a word on arch, insole, and ankle support, I reckon that's what I did.

I wore Red Wing boots when I learned to work. Dad said,
  "Pick a pace you can keep up all day."
I wore Red Wing boots when I learned to rest. Grandpa said,
  "Work on Sunday, fix on Monday."
At times when it took all I had to pull them on, I learned to
  persevere.
Once, I felt them filling with my blood. I was reminded to always
  kick the wedge out before you fell a tree.
They were on my feet when I learned how to hurt, and how to heal.
They were on my feet when I learned to earn, and accept respect.
They were on my feet when I learned to love, and to be loved.
They'll be on my feet when I learn to forgive.
They were on my feet when I learned to live; I ask they're on my feet
  when I die.

They don't call 'em Super Souls for nothin'. ⱳ

Break My Mind

Several years ago, I scored a date with a lovely woman I met on Match.com. We arranged an evening on the terrace at the Edgewater Hotel in Madison. A Mumford and Sons influenced quartet from the driftless, Them Coulee Boys were down from Eau Claire laying down electric folk and Americana in flawless three-part harmony. The crowd was a mellow smattering of crunchy to eclectic. A lazy July breeze rippled Lake Mendota against the breakwater below. I spotted my date from the balcony in the same pose she featured on her profile pictures. I drove my work truck to first dates. I didn't want to seem ostentatious in my '83 Chevy Trailblazer, and if it turned out she was into John Tesh or hairbands, I could fabricate a cow in dystocia emergency and make a run for the Dodge. The downside was my mobile veterinary hospital is twenty-two feet long. There are about three spots on the Isthmus where it will fit. So, I walked, which is never a bad thing. There's always something to see in Madison.

My route took me down State Street, the six blocks most emblematic of the city. The EDM music vibrating the walls of State Street Brats was deafening from twenty feet. In front, a line had formed. Halfway to the door, a group of six young men gathered in a semicircle. Slouching and leaning, with their heads buried on their devices, the only thing moving was their thumbs, furiously swiping never long enough to read a word.

I was so intrigued; I watched them for six minutes. They never said a word to one another.

Facebook's first mission statement: Give people the power to build community and bring the world closer together.

Without argument, social media has its purpose.

 BILL STORK

Wes Coan was our next-door neighbor back home. He was the high school guy who let the fifth-grade kid hang out in the garage and rode me around the backyard in his Volkswagen dune buggy. He helped me build my first bicycle from parts thrown behind the garage. When his father died in a grain dust explosion, my dad took him fishing with us and helped keep him between the lines. Before he moved to Minnesota forty years ago, Wes handed me a custom-made fishing rod and nodded to my dad. "Hand-built for William C. Stork" was monogrammed just above the grip. Last year, Sheila and I took a Saturday night and drove to a dive bar in Winona to see a modern-day bluesman from Duluth named Charlie Parr. We looked Wes up on Facebook.

Social media helps connect people passionate about everything from Huskys to steampunk. Folks can sell lawnmowers, custom coffee cups, and horse hay. Brands have been made in a minute on YouTube.

"Anything in extremes is bad." It was one of my dad's favorite idioms, thirty years before Mark Zuckerberg was born. As I write this piece, the World Health Organization has just declared the coronavirus a global health crisis. I posit the intracellular pathogen will cause a fraction as much havoc as Facebook, Instagram, and Snapchat.

Just ask eighty-eight-year-old World War II veteran Anthony Lenti. After months of being bullied on Facebook, his granddaughter used one of Grandpa's guns to end her pain.

Chamath Palihapitiya (which I learned to spell and pronounce) was the vice president of user growth before he left Facebook in 2011. He confessed to *The Wall Street Journal* that he felt tremendous guilt for his work on creating tools that are "ripping apart the social fabric of how society works."

"The short-term, dopamine-driven feedback loops that we have created are destroying how society works. No civil discourse, no cooperation, misinformation, mistruth."

"I can't control them," Palihapitiya said of his former employer. "I can control my decision, which is that I don't use that shit. I can control my kids' decisions, which is that they're not allowed to use that shit."

Ex-Facebook President Sean Parker went further, "The site is designed to exploit human vulnerability."

The devastation of distraction.

It was my son's senior year of high school. I was making supper, and Calvin was doing homework in the sunroom. Between adding the breadcrumbs, tomato sauce, and eggs to the meatloaf, I watched him study.

He pulled out his phone and swiped six times in forty minutes. Nine times an hour.

There have always been distractions. In the seventies, we had the Mattel Classic Football game. It had six buttons that controlled a red dot—up, down, forward. The simplest smartphone has a television, movie theater, post office, library, and an encyclopedia. You can access trashy tabloids and porn instantly (I've heard).

Thousands of students at three universities in the United States and Europe were taught a curriculum. At mid-term and final exams, they were divided into groups. One was allowed to have their devices on their desks turned off. A second group was required to stow them in their bags turned off. A third was not allowed to have them on the premises. Scores consistently declined according to the proximity of their phones.

The students with the sleeping distraction on their desks scored a full letter grade lower.

In a separate study, researchers found that students who were not allowed to have their devices on their person during lectures also scored a freakin' letter grade higher at test time.

The meatloaf was done in an hour. The kids and I sat down for supper. In an uber-constructive tone, I told Calvin I'd been watching him study. I shared the statistics and research with him. "Good God, man. Can you imagine if you also prepared for the test without your phone?" He was so excited he could hardly eat.

"Damn, Dad, that is awesome. That's like a free letter grade, or more. I can just hear the chancellor reading my name at graduation, 'Calvin Conrad Stork, magna cum laude.' That could easily lead to a prime

BILL STORK

internship and land me a great job. I'll be able to pay back every nickel you helped with my tuition, plus interest. I'll be able to form my own charity by my twenty-fifth birthday."

Yeah, right. Calvin was seventeen at the time. He grunted, "That's cool."

In yet another experiment, researchers found that people asked to perform complicated tasks retained less information and performed poorer in the presence of smartphones and devices, even if they were not their smartphones.

The sound of pings and ringtones and the detection of vibration make subjects' blood pressure and heart rate rise, create distractions, and increase the likelihood of errors.

When asked if they felt the presence of their devices was a distraction, the test subjects responded, nearly universally, that they were not.

A young couple brought their four-year-old tabby cat named Mickey to the Lake Mills Veterinary Clinic. They were deeply concerned. He'd been straining in the litter box, and his urine looked like a Merlot that'd sat at the bottom of the glass all weekend. It was his third visit for the problem. As I explained the change in medications and diet, how to palpate his abdomen, and the specific signs to look for, Mr. Owner serviced his smartphone six times.

Apple expects iPhone users to consult their electronic pacifiers eighty times per day. That's four and a half times per waking hour. Furthermore, studies have shown that thirty percent of young people wake in the middle of the night to check their phones.

In 2017 it was reported that a whopping ninety-six percent of UK residents between the ages of sixteen and thirty-four owned a smartphone of some kind, and the typical user touches their smartphone 2,617 times every single day.

Michelle Powers was in with her red Doberman, Ruby. Michelle is a fourth-grade teacher at Jefferson Elementary School, where devices are not allowed during the school day. She shared the research of a colleague who taught eighth grade. She asked her class to add up all their social media feeds for one class period.

In one hour, during the school day, in a district where devices are not allowed in the classroom, twenty-eight students received in excess of six thousand social media feeds.

Pause to absorb.

Gloria Marks is a professor of informatics at The Donald Bren School of Information and Computer Science at The University of California–Irvine. She is interested in the interaction between people and technology. In her research, Dr. Marks found it takes an average of twenty-three minutes and fifteen seconds to return to the original task after a single interruption. There are nuances. A German study found it takes less time to recover from an on-topic distraction, but her findings have been substantiated in multiple studies.

Kids are experiencing separation anxiety, not from their parents, twin sister Kate, or their Golden Retriever, but from their thousand-dollar pacifiers.

Schools that ban the use of connected devices find that performance on standardized tests rise across all academic groups, with weaker students benefitting the most. Despite overwhelming scientific evidence of the erosive effects of devices in the classroom, when teachers do not allow them, they have to manage against the impact of separation anxiety. Teachers have resorted to putting the phones in clear plastic belts they wear around their waist or locked plastic boxes. The kids can see their phone, even if they can't access it. Others have banks of pockets decorated with names and numbers and equipped with a charging station. Students know where they are, even if they can't have them.

Some districts have chosen to incentivize students who refrain, like a Labrador pup who sits and stays for a rabbit flavored Zuke's treat. Some apps track the number of touches or logins a user registers over a period of time. Students are being rewarded for not touching their phones with everything from Starbucks gift cards to extra credit on tests and study hall time.

My dad would have three words: "[Because] I said so."

One article points out the benefit of smartphones. They are such powerful research tools, and there is so much information at their fingertips, why not let students use them? Not to mention, most students already have them. School districts can save money by not having to provide laptops.

Most kids have them. Some do not.

Research says that easy information is anything but a benefit.

The Google effect.

In a 2011 study, subjects were given statements to type into a computer. Half were told their responses would be saved, while the sentences of the other half would be instantly erased. When asked later to repeat as many lines as possible, those who thought they'd be erased recalled twice as many statements. The ease of access—knowing we can simply Google it—has a profound effect on the energy our brain puts forth to recall, remember, and own.

Psychologists have demonstrated that we can't tell the difference—whether we know it or googled it.

That is a big, frickin' problem.

"Data is memory without history," the novelist and critic Cynthia Ozick once wrote. Her observation points to the problem with allowing smartphones to commandeer our brains. When we constrict our capacity for reasoning and recall or transfer those skills to a gadget, we sacrifice our ability to turn information into knowledge. We get the data but lose the meaning. Upgrading our gadgets won't solve the problem. We need to give our minds more room to think. And that means putting some distance between ourselves and our phones.

Doug Fritsch was in with his cat Mystic, who has chronic feline upper respiratory tract disease and a bad attitude. Doug is a retired history teacher. I had just cracked the cover on the epic WWII novel *Ghost Soldiers*. There's only so much we can do with Mystic without being shredded. The balance of the thirty-minute appointment was a lecture on all that took place leading up to the events written in the book.

Just before graduation, Beth Denzin was in with Benny, who also has FURTD. She had been charged with writing the AP Calculus exam. "Dr. Stork, I'm so nervous. I want them to do well."

Teachers love to teach. Not all teachers are Mr. Fritsch and Mrs. Denzin.

Four years after the sunroom homework experiment, my son is about to graduate from UW–Madison. We were recounting his experience in school over steak burritos at Chipotle. "I had a teacher who was so awesome I got up for an eight o'clock class and sat in the front row. I had other classes where I bought the book and never went."

Ryan Haack and I were warming our hands by the L.B. White heater hanging in the vestibule of his dairy barn. I love to throw open-ended questions at Ryan. He thinks a lot, reads a lot, and milks 150 cows twice every day. I lobbed the notion of online vs. in-person learning at him, "I think there's tremendous value in misinformation. It teaches us to be active, independent, and critical consumers. It helps us sort fact from fiction or opinion." We've all had that teacher who inspired us, but a motivated student can't be deterred.

In an 1892 lecture, pioneering psychologist and philosopher William James proclaimed, "The art of remembering is the art of thinking." It is not until we encode information into our organic memory that we can use it to weave the intricate associations that form the essence of personal knowledge and give rise to critical conceptual thinking. No matter how much information surrounds us, the less well-stocked our memory, the less we have to think with.

The social effect.

The platforms that purport to keep people connected may be accomplishing quite the opposite.

Social scientist Jean Twenge has been studying generational differences for twenty-five years. "Kids these days." Today's youth are far more likely to be in their home, connected to the world around them by social media platforms on WiFi. Yet they report feeling isolated and unhappy.

From 2000 to 2015, Twenge found that young people became forty percent less likely to get together regularly.

A group of researchers at the University of Arizona sought to answer the chicken or the egg dilemma: Does obsessive use of social media lead to depression, or do those with depressive tendencies turn to social media? A paper that's about to be published looks at over three hundred older adolescents. They found that the obsessive use of devices is an extremely accurate predictor of future depression and anxiety.

My friend Ned took chocolate-covered strawberries and carnations to his mother-in-law on her first Valentine's Day alone. They had been talking for a half-hour when his phone pinged. Janet asked, "Aren't you going to answer that?"

"No, Janet. I'm here to talk to you."

Similar to studies on academics and performance, researchers put subjects together and asked them to talk about intense interpersonal topics. You guessed it—half in the presence of their devices, half without. Afterward, participants were asked to score their partners on affinity, empathy, and trust. It was found the presence of smartphones dramatically diminished partners' ability to develop closeness, trust, and understanding.

Yet, some psychologists are prescribing more social media time for kids suffering from anxiety, depression, and separation.

My mechanic Steve would no more try and tell me how to suture his German Shorthaired Pointer than I would tell him how to swap out the fuel injectors in my truck. It is not my nature to question expertise, but seriously?

In a recent article published in *The Wall Street Journal*, psychologists are coaching kids suffering from anxiety, depression, and low self-esteem on how to construct posts in order to garner likes and shares, and therefore bolster their self-confidence.

They're instructed to block and ignore negative responses to their posts. Say what?

To expect the world to treat you fairly and kindly is akin to expecting the bull not to stampede because you're vegan.

Whatever happened to giving our kids the tools to be resilient in the face of detractors and bullies. If you're looking for self-esteem, build something, fix something, or help someone.

Our friends Stan and Patricia have a Mardi Gras party that's like a Lake Mills reunion. I was talking to Eli Wedel. Eli is one impressive young man. He's a fabulously skilled photographer, an active Rotarian, and has a head for marketing. He's just purchased a restaurant in town. He also started a Rotary event that benefitted local drug-free initiatives and is looking to approach local businesses to get marketing materials for alcohol and tobacco off the ground so they are no longer in the direct line of sight of kindergarteners. He may have to add four hours to the day or take a step back from photography.

My friend John always said, "The more pictures you take, the less you see." I shared an exchange from earlier in the week to get Eli's take.

Southern Wisconsin was a postcard. Mid-January, she was tucked under a solid foot-and-a-half snowpack, which sublimated into a haze over the drumlins and valleys in the blinding mid-day sun and twenty-five degrees. When the sun set, and the mercury in the Mail Pouch thermometer dropped below the tin, dime-sized crystals of hoarfrost lit and balanced on every tree branch, farm gate, and fence wire. When the sun rose at six-thirty Thursday morning, she was diffracted into magenta, purple, and gold and thrown into a towering flame-red spire straight to the heavens over County Road B.

The first appointment was in with her four-month-old Golden Retriever. Riley was healthy and sweet. After a hundred kisses and treats, I gave a rabies vaccine and the spay speech. I could not help but ask Riley's owner if she'd seen the sunrise. I described the seminal event as best I could, to which she responded, "Wow, I hope someone posts that!"

Eli nodded. "Oh yeah. I've taken a million pictures and haven't seen a thing."

When we were in grade school, John Paul Snyder was good at baseball, basketball, and football. He had a cool pair of brown suede high-top

shoes with pockets. All the cute girls hung around him. I played tenor sax in the jazz band. I wanted to be like JP.

Now, there are influencers.

It has come to my attention that in a world that begs for tradespeople, truckers, and physicians, there are folks whose primary pursuit is to post on social media. The goal is to accumulate enough followers to court advertising dollars from sponsors. The Dolan twins just purchased a $2.75 million house with over three acres in the hills of California, "Perfect for filming their antics to be posted on YouTube." As close as I can tell, partying in exotic locations, lounging in over-sized chairs, skateboarding in the desert, and posing for butt shots appears more marketable than actually producing anything or performing a service.

Suffering from burnout, twenty-year-old Grayson and Ethan Dolan chose to step away from the platform they've posted to for the last five years and has netted them millions.

"We have a job where you can't just take off because there's the fear of becoming irrelevant," Grayson Dolan said. "I can't even go home to see my mom."

They fear becoming irrelevant?

A number of influencers build a brand and grow it into a career in design, fashion, and often benefit others. That's legit. Not to mention, young boys have been fantasizing forever.

I'm betting there were a fair number of Hail Marys and Our Fathers doled out from behind the curtain at confession as a result of Farrah Fawcett in a red one-piece. Seems like splittin' hairs to suggest the Dolan twins have captivated any more fancy than *Starsky and Hutch* and *Charlie's Angels*.

The difference is that *Starsky and Hutch* and *Charlie's Angels* were on TV, in our living room, an hour a week.

Thanks to social media platforms, influencers are in our pockets, on our laps, and worse yet, in our minds, hundreds of times every day. They are filmed on the beach, on stage, in the mountains, and partying in mansions. The daughter of a truck driver and a nurse living in the three-bedroom ranch in Cleveland feels inferior.

Just when you thought there was no more damage to be done, then came sadfishing.

According to social media data mining firm Captiv8, (which is recognized by spell check), when influencers on social media share their frustrations and vulnerabilities, they see a multifold bump in likes and views. The practice is called sadfishing.

Following suit, the socially-challenged kid in Watertown, Wisconsin, shares her anxiety and depression on Facebook, and she gets bullied or becomes a target for online predators offering to "listen."

Everyone has done it. The day after Sharon Smith dumped me in fifth grade, I walked slow, scuffed my feet, and mumbled when I got to school, hoping my friends would ask how I was doing.

So, Bill, what's your point?

There was a television commercial set in sepia tone and narrow muted light. A young towheaded boy sat at the end of the breakfast table. He anxiously looked toward his mom. "Hey, Mom. I was thinking after school maybe we could bake some brownies!" Mom didn't hear. She was thumbing at her device.

He turned to his dad. "Hey, Dad. How's about this weekend we go fishin', maybe play some ball?"

Dad mumbled, "Just a minute, kid," his head buried in his iPhone.

I shared an exchange with my friend Scott. A client was hoping her son's new girlfriend might "beat a little Christianity into him." In the next phrase, she expressed her frustration with the "idiots at the mall." Twenty years the trial attorney, Scott's response was instant. "Hick, we're all full of contradictions."

In high school, selling nightcrawlers and minnows at Ye Olde Tackle Box, faced with the old-fashioned mechanical cash register with rows of buttons and the plastic bar on the side, I could add a half-dozen items and figure tax in my head. Now, I have a calculator on my iPhone. I have four Facebook accounts and demonstrated the Google

 BILL STORK

effect a half-dozen times cut and pasting passages into this article.

"It is best to rise from life, as from a banquet, neither thirsty nor drunken."—Aristotle

All things in moderation.

Watch the sun rise. Listen to a friend. Ditch the device. ✒

Nurse Lucy

Lucy is really good at weighing fourteen and a half pounds.

Between October 2017 and March 2020, there are twenty data points on Lucy's weight graph. At the urging of the Lake Mills Veterinary Clinic, there raged an epic four-month battle of wills between man and Chihuahua, mid-2019. The guy who feeds Lucy walked her like they were training for Boston, rationed treats, and counted every kibble. They weighed in every fourteen days like World's Smallest Biggest Loser. On July 23, Lucy was down to 13.4 pounds. Our whole staff did a happy dance in the parking lot, but the victory was fleeting. By Labor Day, she'd beefed back up to 13.9. On Christmas Eve, she was back in her comfort zone, just a tick under fifteen pounds.

An eight-year-old Chihuahua, her tenacity would pale that of a Bulldog. The AKC microchip between her shoulder blades legally identifies her, but the chip *on* her shoulder defines her. Lucy's ideal weight would be little over four and a half kilos, but when you save the biscuit of the guy who walks you—three times—you might get an extra Charlee Bear now and then.

The guy who walks Lucy.

Bill Street skipped out on his high school graduation. He was on a plane bound for Orlando with his show choir to perform in Disney World, a gig that would take him to the set of two Frosted Mini-Wheat commercials and the stage of the Pabst Theater singing with the Milwaukee Symphony Orchestra, conducted by the legendary Margaret Hawkins.

Through college, it became glaringly apparent that show business was no business for the boy from Greenfield, Wisconsin. For eight years, he worked food management and sports services in and around the venerable Milwaukee County Stadium, which could explain his wardrobe. Every visible piece of clothing Bill's ever been seen wearing bears the Milwaukee Brewers logo. The tag on his Jeep Grand Cherokee is BATBOY. By the mid-eighties, he transitioned from food management to delivery. For thirty years, Bill racked out by two forty-five in the bloody a.m. to keep Southern Wisconsin taverns stocked with Miller Genuine Draft, Friskies flush with Salmon parts to make cat food, and Scientific Protein Labs in Waunakee supplied with reagents.

In 2012, the crank handle on a trailer jack sprang backward and nearly did a Captain Hook on his right hand. As Bill puts it, "There began my career as a professional surgical patient." After five procedures on his pitching hand, he was declared disabled, a designation that does little for a man's pride.

Bill stepped off the stage in his early-twenties to support his family. For three decades, he was relegated to serenading the dashboard of a Freightliner day cab. His voice dropped an octave or so, and his knees would no longer powerslide or grapevine. Looking to serve his artistic side, he found his way back to the stage this time in turnout gear, acting in a Penguin Productions adaptation of Michael Perry's *Population: 485.*

Bill's a storyteller. He phrases and pauses thoughtfully with a twinkle in his eye. His voice is an instrument, like Bailey's over ice with a splash of bourbon. Looking to debunk the adage of old dogs and new tricks, at sixty-four, he enrolled in a program and earned a certificate in voice work.

Still, there was a void.

When his kids were young, they had a pair of comical Italian Greyhounds, Dino and Desi. Then the nest emptied, and Bill was on the road fifty hours a week. Way too much crate time for a pup. In 2012, he moved to Lake Mills, and his daughter hounded him. "Dad, it's time to get a dog."

Dads listen to kids like they listen to us—in a time-lapse fashion. He found himself facing another Wisconsin winter in a lonely house. The "yes I shoulds" drowned out the "no I shouldn'ts."

Bill drove to Waukesha, just to take a look.

On that late-October Sunday afternoon, the kennels at the Humane Animal Welfare Society were bare as the toilet paper aisle in a pandemic, clearly a sign that it's not meant to be. He turned to leave when he saw two buggy eyes and a cream-colored head just above the reception desk. When Bill asked to spend time with her in the meet-n-greet room, she trembled in the corner.

The volunteer explained that Sunny had no social skills. They were simply looking to expose her to people.

Mission accomplished.

Back on East Washington Street in Lake Mills, Bill collapsed on the couch with, "What in the hell did I get myself into?" looping in his head. Sunny, now Lucy, scaled his belly and gave him one kiss on the cheek.

It was the beginning of Bill and Lucy.

He's still wondering what he got himself into.

Lucy is fourteen pounds of opinions.

Lucy has rules. She does not pee or poop where she plays. Realtors, and Lucy, say it's all about location. The spots she chooses are curated like a gourmet and his spices. The spot will be the correct consistency, texture, lighting, temperature, topography, and ventilation. The spot may be on the other side of town by the fish hatchery.

The when is no more predictable than the where.

Timing is everything, say actors, and Lucy Street. Her desire to defecate is not dictated by proximity to her last meal, or the clock on the wall, but the one in the stadium. Without fail, nature will call with a minute and a half left in the fourth quarter of the Packers game, or when Columbo is just about to crack the case.

There is no negotiation. Any effort to empty her tank in anticipation will make for a fine walk, void of any attempt to void. Our behavioral staff instructs clients to ignore demanding dogs. Attempts to postpone her will result in Lucy barking and dragging her hinder from one end of the house to the other.

They bicker like an old married couple. Paused in front of The Corner Mercantile, Bill wanted to see what was happening in Commons Park. Lucy smelled something on the wind from Rock Lake. They turned right.

At sixty-six years old and two hundred pounds, it's not that Bill is submissive to a fourteen-pound Taco Terrier. He figures he owes her. Friends and family don't keep score, but if they did, she'd be up on him, 4–1.

Shortly after the pup, formerly known as Sunny, came home from HAWS, she established the business hours of Sir Winston Churchill. Sleep all afternoon, up until the wee hours. Bill and Lucy were walking Washington Street as the rest of the city slept when Bill felt a breeze lift the Brewers cap off his head. He snatched Lucy from the end of the leash as a great horned owl swooped in for a midnight snack. At the time, Lucy was well within his cargo capacity.

Since then, it's been all Lucy.

She's saved his life three times.

In 2015, Lucy started to lick the right side of Bill's nose obsessively. He felt nothing; there was nothing to see. After months there came a raised, fleshy mass the size of a wood tick. Upon the first sight, and Lucy's insistence, Bill booked the first available with his GP. His doctor took one look and referred him to a specialist at UW, who diagnosed a basal cell carcinoma and scheduled a surgery to disentangle the malignancy from the nerve roots it had wrapped around.

Bill had managed asthma with inhalers, bronchodilators, and steroids his entire adult life. The common cold can be fatal. In 2019, Bill was hospitalized with a case of the flu. Discharged from the hospital, he became lightheaded and hypoxic. He fell between the wall and the toilet, where the coroner would have likely found him were it not for a persistent Chihuahua licking his face and barking like Lassie when Timmy fell down the well.

Lucy has not allowed Bill in the bathroom unsupervised since.

Bill started struggling for air in February 2020. Hell-bent on not repeating that horror show, Lucy wedged herself behind the toilet tank. Bill got the hint and made an appointment with a pulmonologist. He was diagnosed with COPD on top of his asthma.

To reward Lucy, Bill brought home a Benny.

Bill describes Benny. "He'd rather sleep than eat a rack of ribs, and Lucy and I are good with that." When he is awake, he eliminates in the house and has zero concept of personal space. Lucy's solution is to give him a couple of shake-n-bake play bows to wind him up, then watch him fly around the house like a BB in a boxcar until he's tired and goes back to sleep.

The CDC likens the physiologic effect of loneliness among the aging to smoking two packs of cigarettes and imbibing six alcoholic drinks a day. I asked Bill about not going for Lucy's walks when he felt poorly or when it was eight below zero. "Not an option."

Drive through Lake Mills on a Wednesday afternoon, and you'll see Bill and Lucy chatting with the salsa guy and Doug Jenks at the farmer's market. You will not see Lucy getting butt scratches from school kids or giving kisses to Shelly Perry. Among her opinions is that she does not care for little kids and certain people. Shelly loves everything that breathes and runs a pet sitting and dog walking business.

Shelly is not on Lucy's list.

So, if you see a jovial guy in shorts and a Brewers cap walking one dog forward and the other backward, wave and say hi; that's Bill, Benny, and Lucy.

She might like you, or she might not. ꝗ

BILL STORK

Manifest Destiny

In twenty-eight years as a country veterinarian, I have seen my mom's dinner table doctrine confirmed on a daily basis.

Alma Ann Stork only saw good.

There was the repentant Milwaukee slumlord—near-sighted, daffy, and a dead ringer for Mr. Magoo. You can call it penance or payback, but after serving ten years in Milwaukee County Jail, he found himself living in an abandoned mobile home at the dead end of a farm lane in southern Dodge County. He had no heat, lights, or running water. Two cylindrical Shi Tzus, who he fed before himself, were his only companions and source of warmth through six months of Wisconsin winter. Their coats were matted, skin infected, and molars rotting out of their heads. We clipped their coats, cured the skin infection, and extracted the rotting teeth. He paid us what he could and thanked us with two packs of dollar store sandwich cookies.

I've watched a man I'd thought was the town drunk kiss a kitten. His daughter told him of a farm dog with a broken leg in Iowa. He searched half the Hawkeye State, rounded him up, and drove him back to our clinic for treatment. I peered over the top of my glasses at the monitor, arms crossed, and stroking my chin. I could not believe what I was seeing on the x-ray. Tom grumbled, "Wow, Doc, as completely displaced as that fracture is, we've got some pretty impressive calcification going between the proximal and distal ends of the tibia. Do you think that thing will heal as a non-union?" It was easier to hide my surprise in the dark. Tom had done three tours in Vietnam as a combat medic and saved a hundred soldiers and a senator's son. Another first impression annihilated.

I call it faith; you can call 'em miracles. Mary, the six-month-old Lab pup, was romping in the living room with her family on Christmas Eve. Minutes later, she jumped on her owner's arm and dislodged the barrel of a .357 from his temple—on the porch. No one had let her out.

There was the sixteen-year-old Cocker Spaniel named Sally who spent her last breaths barking at a stove, saving two teenage boys and a widowed husband from a house filled with carbon monoxide.

Hardwired with the git-'er-done ethic I learned in my dad's garage and on the end of a chain saw, and armed with a college education my family busted ass and pinched nickels to pay for, I've been blessed to work shoulder-to-shoulder with the most purpose-driven people I know: the family farmer.

When I finally hang up my stethoscope and coveralls, I hope to have given a fraction of what my profession has provided.

That said, my path was anything but manifest destiny.

I was always *that kid*. In kindergarten, our family insurance man mentioned his litter of six-week-old Collie pups. "Little Bill can just come out and play with them." Dad knew better. For the next week, I slept on the basement floor so that Sugar wouldn't whine.

Our family vet was Dr. Bill Van Alstine at the Brush College Animal Hospital. Before I could see over his exam table, I begged for a job. He'd put his stethoscope in my ears so I could listen to Sugar's heartbeat and promised I could start when I was fourteen. My first day was March 4, 1979.

Folks in my family knew how to build, fix, and grow things. I was the first to even think about college. I got a twenty-seven on my ACT and graduated well off the podium at Eisenhower High School, where kids dreamed of the Army, Navy, Marines, or a plumbing apprenticeship. We didn't know the Ivy League from poison ivy. The few of us who thought about college went to Eastern, Western, or the University of Illinois. I knew I wanted to be a veterinarian, and the school was at the U of I in Urbana–Champaign. Oblivious that my application was underwhelming, and ignorant to the concept of a "safety school,"

BILL STORK

I snuck in under the wire.

I had three years of Spanish in high school, but by the second semester of college, I still couldn't order a beer in a border town, so I transferred from Liberal Arts and Science to the College of Agriculture. The aggies had no foreign language requirement. At the end of my third year, I took my first swing at the Veterinary Aptitude Test. I scored in the seventieth percentile, which would barely qualify me to clean box stalls in the horse barn. I reloaded. Senior year I brought my score up twenty points. I graduated from college with no kinda cum laude and a degree in animal science, but the seas parted. Fall of 1987 saw the fewest applications in the history of the University of Illinois College of Veterinary Medicine.

Still, I was number thirteen on the waitlist, which was good enough to get an interview. The door was open, if just a crack.

They said it'd take twenty minutes.

I walked into the academic interrogation knowing the alma mater, hobbies, and shoe size of everyone on the board. For two hours, we talked about everything from pulling calves out of the mud to Muddy Waters. I had worked for a diminutive Lebanese immigrant named Boonton Syalavong, cleaning cages in a rodent research lab, all four years of undergrad. Doctor Dave Smetzer was the professor of cardiology. Thin as a fence wire, he wore black polyester pants and red and white striped Oxfords. He spoke with a wicked witch smoker's crackle. Pointing at my application with the earpiece of his glasses, "Mr. Stork, you worked for Boon," he questioned in a statement. He nodded to his colleagues and closed my file.

I was the last one accepted.

Day one, the incoming class at the University of Illinois College of Veterinary Medicine was poised with pencils in hand and minds ready to absorb, except for my classmate Mark Revenaugh. He'd been busking in Seattle, blanked the date, and showed up a day late. With round black horn-rimmed glasses and the stature of a two-eyed Minion, our anatomy professor Dr. Mark Simon lectured us on the devastating physiologic and psychological effects of exhaustion, complete with graphs, stats, and slides. His advice: "Don't get tired."

That year I was an hour early to every lecture and never missed a study group. Taking Dr. Simon's wisdom at his word, I drank black coffee by the gallon and chewed tobacco by the bushel to stay awake. I carried solid Cs in parasitology, pharmacology, and histology, but in anatomy, a D was the best mark I could muster. The administration was not impressed. The assistant dean was a lady named Nancy Bailey. She wore navy blue sweaters, khaki skirts, and an expression to match. Dr. Bailey spoke in measured diction and feigned sincerity. "Mr. Stork, you are clearly not happy here." Her recommendation was that I drop out. Few things piss me off more than presumption, and I'm not much on quittin'. I suggested she come up with plan B.

She reluctantly offered that I could repeat my freshman year. An additional year of vet school would cost our family another 25,000 blue-collar (1989) dollars.

I broke the news to my parents in the garage on a Sunday afternoon. Standing at the workbench, Dad pointed with a half-inch ratchet. "Son, did you try your best?"

Mom was on the stoop. "How can we help?"

My mates who moved on were supportive, but I started my second-go at my first year with my tail tucked.

There was some consolation. My friend Dave Rosen was the second-ranked full-contact karate fighter in the world and a bartender at my favorite music dive. Dave has resting sad face, but he was looking even lower. He'd applied to vet school seven times. He slid a Budweiser longneck at me while Otis and the Elevators sound-checked. "Yeah, Bill. I'm giving up. I applied to law school." I told him numbers were down, "Hell, Dave, I got in." He applied, and we became classmates.

Tail-winded by my parents' support, after a year-long review, I arrived at my sophomore year of vet school with a firm grip on anatomy, physiology, and histology.

On the first day of my second year, I ran into a buzz saw.

Harry Reynolds was a silver-haired ex-Marine and Golden Glove boxing champion. The crook in his nose suggested that he didn't dodge every right jab. Dr. Reynolds taught clinical pathology. Clin

Path required a functional mastery of biology, pharmacology, histopathology, and anatomy. The treatment protocol and prognosis of every vomiting cat and PUPD Pug in practice were dependent on the accurate interpretation of their CBCs, chemistry panels, and urinalysis. Harry was fair but merciless.

I carried a comfortable C and a cautious measure of confidence for two semesters, and then came the final exam. The wheels fell off. Black bifocal half-cheaters resting on the crook in his nose, Harry taped the grades to the cinder block by our lockers. The bell curve looked like a plowed field. I'd missed a C by two percentage points. My buddy Hal Leonard and I were on the outside looking in.

Two strikes and you're out.

Hal and I called a meeting at Murphy's Pub. Over bacon cheeseburgers and three Guinness stouts, we planned our plea.

The benevolent board who'd granted me admission and my first second chance felt like a firing squad. Hal let me do the talking. Academia is a brutal business, so I did some math for them, "If Hal and I are not allowed to go on, you won't be able to replace our tuition dollars. At eight more semesters between the two of us, you're forfeiting a solid $80,000. That's enough to buy anatomy dogs for the entire incoming class, or a pair of matching Mercedes." I caught a glance between professors Smetzer and Sisson. I laid it on thicker as I went. "We've worked on beef farms, slopped hog pens, mixed feed, milked cows, and cleaned dog cages since we were kids. Hal and I have paid our dues.

Their hands came down from their mouths. Smetzer leaned in. I sensed I had one more round before I'd lose 'em. I pulled an excerpt from the Veterinary Oath, "Ladies and gentlemen, when we turn our tassels, we will swear to use our scientific knowledge and skills to promote animal health and welfare, relieve animal suffering, and protect animal health. The fact that Hal and I are standing before you, in my case, after having repeated a year of vet school already, speaks to our dedication. We are not looking for a free pass. We're asking for a second chance to secure the competence our noble profession requires. There will be two more years of opportunities to weed us out if the powers-that-be feel we're not capable. Not to mention, we have to pass the National Board Exam. For the betterment of the profession we aspire to and the animals we love, if we are to be a detriment, then ask us to leave, but please do not eliminate us for a few points on an exam where the best and brightest also struggled. Our travails will be tools and only make us stronger."

Hal had a tear in his eye. The room collectively exhaled. I had initiated an all-school blues and barbecue tradition to end each school year. "One last thing, guys. Who's going to hire The Mudhens and cook the pigs?"

They granted us a retake in mid-July.

I had no Plan B. For six weeks my future hung in the balance. A cradle Catholic, I bargained with God. I didn't drink a beer, water ski, party, or sleep with my girlfriend. I studied CBCs, chemistry panels, urinalyses, and blood gases before work, during breaks, and after work, seven days a week. I dissected case studies, midterms, and final exams.

Test day arrived in the middle of a three-day monsoon. Dr. Reynolds escorted us to a windowless meeting room deep in the bowels of the basic science building. Not a word was spoken. Looking to break the tension, I said, "Well, Dr. Reynolds, if Hal and I don't pass, let us know, and we'll get to work on an ark tomorrow morning."

Not even a smirk. With tobacco-stained fingertips, he laid our future on the table in twelve stapled pages.

Hal and I flexed our brows like a couple of prizefighters, nodded, and went to war.

Three and a half hours later, the bell tolled. I tried to stand but forgot I had legs. I staggered to the vestibule and stood framed by the floor-length windows. Minutes before the next deluge, the clouds roiled like creamer in a coffee cup, and the trees danced like car lot inflatables in a hurricane. I looked to the sky and asked for a sign.

For a second and a half, the clouds parted, and the sun shone on my face like a stage light.

I can still feel the warmth.

I passed by one point.

Paul Harvey would say, "And now, the rest of the story."

Before our first lecture in vet school was orientation week. The day before classes commenced, there was a beer-n-barbecue back porch gathering. I met a classmate who was into water skiing and blues. We began to study together and realized that music, and being dragged behind a boat, was not all we had in common. I had dated with minimal success in high school and undergrad and never had a steady. It soon became apparent she absorbed things more quickly than I and would go to bed after the ten o'clock news and *MASH*.

I should have kept studying, but I allowed pleasures of the flesh to supersede the business of the brain.

She graduated from vet school in 1991 and moved to Wisconsin to practice dairy and small-animal medicine. I followed a year later.

The very same relationship that cost me an extra year of veterinary school would last for eighteen years and yield two of the finest young people I know. The first years were spent building a business, a family, and a home. The last were spent tearing them apart. I was left with a broken heart and a decision. I could believe I was the poorly-dressed, inarticulate oaf she worked to convince me I was or a flawed man in need of a little polishing up.

I had been in practice for twelve years at my fortieth birthday party. I looked around the room and took stock of my friends and clients. I decided that I must be okay.

I'll take credit for some measure of resilience, but all I am, I owe to a dad whose first requirement was that I give it my best shot and a mom who only wanted to help. ⟨

From Aristotle to the Amazing Dick Bass, and the Seven-Minute Nap

Aristotle, Gary Edmonds, Leonardo da Vinci, JFK, Thomas Edison, Winston Churchill, Albert Einstein, William E. Stork, and the Amazing Dick Bass—a shortlist of impressively productive, thoughtful, and influential people in history. None of whom had a single follower on Instagram.

They are also obligate nappers.

Margaret Thatcher was known as "The Iron Lady," often working more than twenty-hour days. She would take multiple snooze breaks throughout the day.

Churchill was said to work third shift. He'd work until the wee hours of the morning, then conk out for two to three hours in the afternoon. John and Jackie Kennedy built their schedules around a two-hour midday siesta.

Salvador Dali was famous for his eccentricities, as well as his artwork. He'd execute one-second micro-naps by pinching a heavy key between his fingers. As he lost consciousness, the key would fall to the floor, signaling the end of the slumber.

Thomas Edison was famously critical of people who slept more than three to four hours daily, calling it a waste of time and productivity. He was considerably less vocal about his own two-hour timeout in the afternoon—more than a hint of hypocrisy for the man whose invention forever dismantled our circadian rhythms.

Humans and, more specifically, modern Americans, are among the few animals on the planet who seek to be monophasic sleepers, accomplishing all our sleep in one session (the effect of aging prostates

BILL STORK

and consumption of alcoholic diuretics notwithstanding). It flies squarely in the face of our neurophysiology to maintain productivity through the middle of the day. Yet, we fear being stigmatized as lazy or nonproductive if we're caught with our eyes shut.

Let's rethink that paradigm.

The science is overwhelming. Researchers at NASA found astronauts and pilots were thirty-four percent more accurate and one hundred percent more alert for up to two and a half hours after a twenty-minute nap—specifically twenty minutes. (More on nap duration later.) In a peer-reviewed study, four hundred subjects were given a task to learn or a series of images to memorize. Half were instructed to take a thirty-minute or less nap, while the control group was kept busy and awake. The nappers performed nearly one hundred percent better on both tests. Thankfully, I was in neither group. My kids could beat me ten out of ten times in Go Fish and Concentration from the time they were in kindergarten, whether I slept, swam, or stood on my head.

It's physiology.

They say, "practice makes perfect." Unless *they* happen to be neuroscientists who explain, "neurons that fire together, wire together." Think of your brain at rest (contradictory, I reckon). There are billions of nerve cells. When we form our fingers on the frets to play a song on the guitar, we begin to recruit and fire the required neurons. The more times we play the same chord, the more completely that bundle of neurons becomes bonded, a concept called potentiation. With each repetition, neighboring interneurons are recruited, and the neuronal pathway becomes more established. This high-intensity neuronal firing results in even more durable bonds, a process called long-term potentiation LTP. The specific electrical activity that defines phase two sleep solders these neuronal pathways and enhances LTP. Long-term potentiation, and therefore long-term learning and skill building, can take place without it, but it is dramatically enhanced by phase two sleep.

So, let's take a Cliffs Notes cruise through the science of sleep. No worries if you nod. All the better to ensure you never forget a word.

Dr. Sarah Mednick does research and teaches at Harvard and gets paid to lecture for big companies. She's published *Take a Nap! Change your life.* She must know what she's talking about. Dr. Mednick explains that sleep takes place in repeating cycles of approximately five phases.

Stage 1 is the sleep-induction phase. We are still aware of our surroundings but begin to become detached from them. It is in Stage 1 that we are hyper-reactive to subtle sounds. I read this aloud to my wife. She takes great delight in hitting the light switch 0.4 seconds after my head hits the pillow and watching me nearly leap out of bed. Stage 1 is also referred to as the hypnagogic (the converse of which is hypnopompic) state of sleep. We start to lose grip on the conversations and interactions of our awake selves. Some report feeling paralyzed when still awake. We can experience non-linear thoughts, hallucinate, and make associations we wouldn't have access to when awake. Mystics, mavericks, and hippies have long sought access to prolonged periods mimicking Stage 1 by any means possible. I call Stage 1 "rookie time." Dr. Mednick says Stage 1 lasts two to five minutes; I can knock it out in a wink.

In Stage 2, we are truly unconscious. Our heartbeat, respiratory rate, blood pressure, and body temperature begin to drop. Our muscles begin to relax, hence, the nap nod. (We will address specific countermeasures later.) We also disconnect from external stimuli. It is in Stage 2 that we assign appropriate context to events we have reacted to. I'm pretty sure my wife suffers from Stage 2 sleep deficiency. She gets disproportionately frustrated at me for returning empty cereal boxes to the cupboard.

On an EEG, Stage 2 sleep is characterized by a series of lightning-quick spindle waves, all within a fraction of a second. A series of spindle waves conclude with a higher amplitude K-complex. Spindle waves and K-complexes are the specific electrical activity that help hardwire skills, processes, and memory. Stage 2 sleep reliably lasts for about seventeen minutes.

My dad and I, the Amazing Dick Bass, Kishan Khemani, and Gary Edmonds, have all independently concluded the optimum period of

time for napping to be at or near seven minutes. We have just learned that scientifically speaking, we could punch that out to anything short of twenty-five minutes without harm.

We'll refer to any event that has us safely in Stage 2 sleep as the seven-minute nap (SMN).

My intent is to celebrate the science and benefit of the seven-minute nap. Later, I'll give you some tools and techniques for the execution of a successful siesta. Though not immediately relevant to this piece, the final three phases of sleep are fascinating. So, for the sake of completion, a few words on deep nighttime sleep.

Stages 3 and 4 are the repair and maintenance phases. It is when our body changes the oil and filters, greases the U-joints, checks the air in our tires, and makes sure the lights are all working. Our heart rate and body temperature drop further. Noises like a cough and conversational tones will not wake you. I must have been in Stage 3 on January 19, 1974. Two railcars full of isobutane collided six blocks from my house. I knew nothing of it until my dad was dragging me down the stairs by my arm. I recall a ball of fire outside my bedroom window. In Stage 3, the stress hormone cortisol is shut off, and the pituitary gland starts cranking out growth hormone to repair bones and muscle and metabolize fat and cholesterol. Yes, to lose weight, we must sleep. My son will be able to eat ten thousand calories a day and stay below two hundred pounds for life. Stages 3 and 4 are also called slow-wave sleep.

After Stage 4, there is an obligatory seven- to eight-minute rebound into Stage 2. Then REM— the party in your head—begins. Our heart and respiratory rate increase by up to forty percent. Our body temperature drops further, to the point that we don't regulate it, but the temperature in our head increases. It is essentially a reptilian state. Our body temperature is no longer regulated and varies with the environment. Interestingly, we won't shiver when we're cold or sweat when warm. We breathe irregularly in fits and starts. Our body convulses, and we get the characteristic rapid twitching of our eyes. For better or worse, REM is when our most vivid dreams take place. Yet, thankfully, our body is paralyzed, explaining why our legs feel like lead pipes, and we can't run from the Tyrannosaurus with the face of our eighth-grade English teacher, but she never seems to catch us.

It is also in REM that emotional memory is formed. We associate the jingle of the ice cream truck with the pleasure of eating a chocolate sundae. In addition, our brain searches for stimuli and responses that are no longer useful and uncouples them. Think about soldiers and victims of abuse who are battling PTSD. We once had a client who was a retired Marine, having seen combat in Desert Storm. He lived in fear and could not sleep longer than twenty minutes until he bought a Great Pyrenees to stand guard.

It is in REM that long-term memory, complex learning, and creativity take place. Michael Perry must only REM sleep. If I ever crank out one chapter on the same plane as *Population: 485*, I'll do a Lambeau Leap.

The intricacies of effective napping, in my experience.

I have no illusion that more time in Stage 2 sleep will make me play guitar like Joel Paterson, but we have established that the SMN will enhance our alertness, accuracy, and memory. Still, some won't, don't, or say they can't.

My editor, Mittsy Voiles, says she cannot nap, and never has. Science does not apply to Mittsy; I'll make no attempt.

Potentially the greatest impediment to effective napping is the siesta stigma, whether real or perceived. I've long felt that a significant percentage of human behavior revolves around managing our insecurities. Most mental health professionals I've asked say, "Oh, about 125 percent." In the absence of any sort of superpower, the best I can do is work longer and harder. If I'm caught with my eyes closed, I surrender a measure of my iron man status.

Does it have to be that way?

We know the folks mentioned earlier first as fathers, philosophers, authors, artists, politicians, statesmen, and folks who simply get shit done. So then if we are looking to emulate their productivity, should we not view their tendency to slumber in the same way we would the trucks they drive, the hammers they swing, or the boots they wear? Now we know that they are all expert nappers.

BILL STORK

Ryan Haack is a paragon of productivity. He's in the barn by five every morning and hopes to spend an hour reading or writing to get to sleep by eleven at night. Ryan has worked a forty-hour week by lunch on Wednesday. He naps to survive. I asked him about the perception of the lazy napper. Ryan spent some time in Japan, where they take napping very seriously. He explained that if the man or woman is hardworking and productive, they are revered in their nap habit. Only Ryan Haack could learn this in a country where he doesn't speak a word of their language, and he was only there for a week or so.

Two factors drive our bodies' craving for sleep. The need for Slow Wave Sleep, (Stages 3 and 4) is dictated by a phenomenon called sleep pressure. Sleep pressure is dependent on proximity to our alarm clock. Sleep pressure is at a minimum immediately after we wake up and peaks near bedtime. The other factor is circadian rhythm, which wants us to lay down six or seven hours after we've woken up. Which answers, "I can't stay awake from one to three in the afternoon, but after work, I get my second wind."

Yup.

Throw a Cowboy Barbecue sandwich in your stomach and a lunch and learn event from a drug rep, and any attempt to stay awake is flying in the face of a thousand years of evolution.

Research shows that the benefits of the SMN can last for up to two and a half hours

"I don't have time to nap." Oh, really?

My wife worked at a high-end referral equine hospital. The nearest fast food or convenient store was five minutes, one way. The nearest Starbucks was a seven-minute drive. Yes, I know, primitive. With the app, the average wait at a Starbucks is three to five minutes. Alternately, pack a ham sandwich in a soft-sided cooler with an ice pack. Depending on whether your style is urban-chic or old school, a Yeti or Stanley thermos will keep your coffee hot all day long. You've likely saved five hundred calories, two hundred grams of cholesterol, a ten-dollar bill, and ample time for a SMN. Pull up a bale of shavings on the south side of the barn and kick back. In doing so, you can improve everything from your memory to your sex life and skin tone by spending a solid ten minutes in Stage 2 sleep.

"I don't have a place to take a nap."

First, a disclaimer. Subject to my ramblings on a daily basis, my staff has yet to read a word I've written. I'm good with that. Often, they've lived the stories or been captive as I regale clients with them. If this little essay would ever make it to their eyes, there could be a protest. The Lake Mills Veterinary Clinic was built in 1977 by a stubborn German-Scotsman (yes, redundant) on a tight budget. Our physical plant doesn't have a break-room where haggard veterinary nurses can escape the telephones, let alone space to recline.

To this point, we've explored the scientific benefit and ideal timing of the SMN. I've attempted to dispel the siesta stigma, and we've spoken briefly on creating the time to do it.

This, dear reader, is where the rubber meets the road. My dad was one of the most productive men and skilled nappers who's ever drawn a breath. After nine years in higher education and over twenty-five years of veterinary practice, I have developed skills organically and learned by observation from some of the best in the business. I've read articles from The National Sleep Foundation, Mayo Clinic, and Web MD, and the relevant chapters of Dr. Sarah C. Mednick's book. At this point, I feel exquisitely qualified to expound on the proper execution of the SMN.

I'll introduce techniques perfected on job sites, offices, and the cab of pickup trucks. I'll be largely in lockstep with the learned, but on the topic of comfort, my people do not line up precisely with Dr. Mednick and Mayo. Finally, I'll plug what I consider to be a gaping hole in what's published on effective napping, the post-seven-minute nap (PSMN). This is a master class. If it takes you a full five minutes to get through Stage 1, or if you slip into Stage 3 and succumb to inertia, do not get frustrated. Joel Paterson did not nail "El Cumbancharro" the first time through. It takes practice.

We've established the profound and long-lasting effect, and therefore, the need to nap. For some, the consequences can be dramatic. If I nod off during a lunch and learn, I miss out on the molecular mechanism

BILL STORK

of fluralaner and have to look it up later. My dad was a heavy equipment operator. He ran everything from a bulldozer to a five-hundred-ton tower crane. A Cat D-11 weighs over a hundred tons and is close to one thousand horsepower. If he nodded off on the levers, he could take out a twenty-foot swath of Watertown.

Dr. Mednick and others posit that a comfortable, quiet, dark space is required for proper napping. I beg to differ.

At his retirement party, I met some of the guys Dad worked with. The first thing they told me about was his napping habits, "That old man of yours can fall asleep anywhere." If there had been cell phones in the seventies, someone would have a collection of photos of Dad on the catwalk of a Manitowoc crane, on the tracks of a Cat dozer, or in the bucket or a rubber tire end loader. On the job, he always kept his lunch bucket and thermos under his seat. He'd throw down Mom's meatloaf sandwich and a bag of chips, prop his head on his hard hat, and be throwing K-complexes in seconds flat.

For those of us in an office setting, Dr. Mednick recommends a functional or physical Do Not Disturb sign.

That's an awesome option if you can get it.

There are times when an uninterrupted SMN is going to disrupt workflow. When Indie Jones hits the front door of the clinic, he's lunging for jugular veins. "We'll get him settled as soon as Dr. Stork wakes up to calculate how much Dexdomitor and Torbugesic," is not consistent with low-stress handling techniques and the longevity of technicians. When Jennifer DeKrey phones after letting Riley out eight times overnight to relieve his loose stool, if Dr. Stork had his Do Not Disturb sign up, the subsequent game of phone tag could trash an expensive oriental rug.

Rather than a Do Not Disturb plaque on my office door, I'll simply close and latch it. My office chair has sturdy arms and reclines to seventy-five degrees. I can bury my chin in my chest, cross my right leg over my left, and let my toe touch the filing cabinet to prevent further rotation. Technicians with questions will tap once—or not—on their way in. Much like Dali's key hitting the floor, the click of the latch will jolt me to sufficient awareness to calculate a dose of

Metra-whatever-i-zone for a sixty-five-pound Golden Retriever with lingering diarrhea.

Truck napping.

Sheila chuckled smugly as the nice lady at Culver's gave us (me) a senior discount. As country veterinarians go, I'm a bit of a dinosaur. My first day on the job was June 15, 1992. At that point, our distribution was 70:30, farmwork to pets. As of EOY 2019, the pendulum has swung, and then some. Farmwork constitutes less than three percent of our work. My accountant recommends that we have an appreciation luncheon with the farmers and hang up the coveralls. To this point, I don't take days off. I'd rather talk politics, the NFL, and dairy economics with Rick on Monday mornings. Ed will often bring donuts to the Wollin herd check, and Ryan Haack always has a fresh quote from Margaret Thatcher or his buddy Brian from Alaska.

It also sets the stage for the crown jewel of the SMN, the truck nap.

If we are to achieve the thermo-neutral and physically comfortable environment Dr. Mednick recommends, there is both art and environmental concerns.

In the wintertime, find a southern exposure. Especially dressed in coveralls, fleece, and a stocking hat, the UV on the windshield will render the cab an optimal fifty-eight degrees, without idling the engine. May through September here in Southern Wisconsin, the average midday temperature is eighty degrees. In order not to bake yourself to medium-rare, you're going to need to face north, with a healthy cross-breeze through the cab. Regardless of the time of year, angle is everything. On any given county blacktop, you'll find an excellent selection of field roads. To get tractors and implements into the field, they'll usually have a nice, soft approach. Back down to the point that the angle of your seat counters the gravitational pull of the nap nod when you slip into Stage 2. Always be aware of footing. You never want to rut a farmer's field, or worse yet, call Steve for a tow.

For those in urban settings, you may not have access to the environments described above. The circle drive at Tyranena Park on the northeast corner of Rock Lake is one of the most pristine spots I know. Seven-minute nappers who have not come to grips with the siesta stigma will try and not make eye contact as they idle in like lovers on a noon rendezvous. Depending on the month, the little lot can provide proper exposure, cross-breeze, and the thrum of the water against the shore. It is also flat. In which case, I encourage you to use the recline lever on your seat. This is a fine option, but it leads us to an issue that I found to be overlooked entirely in the literature.

The post-seven-minute nap.

The perils of sleep inertia are well-documented, and we've all experienced it. What I can find no mention of is the benefit of post-nap momentum. The fewer adjustments you have to make when your eyes open, the sooner you'll return to productivity. In the case of the truck nap, you'll have to fumble with the lever to get your seat back to just right, unless you're a fancy-pants equine vet with a Euro SUV with presets on your leather seats. For office naps, I'll have the record I'm writing across my lap and the pen in hand.

On Saturdays, I often work until noon or so. I'll go home and put two slices of bread and cheese on the griddle. Cheese toasties are my favorite lunch treat on weekends. While I'm waiting for the bread to brown, I'll set up my sawhorses, make sure the batteries on the drills are charged, put the T-25 bit in the chuck, and lay out my star-headed screws. After I finish my milk and do the dishes, I'll put my Red Wings back on. We have a dog bed in the laundry room that always has an empty jar of Jif that makes the perfect head prop.

With all due respect to the research, I feel the need for comfort is on a sliding scale. It seems excessive comfort can present a gravitational pull similar to sleep inertia.

Sheila has become my test subject. She says she just can't wind down as quickly as I do. It'll come to her.

Research is pending.

Gary Edmonds will read this and say, "No shit, Willy." He'll likely have wisdom to add. He's retired to the point he has time to both nap and read my ramblings. He might even say that one necessitates the other. If there is a single pearl on these pages that contribute to your rest, well-being, productivity, and safety, then I've done my job.

Dad always said, "I never learned a thing with my mouth open." If there are techniques you've developed, please do share at author@drbillstork.com.

In closing, I'll mention a subset of the SMN. I reckon we could call it the bonus or the special occasion SMN. We've all envied our dogs sleeping fitfully in the yard. Ryan waxes on how comfortable it would be to lay in a fresh-cut hayfield. Alas, there are bugs. If we tried that, we'd be inundated by mosquitoes, flies, and fire ants. There are a few days in early spring and a couple in September, or shortly after a quick cold snap, or days before the first hatch, when you can find a patch of grass, often aided by a crosswind, and lay down in the lawn just like Tugger and Token.

It's supposed to start snowing this evening through tomorrow. A total of six to ten inches is possible. I hope it comes through. It takes an hour or so to plow the three drives and the dooryard at the farm. Then there's just enough shovel work around the tracks of the machine sheds to just about break a sweat. Bundled in snow pants, boots, and my Carhartt hat, there's nothing more peaceful than falling into a south-facing snowbank and shutting your eyes.

You'll never get a full seven minutes around our house, though. Token L-O-V-E-S to chase snowballs, and she does not take no for an answer. ⸱

Learning With My Mouth Shut

Uncle Erv and I walked to the end of the driveway. I'd dug a chest freezer-sized stone we call Big Pink and a dozen of her friends from the fence line to form a raised wildflower garden. In retirement, Erv taught a college course on geology. He scratched the surface with his fingernail, speculating on their mineral makeup and origin.

"I just love rocks," he quipped. "I figure I'll always have cheap entertainment."

And so it goes for those of us addicted to sunrises, sunsets, and storytelling.

The Moth is a nonprofit organization founded in 1997 by George Dawes Green. He wanted to create an environment reminiscent of his front porch in Georgia. Moths would flutter in the heavy night air 'round a single fly-stained bulb, and neighbors would gather to tell stories. The website defines The Moth as a group dedicated to the art and craft of storytelling.

I find that description a bit humble.

I've come to realize that story*telling* rides my chromosomes like chicken legs, snoring, and getting up early.

But first, I was a *listener*.

A high point of summer was a 150-mile sojourn to southern Illinois with my grandma to visit Aunt Mary and Uncle Kelsey. We'd load a Coleman cooler wide as the vinyl seat in the back of her shit brown '74 Plymouth Valiant with enough powdered sugar donuts, whole milk, and iced tea to get Christopher Columbus to the New World.

The week on the farm would be swimming in the creek and playing baseball with my shirttail cousins. Early mornings after breakfast, we'd cake ourselves with yellow powdered sulfur from a gallon glass jar to repel the chiggers. We'd pick blackberries 'til noon and butcher chickens after lunch.

I'd ask Grandma and Aunt Mary, "Are you gonna sit outside tonight?" Some nights a neighbor would stop by. They'd gather the rusty back porch farm chairs—legs brazed, arms taped like a candy cane—in a circle. Us kids would climb trees, swing, and catch fireflies, while parents, grands, and neighbors drank near-beer, spat watermelon seeds, and told stories.

Uncle Kelsey had a half-dozen milking Shorthorns and an old Jersey cross named Big Red. He'd drink one beer on the back porch, then sterilize his buckets and strainer. When the bottle hit the crate, he had a dog, always named Butch, that'd let themselves out the screen door, jump the fence, and have the cows waiting to be milked when Kelsey got to the barn. His International L-180 wandered the county blacktop like Otis the Drunk. There was a hole in the seat he covered with a feed sack and one in the floor he spit Mail Pouch tobacco bullets through.

Prone to embellishment, but firmly rooted, their tales were straight out of the Woody Guthrie and Fred Eaglesmith songbook: summertime sermons of family values, faith, and grit.

It's been forty-some years from the four-acre alfalfa field north of Greenville, Illinois. At every transition, graduation, and relocation, there's an opportunity to reinvent, redefine, and progress. For better or worse, every aspect of our persona affects how we are perceived. We choose how we walk, talk, and dress.

And we tell stories.

The stories we tell, and the ones we choose not to, speak as much to our makeup as our handshake and hairstyle.

I've long held the notion that animals evolve in the likeness of their people. Jim Kassube had a cow with a sore foot he called "Thelma Lou," and she bawled from behind a tree. We walked up to her standing in the pasture. We put a halter on her head and wrapped it around the nearest box elder, but she would have stood stock with

 BILL STORK

Jim rubbing her ears. I picked up her right front foot and opened a painful abscess.

Afterward, Jim hobbled back to the house. I asked if I needed to pick up his foot.

"Oh," he said, "you didn't hear. I got hurt at work."

At which point, he proceeded to drop his drawers in the middle of the driveway. He was missing a pot roast-sized chunk of quadriceps from his thigh.

"Oh, my God, Dr. Stork," he shook his head. "I am so lucky. A piece of grinder wheel flew off my machine. It happened ten minutes before the end of my shift, and the little gal who works second is barely five feet tall. It would have killed her for sure."

Jim Kassube has a high school education and a million dollars worth of antique John Deere tractors sitting in the weeds. He does not know the meaning of martyr.

Tom Carpenter had a Ford GT. He'd written a check for it as-is and probably didn't know where the dipstick was. He'd take it to car shows and stand beside guys who'd restored theirs from the ground up. I'd just pulled a calf at the Strasburg farm. We were deep in the middle of the '08–'12 downturn, and the heifer calf was DOA. Tom roared into the drive, got out of his Hot Wheels car like a sixty-five-year-old Ken doll, and bellowed, "Damn it, I gotta pay $40,000 in income tax this year from that land I sold to the power company."

"Most people do not listen with the intent to understand; they listen with the intent to reply."—Stephen Covey

(It comes as no surprise that I only made it through the first three-and-a-half habits of The 7 Habits of Highly Effective People. I did come away with one pearl.)

Dr. Martin Seligman is widely considered the father of positive psychology. He explains that connections between people are accomplished by establishing deep and meaningful relationships through effective and positive communication. Connections reduce the number of social stressors and render us more resilient in the face of adversity.

In challenging times, our connections can help assuage our need to be cared for, understood, and validated.

Central tenets of every Moth event are respect and support. I can think of no environment that better nurtures connections than The Moth.

Nestor Gomez migrated to the United States from Guatemala. To learn English and defeat his stutter, he began to tell stories at The Moth. Today he champions immigration reform, leads his own troupe of storytellers, and is the process of publishing three books. Nestor has won more StorySLAMs than Brett Favre has interceptions.

Haywood Simmons Jr. played defensive end for the Wisconsin Badgers and the Dallas Cowboys. His upbringing was not always warm and supportive. He tells stories just above a whisper, but his messages should be shouted from the rooftops. In storytelling and in life, Haywood is all about supporting at-risk kids.

Patty calls herself a trophy wife. Her stories are delivered with Robin Williams' frantic lack of apparent organization and ninja humor—a poorly concealed attempt to hide the anguish of having lost her husband (and partner in the award business) young and suddenly.

Charles "The Voice" Payne has taught impoverished kids in southern New Mexico. He manages depression and anxiety by telling self-effacing stories of his anatomical peculiarities, struggles with race, and about those who have supported him. Many of his stories conclude with, "I'll be there for you." I have no doubt.

Research also shows that having someone to share with in times of triumph magnifies the positive effect of the victory, a term called capitalization. Under-trained and physically broken first-time storyteller Tom Barry carried us through every harrowing inch of his first Ironman. The crowd barked and fist-bumped as he crossed the finish line.

Though eloquent, poetic, and profound, Clemmons, Buddha, and Montaigne don't have a gram more common sense than my dad. Dad's diction was that of the working man, "Son, I ain't never learned a thing with my mouth open."

In the past year, I've told a few stories, but more importantly, I've heard nearly two hundred. There are those of us who love to tell stories. There are at least as many who have a story to tell. Some have literally been pushed on stage by friends and daughters. Those are the stories they have to tell, and more importantly, the ones we really need to hear.

It is when I'm in the darkness of the footlights, out front of the microphone, that I've been enlightened, grown, and come to understand.

On September 20, 2019, along with nine other monthly winners, I'll be telling my story in the Madison Moth GrandSLAM at The Barrymore Theater. Tickets are available at The Barrymore Theater website.

The Moth defines itself as devoted to the art and craft of storytelling. I'd have to add therapy, history, community, support, acceptance, tolerance, understanding, desegregation. ⌕

The Moth:
Gratitude

You may get the impression that I feel strongly indebted to Certified Nursing Assistants. There could be something to that. The topic at The Moth in November 2019 was Gratitude. I told the following story to a standing-room-only crowd at Colectivo Coffee House on the southside of Milwaukee. We're given a six-minute time limit. Most of us can do around eight hundred words before the bell tolls. Though I've been criticized, prodded, and prompted for what I consider thoughtful diction, I laid down the following 1,100 words with time to spare.

To live on in the hearts of those you leave behind is not to die.

In over twenty-five years as a veterinarian, I've pushed the plunger on pets who were their owner's soul and salvation. I've lost both parents, and way too many friends, before their time.

Possibly the most depressing first stanza in Moth history.

Friends, I assure you this is anything but a tale of woe.

Whether by my father's bedside, or in the congregation of Cobb Creek Missionary Baptist Church at the funeral of my friend Dick Bass, when the time is nigh, I open my ears and my eyes, my pores, and my soul in a conscious effort to absorb and incorporate all that is strong, beautiful, and unique in that moment, and the person we celebrate.

That trait has contributed to the man who stands before you and developed a deep appreciation and respect for a group of people. I'm about to tell you about six of them.

BILL STORK

Dad always said, "If a neighbor had a heart attack, the ambulance better be quick, because your mom would be there first with a casserole and a pitcher of iced tea."

When she was overtaken with the god-awful affliction which is Alzheimer's and dementia, my construction working, git-'er-done, 'til death do us part dad, cooked, cleaned, fed, bathed, and dressed her. He preserved every fabric of her dignity.

Until he could no longer. She struggled for years; she only spent three months in a home.

In those last days, she was soiling her bedclothes hourly. She didn't know Dad and me from Garth Brooks and George Strait. She'd lay there babbling while Carol and Jocelyn gently rolled her over, bathed her, and gave her clean sheets. They'd kiss her on the temple as they departed.

After Mom passed, Dad had ten good years.

Dad was one of those old guys who drove used cars from an auction in Indiana back to the dealership in Decatur. I got *the call* from Cousin Jim at six-thirty on a Wednesday morning. Dad had a massive stroke and launched a Buick into a bean field in Indiana.

That night was from hell.

He had a violent reaction to the morphine they had given him for pain. He thrashed, pulled at his catheter, and attempted to relieve himself off the side of the bed. I got to know my dad more personally than I ever hoped. Blind and ataxic. I propped him on the left. Under his right arm was a thirty-five-year-old mother of three named O'Meka.

After a week in the hospital, he was discharged to a nursing and rehab facility. The nurses set about the business of arranging an ambulance transport four hours to Wisconsin. As they scrambled, I pulled my work truck to the exit.

"You can't do that, Mr. Stork. What if something happens?"

"Then it'll happen in the passenger seat of my pickup truck, exactly where he'd rather be." I pointed to the commode I'd borrowed from St. Vinny's in the back seat. "Don't worry. We've got this covered."

I drove a couple of miles out of my way, so we didn't have to go past the home I feared he'd never return to.

I moved him into Lilac Springs Assisted Living Facility in Lake Mills.

I particularly remember Karen, Christie, and Stephanie.

Karen was built like a refrigerator with a head. At fifty-six, with thirty years in health care, she could no longer stand fully erect. She walked like a constipated Herman Munster. Four days a week, she worked back-to-back eight-hour shifts at two different assisted living facilities. I had gone back to my clinic to see a couple of cases. When I returned, she was sitting next to Dad, holding his hand, combing his hair, telling him that she loved him—after she had clocked out of her third consecutive sixteen-hour day.

Christie found out my dad liked big band and swing music. She had two kids and a husband but somehow found time to record a mix CD and found an old boombox she brought in to play for him.

Stephanie was middle-aged, trim, and attractive. She moved crisply, and her scrubs were always pressed and tucked. When Stephanie was on shift, things would be handled. I sat vigil with my dad during his last week. Somewhere in the wee hours, Dad stirred, and Stephanie attended. We settled him, cleaned him, and she wet his lips with the sponge swab.

I picked a subtle y'all from her diction. When I asked, "Where's home?" she first said it was Wisconsin. I pressed just one more round. She admitted she was originally from Louisiana. When she was twenty, she loaded her special-needs son and her eighteen-year-old boyfriend in the car and drove north because she knew there was a better life beyond that damn bayou.

Carol, Jocelyn, O'Meka, Karen, Christie, and Stephanie are all Certified Nursing Assistants.

After my dad passed, I went back to thank the staff at Lilac Springs. "Your dad was one of our favorites. He was so kind and funny."

Yes, he was, but not when they knew him. He was cantankerous, mad, and bitter.

  BILL STORK

Carol and Jocelyn were at my mom's funeral. When they first knew her, she was a sixty-eight-pound babbling mannequin where my mother used to be. I thanked them, and they cried. "She was the sweetest lady. Her last words were 'I'm sorry, and thank you.'"

I hugged and thanked O'Meka. "Oh, Mr. Stork, that's okay. I just want to make sure that every one of my patients gets the kind of care I'd want for my own mother."

In our health care system, CNAs are at the bottom of the pecking order and pay scale, yet they are often the point of care. They do the most physically and emotionally draining, organic, dehumanizing jobs for people they never got to know when they were at their best and benevolent. And, their average pay in the state of Wisconsin is less than a cashier at Kwik Trip, often, without benefits.

If you have ever been a CNA, or if you are one now, I thank you.

If you ever need a voice or an advocate, I will tell this story and a hundred others, in full-throat, before Congress, the American Medical Association, or from high atop the tallest mountain.

If you know a CNA, please tell them some old bald guy at The Moth appreciates them immensely.

P.S. Moth stories are judged by three teams, on a scale of 1–10. For the first time in Moth history (at least in Milwaukee), I tied with my friend Dave Nelson for the victory. ✑

SCAN ME

The Moth:
Love Hurts

The topic of the February 2019 Madison Moth event was Love Hurts. A few things of note, the slam took place on February 12, two days before Valentine's Day. Anyone who had someone was with them. Those who did not, wrote stories about being left at the altar and cheated on and brought them to the High Noon Saloon. To that point in my career, I had told heart-wrenching stories about dogs and cats, most of the time, as I euthanized them. I was called eighth out of ten. As Dr. Death mounted the stage, I looked to our producer, Jen Rubin. She buried her head on the desk.

Evidently, the judges were grateful for a six-minute break from gloom and doom. They were kind, and I qualified for the Madison Grand Slam, which gave me the opportunity to tell a story called, I Think I Can.

I met my first wife at orientation before our first year of veterinary school at the University of Illinois.

The first difference, of many to follow, was academic. She could knit sweaters during lectures, study for an hour, and ace a test. I sat in the front row, took notes like a madman, pulled all-nighters, and prayed for Cs.

Sadly, I let affairs of the heart supersede those of the head. In doing so, I achieved a GPA the administration was not in the least bit impressed with. As a result, my girl graduated a solid year before I did and migrated to Wisconsin to become the next great dairy vet.

I was left behind, but not alone.

  BILL STORK

My good friend Arlin Rodgers was in need of a roommate. We rented an apartment in a graduate student commune called Winfield Village. Between the two of us, we never had fewer than three dogs, a stereo system I did DJ jobs with, and four hundred compact disks.

On any given night, the dogs would be doing hot laps around the backs of the couches, up the stairs, down the stairs, and off the walls. We'd be cranking Stevie Ray Vaughan's *Couldn't Stand the Weather* at volume 11 or drinking beers and singing "The Front Porch Song" aka Robert Earl Keen and Lyle Lovett.

Our poor neighbors.

They were a lovely family of five we affectionately referred to as "the Baptists." So called because every Sunday morning, Sunday evening, and Wednesday evening, they departed their apartment. Properly dressed and in formation from Papa Bear down to the youngest son, Bibles tucked under their arms, they headed for worship.

Long-distance love is a challenge under the best of conditions. Given there were 240 miles between us and attempting to navigate on-call and clinical schedules, there were times we did not see one another for a month at a time. On the heels of one such drought, she decided to come visit, though she was on call Friday night, which bled into Saturday morning and afternoon. Long story, she didn't arrive in Champaign until midnight, exhausted. But still, we celebrated our reunion as young lovers will do, and fell into peaceful slumber, wrapped in one another's arms.

I woke shortly after dawn the next morning and carefully extracted myself so that she could continue the restoration she so desperately needed. I squatted next to the bed to gather the spoils of the previous night of passion. Nothing. I dropped and swept my arm as far under the bed as my arm could reach. I harvested three dirty socks and the early onset of panic.

Cooder, my nine-month-old yellow Lab, had his head pressed into the carpet, pretending to be asleep. You see, Cooder's power-eating resume included a half a crate of oranges, six pounds of dog food, and an entire Thanksgiving pumpkin pie.

Fear not, animal lovers. Cooder would be fine. Even if it came to that, an uncomplicated foreign body is a fairly straightforward piece of surgery. The source of my anxiety: the student on call for small-animal surgery was ME. I would be assisted by two phenomenal technicians, one, if not two, of my classmates and a clinician. One cannot simply make an incision and quickly extract a used contraceptive from your dog's duodenum and stuff it in your pocket, hoping nobody noticed, without breaking sterility.

So, I stuck with plan A.

Cooder and I flew down the stairs two at a time and into the kitchen for the brown bottle. The sight of which sent Cooder to his corner. He sat and raised his head. I told him, "Chug like a frat boy," and after forty-five cc's, his stomach started to churn.

We flew through the living room and flung open the front door and introduced the reluctant little Lab to the front porch.

At precisely that moment, the Baptists emerged, bound for glory.

I had a split second to decide which would be less scarring on these poor kids—what my dog was about to vomit on the sidewalk, or a six-foot-four Sasquatch in tighty-whities attempting to shield them from it.

I slammed the door and parted the blinds. Cooder ran six feet in front of them and heaved twice. He vomited three Kleenexes and a Trojan receptacle tip condom onto the sidewalk.

Papa Bear lifted his chin, planted his left foot, and step-step. He planted his right foot and step-step and marched his family in a perfect military square around the scene of the crime.

To this day, I wonder if it hasn't been the prayers of those good people, for the salvation of the heathens next door, that has saved me from significant harm. ⌕

BILL STORK

The Moth:
Family

I told this story at a standing-room-only Moth event at Anodyne Coffee Roasters, on the southside of Milwaukee in December 2019. The topic of the night was Family. The beauty of a Moth storytelling event is everyone has a unique and beautiful take on any given topic. Mine was a little out there. I was a bit nervous until a guy in the thirteenth row let out a guffaw when I got to the "Teflon off a teapot" line, then I knew I had 'em.

The judges were kind. I won the event and qualified for the next Milwaukee Moth Grand Slam.

Family: Judy B

I can't say it was love at first sight. I fell in love with my wife between Tyranena Brewing Company and the Deerfield exit off Highway 94. That's about eighteen minutes. Sheila is gorgeous, accountable, and loyal to the core. Still, they say to take a good look at Mom before you say, "I do." Well, I did, and I'm all in.

With one sliver of reservation.

My mother-in-law, Judy Barnes, is well over seventy years old and barely five feet, four inches with her hair in curlers. She walks softly, speaks softly, and carries no stick. Her husband of over fifty years calls her The Boss, with a glow in his eye.

Her left foot is as comfortable on the pedal of a Singer sewing machine mending overalls as on the clutch of an '02 Peterbilt. No one has ever pushed back from her holiday table hungry, heavy-hearted, or empty-handed. In a world where common sense and accountability are at a premium, you needn't look any farther than my wife, her sister, and her brothers. It is glaringly apparent where they got it.

Judy is the corner post of our family. It is not the trait that defines her.

Butch and Judy drive truck. They'll take a six-day West Coast run, get out of the truck, climb on the four-wheeler, and visit the neighbors together. Early in our courtship, they were hauling a load of cheese to California. Somewhere around St. George, Utah, outbound, she started to feel a little rumbling in her stomach. By the time they made their drop in LA, the rumbling had escalated to a full-on urgency, and the effluent was anything but organized. Their niece was a nurse at Los Angeles General. She could get her right in. Judy waved her off. It was only 2,100 home; she'd be fine. By the time they made Barstow, she was doubled over in the passenger seat. One hundred sixty miles out of Vegas, Butch was on the phone with my wife. In an hour, Sheila had a first-class seat on the next outbound plane to Madison or pre-admission at Vegas General ER.

Judy thought about it, then politely declined. There were forty thousand pounds of fresh veggies in the reefer that Woodman's expected by Wednesday. That Peterbilt won't drive itself, and there wasn't enough caffeine in California to keep Butch's eyes open another mile. Judy said, "I'll take a turn."

"Judith, just give me 150 miles, and I'll be good to go." He may as well have been talking to Abraham Lincoln.

Eight hours later, he rolled out of the sleeper, fifty miles east of Cheyenne, Wyoming.

Fourteen hours later, my wife and her sister met the rig at the dock in Sun Prairie. Incoherent and barely able to walk, they poured her into the back seat and rushed her to St. Mary's. The gastroenterologist ordered an MRI. She had diverticulitis, a nearly perforated bowel, and was septic. After three days in ICU, she was strong enough for surgery.

Post-op, the doctor met with the family. The surgery went well. She could go home when she was able to pass gas, to which Butch responded, "Doc, you better be darn careful what you ask for."

BILL STORK

He could not have been more serious.

Any given holiday or family gathering, sometime after dessert, in-laws and grandkids will come pouring out of the kitchen gasping for air—windows and doors propped open for cross-ventilation.

The woman could take Teflon off a teapot.

And it is not all about BTUs and cubic feet. The woman's got finesse. She can crop dust, one cheek sneak, or—her specialty—the staccato musical walking fart. One Black Friday, it lasted the entire length of the appliance section at Kohl's.

She doesn't laugh. She also doesn't apologize. And why should she? It's biochemistry 101. Mammals cannot convert a quinoa salad or a cheeseburger to purposeful movement or meaningful thought without the obligatory production of methane. Yet, we live in fear of being stigmatized if we get busted.

We once thought evil spirits entered us when we sneeze, so we say bless you. It seems obvious when they escape.

No one is spared. The great James Gordon told a story at the Milwaukee Grand Slam of a first date that was altered as a result of lactose intolerance. One can't imagine how many inauguration and valedictorian speeches have been affected by a few too many cauliflower florets and an overly-sensitive microphone. I'm a veterinarian, and I live in fear. Imagine a family gathered to say goodbye to their fourteen-year-old Golden Retriever. The exam room is silent, except for the sobs. I'm trying to hit the vein, all while fighting against a chorizo burrito with rice and beans.

So, I am here to propose that we de-criminalize the fart. It is not to be celebrated, nor apologized, rather, glossed over and ignored like a mismatched pair of socks. For the love of the unstoppable Judy Barnes, please, give gas a chance.

*P.S. For a couple of hundred strangers in a coffee shop in Milwaukee, I had only minor trepidation telling this one. I was later **required** to tell it in the kitchen with the family gathered around at Christmas time.* ☖

SCAN ME

The Moth:
Traditions

I've said in many places, "There are people who come into our lives at a time when we are vulnerable or in need. They bring to us an energy, spirit, or perspective that forever changes every interaction from that moment forward." I've been fortunate to know a few of those people, but the Amazing Dick Bass and my parents are at the top of this list. This chapter and the story to follow have been in my head since the day I first put pen to paper—ten years and 750 pages ago. It's all been practice up to now; I wanted to get this one right.

I attended my first Moth event in Madison in the fall of 2018. A month later, I worked up a story and threw my name in the hat. In the past year and a half, I've heard some awesome stories from some amazing people. I've told a few I was proud of, and occasionally, the judges have been kind. I've notched victories in Story Slams in Milwaukee and Madison, but the microphone I craved to stand behind was on the stage at Lincoln Hall in Chicago. The topic of the Chicago Moth on April 13, 2020, was Traditions. The Amazing Dick Bass and I would go for donuts every Saturday morning when we were in college at the University of Illinois. I prayed for my name to get pulled from that hat and to tell the story of the man who'd meant so much to me, in front of my friend Kish, who introduced me to him.

Alas, came the coronavirus.

I was disappointed, but there are much bigger problems in the world. Though I've yet to tell this story to a live audience, I told it to my dogs, cats, and horses. It can be found on my YouTube channel. Here is the script.

BILL STORK

Traditions: The Amazing Dick Bass

My friend Dick Bass envied Kermit the Frog. "You know, Billy Stork. He could squat right down on a lily pad and pick his banjo and sing and never fall in the water."

Dick Bass was well into his doctoral research, and I was a second-year veterinary student. We'd meet at The Ye Olde Donut Shop at six every Saturday morning. Dick would have a sour cream donut and chocolate milk. I'd have a white long john, and we'd talk to the locals. We'd debate the merits of *The Andy Griffith Show* with a plumber named Bernie. There was a retired asphalt foreman named Porter Kaise who'd regale us with the intricacies of courting women, from a front porch, with a pitcher of iced tea.

Walking home one Saturday, we stumbled on a garage sale. Dick moved a blender aside and held up the broken neck of a flat-black mandolin, the bridge and body hanging from four rusty strings.

He tucked the sad little instrument under his arm like Bill Monroe himself had played it.

We got home, and I asked, "Dick Bass, you know anything about the mandolin?"

"No, Billy Stork. But it seems when folks down home get together to play, we're always missing a mandolin player."

Dick Bass played guitar, banjo, piano, and sang. He was well on his way to his PhD in EE, but his superpower was that he simply made every person and every minute of every day special.

At two o'clock every Tuesday, he'd rally the entire IEEE department—students, staff, faculty, and administration. They'd high-kick down the hallowed marble halls for a soda break singing, "I'm a Pepper, you're a Pepper, he's a Pepper. Wouldn't you like to be a Pepper too?"

We'd host Thursday and Sunday family dinners with meatloaf, turkey, and stuffing; you name it. Come one, come all. After dinner, we'd retire to the front porch for a sing-along from the Big Square Grey House songbook.

The last weekend before fall semester, we'd invite everyone we knew to Lake Shelbyville for waterskiing, camping, and crawfish etouffee.

The boat was getting full, so we dropped Dick Bass and others off at a beach with an inner tube and his banjo. When we finally went to pick him up four hours later, it was like an armada with houseboats, pontoons, johnboats, and ski boats. Folks were clapping and singing, and in the middle of it all was the Amazing Dick Bass. Kicked back on an inner tube, pickin', singin', and taking requests. He smiled with his whole head. "Billy Stork, Kermit the frog ain't got nothin' on me today!"

His PhD work applied to adaptive and mobility devices for the disabled. His defense drew interest from the Veterans Administration and General Electric. Several hours in, he paused. "Man, I'm getting a little tarred in the head." At which point he passed out boxes of donuts, gallons of chocolate milk, and read Dr. Seuss:

Sam-I-am,

I do not like green eggs and ham.

On April 14, 1999, I got the call. En route to the hospital to see his dad, he rear-ended a semi and died.

We rented a van, gathered the guys, and made the odyssey to Cobb Creek Baptist Church in Atlanta.

Dick had sent a letter when he and his wife, Cathy, joined the choir. "Yeah, Billy Stork, they had to teach us rhythm." Minus the only two white faces in their membership, the Cobb Creek Gospel Choir swung slow in their flowing robes, singing "I Can't Even Walk" on low. Their voices like a hug, filling every space not otherwise occupied by a person, pew, or Bible.

Dick had told me about his bluegrass gospel outfit.

Around no microphone, they gathered. At the bottom of their U, in missing man formation, a chrome stand held a two-tone Sunburst Gibson A-12 mandolin. One white rose was wedged under the tuning pegs. The guitar player tried to speak.

"Not only did we lose one of the finest man-a-lin pickers and tenor singers I've ever heard, we've lost a spirit. The minute that man stepped into our circle, it was like songs we'd been singing for twenty years were brand new."

BILL STORK

The stained-glass windows propped wide, the congregation swelled with faculty, friends, and kinfolk. The minister shuffled the ribbons in his Bible. The silence was broken by the screech of the brakes of three city buses. In filed residents of group homes, shelters, and the street. Like prisoners of war, they stared at the floor and gathered in the back of the church. Because loss knows no education or ethnicity, in the likeness of the man we'd lost, the minister spread his arms wide and beckoned the men to sit with us.

Among the suits and ties, there were wrinkled noses and murmurs. I leaned to the dean of Dick's department, "Have you ever asked what Dr. Bass does before he commences his research and teaching each day?"

He did not.

"He serves them breakfast."

So, traditions. Every Saturday morning, I drive to work listening to bluegrass music. I stop at Kwik Trip and get a sour cream donut and a bottle of chocolate milk. ⌖

WATCH NOW

The Moth:
I think I can

Each of the area Moth locations host monthly StorySLAMs. They take place in spacious bars and coffee houses in their host cities. Ten winners of local slams are invited to compete (participate) in The Grand Slam. I had won the February 2019 Slam with my story about my dog Cooder vomiting a condom on the sidewalk in front of our apartment.

The Madison Grand took place on September 8th, at The Barrymore Theater. The historic old cavern was standing room only; I was humbled to have a number of friends in attendance.

My goals for the night were to enjoy every minute and nuance of the event, and to tell my story. If there is one story I'd like to be defined by, it would be this one. I had rehearsed in my truck and on the hill out back, and invented or employed a handful of nerve-settling tactics. I circulated in the crowd as guests found their seats, so that staring into a thousand people, foot-lights in my eyes, I could speak to spots where my friends were seated.

We arrived for sound check two hours before show-time. We were allowed to save as many seats as we wanted. I saved ten, in the third row. Scott had come up from Chicago, Gary and Dianne from central Illinois, Linda and Charlie from Lake Mills. Above all else, I wanted my son and daughter to hear this story. I put my wife, Sheila, on the aisle.

  BILL STORK

The Story

I had been on-call and dad-duty for the better part of five straight years as my wife played for every co-ed soccer team in Madison, often until three in the morning. In order to placate my plea for a break, and possibly reconnect, she booked us a back-country biking trip in Colorado.

I had a pretty good idea how this story would end, but I was a 'til-death-do-us-part Cradle Catholic and I did not want my kids a statistic, so I asked for a seven-day-cease-fire and prayed for a miracle in the mountains.

Hopes crushed, day one.

Forty minutes out of Denver International she took a detour. Red Rocks Amphitheater has hosted everyone from Beatles to Brandi Carlile. Staring at the stage, "When we get back from this trip, we are through."

She spoke but a whisper, yet the words felt like a splittin' maul, right between the eyes.

We spent the week sleeping in separate tents.*

Our group met in Telluride the next morning.

Our lead guide was a man named John Humphries. John <u>revered</u> the Rocky Mountains like a farmer his back forty. He treated me like a broken-hearted big brother. He always had a shoulder to cry on and a bottle of fine agave. At night, we'd sit, and he'd listen 'til the flames faded.

Days would start before dawn, John beating a soup pot with a wooden spoon bellerin C-o-f-f-e-e. The dark roast fog wafting through the walls of my tent would induce a peristalsis that would deliver me first to a device we called, the groover then huddled around last night's embers, shoveling down 3000 calories of road-kill omelets, steel-cut oats and OJ.

It'd take nearly two hours to break camp, then, we'd clip in and climb.

Wednesday, we rode the Indian Ridge Trail. There were creek crossings, herds of elk, and handlebar-high monument flowers. We ate lunch at the top of the world, looking down through clouds at neighboring mountain ranges.

Day's end was in a family circle 'round the cave man TV. The flames would flicker a face, conversation was measured, muted, and reflective. If I sat at three o'clock around the circle, she'd sit at nine. At fourteen-thousand feet of elevation and fifteen miles long, Indian Ridge was but half the distance between her and I.

Critical Thursday we camped at a site known to locals as The Vortex, at the trailhead of the legendary Hermosa Creek Singletrack.

Friday morning John delivered one final lecture, "If in doubt, chicken out."

Three hours of climbing, and one cliff-hanger, delivered our expedition to the foot of a fifteen-hundred-vertical-foot obstacle course the guides call, The Beast.

To clean is to conquer. To clean-the-beast was unthinkable but in less than twenty-four hours I'd be wedged into the window seat of a 737, Milwaukee-bound. Elbow-to elbow with the mother of my children, searching Craig's List for a new place to live.

I wasn't holding anything back.

John went up first. He punched the cobalt sky and gave out a yee-ha!

I dropped my chest to the crossbar, levered my tire tight to the trail and pedaled like a man possessed, around switchbacks, over rocks and roots. Redlined, The Beast gave me twenty-five feet of scrabble, I soft-pedaled slow as I could stay upright.

I made the first three switchbacks and started to fail, the fourth seemed a mile. I bargained my body for a hundred more pedal strokes, then fifty, twenty-five, ten, until I was begging the engine room for every turn of the crank.

That's when I heard John.

"Big Man of the Dairyland, You Will Not Quit."

I'd lost my peripheral vision, and couldn't lift my head. I was honking like a goose, legs on fire. I had taken my last pedal stroke 250 times.

At one point relaxing my right eyebrow to save the strength.

I have precious little memory of those last 200 meters, but I know one thing: my fucking foot never touched that trail.

I punched my front tire over the rim of that canyon, got lightheaded and started to fall back. Then came John's hand on my headset. He hauled me over the precipice. I coasted to a stop and passed out.

They say home is where the heart breaks. Back in Wisconsin there were lawyers, counselors, and a guardian ad laduma I'd still like to strangle. I lost my home, nearly my business, and thirty-five pounds. Nights I drank myself to sleep and mornings I struggled for the strength *or* motivation to get out of bed. It was then I put my mind back on that mountain.

I'd put my feet on the floor, I'd get my feet to the breakfast table. From the breakfast table to my pickup truck, and from the truck to work, until I'd conquer another day.

At the bottom of that mountain I was consumed with fury, hurt and fear. Going up that mountain, I had a hundred chances to quit, but I refused.

And that, is where this story used to end.

(Still speaking into the microphone, I turned my head and body to where my wife was sitting, in the third row.)

But, ten years ago, with the help of some friends, I talked a Redheaded Farm Girl into going swing dancing with me on a Saturday night. Two years ago, standing in our barn, she agreed to be my wife. As a result, I can say there is one source of strength greater than facing failure, and pushing past: being unconditionally loved, respected, and accepted without condition — by your best friend in the whole world.

An important P.S. that I did not have time for at the Moth GrandSLAM:

Some years later we were back in Colorado for another trip. John found me huddled over a trail map pointing with a stick. "What's up man, I've never seen you look at a map?"

"You know that trail with all the rocks and switchbacks?"

"Yeah, The Beast."

"That things gotta be coming up pretty soon".

The corner of his eye crinkled behind his riding glasses and he gave me a full-on bear hug, "Brother, that was a mile-and-a-half back".

*Which sounds a bit like a killjoy. The reality is, on a back-country bike trip, we spend eight hours a day in the saddle. The only shower is from a bag hanging next to the truck, or an ice-cold mountain stream. It's not quite as romantic as the Holiday Inn. 🐾

BILL STORK

About the Author

Dr. Stork is a cradle flatlander from central Illinois. He was raised around a dinner table under a starving-artist rendition of The Last Supper. His mom was an incurably kind, comfort food gourmet. Dad was a git-'er-done construction worker, welder, and shade-tree mechanic. There was always an extra place at the dinner table for a neighbor with a trailer hitch or a carburetor to rebuild.

He was first moved to write by John Boy Walton on Thursday nights. An aunt gave him James Herriot's *All Creatures Great and Small* as a Christmas gift. At speaking engagements he jokes that book cost his dad a thousand hours of overtime, because there began his mission to become a veterinarian. His horizons began to expand beyond 1195 Nickey Avenue when he was accepted to The University of Illinois. He ate dinner and roomed with friends who would go on to become doctors, lawyers, rocket scientists, and engineers. His friend Eric helped write Google.

He first crossed The Cheddar Curtain in 1986. A friend invited him to spend the weekend with her family on the river near La Crosse. The sun rose between a Lutheran Church nestled in a valley, and a hip roof dairy barn. Six years later he delivered a Guernsey heifer calf in that barn, two days after he graduated from vet school.

On June 16th, 2021, there will be a party. He will have spent one more day in Wisconsin, than The Land of Lincoln. He will officially declare himself a Cheese Head.

Dr. Bill claims he does not recall many of Herriot's stories, but he was impressed upon by his heart, his passion for his patients, and reverence of his beloved England.

He can relate. In twenty-eight years, he's come to love every-square-inch of Wisconsin, and most of her people (a few took a while).

He is fascinated by perspective and obsessed with the artful exchange of images in any form. That is what the HS series attempts to capture.

Dr. Bill resides—figuratively and literally—at the top of a hill in Jefferson County, Wisconsin. He calls it The Compound. He lives with his wife Sheila, dogs, horses, a twenty-seven-year-old cat, and The Big Stink. Down the hill are Sheila's parents; her brother and sister-in-law are a hundred yards to the west; and the rest of the family that has treated him like blood since day one, is just around the corner (later he learned that his sister-in-law Debbie was looking for someone 'a little younger' for Sheila.) ◵

Acknowledgments

My wife, Sheila. In one of my favorite stories about Grit and resilience, I wrote something to the effect, "I have found there is one source of strength greater than having arrived at certain failure, and pushed past. That is being loved unconditionally, respected, and accepted as you are, by your best friend in the whole-wide-world." That's all there is, ain't no more.

My editor-sister-friend, Mittsy Voiles. She has now sorted through, cringed at, and attempted to make sense out of nearly seven-hundred-fifty pages of my drivel. No Mittsy, no books, period.

My illustrator-brother-friend, Glenn Fuller. He has made these books feel like the people and places I hope to celebrate. This book likely would not have been printed without Glenn; he would not allow me to walk away. He has believed in me and believed in us. I pray someday he can believe in himself.

My brother, Scott R. Clewis. We are closing in on our fortieth anniversary of friendship. Scott is a paragon of Grit and a self-made man.

My brother, Jay Walker. No man has ever done father and husband better than Jay Louis Walker.

My brother, Gary Edmonds, who has done father and husband as well as Jay. He's also kind enough to take the red pencil to my ramblings and *attempt* to make my writing as succinct and relevant as his.

My brother, Kishan Khemani. Before we were old enough to legally drink, he rendered the most succinct and inclusive piece of advice I've ever heard, "Do the right thing."

My brother, John Humphries. An alternate title for this book was to be *No Bad Weather*. Embrace of that Norwegian philosophy, figuratively and literally, has changed my life. John owns and operates Lizard Head Cycling Guides. He has delivered me to the most spectacular points on earth, at the cost of many hours of suffering. Through him I have met some of the most exemplary people.

The staff at the Lake Mills Veterinary Clinic. Their hard work and compassion is without fail, and requires me to do all I can to dignify and equal their energy.

The clients/friends of The Lake Mills Veterinary Clinic. Their trust requires me to get out of bed every day and go earn it. ᐊ